D1613545

A Concise Companion to
Contemporary British and
Irish Drama

Blackwell Concise Companions to Literature and Culture
General Editor: David Bradshaw, University of Oxford

This series offers accessible, innovative approaches to major areas of literary study. Each volume provides an indispensable companion for anyone wishing to gain an authoritative understanding of a given period or movement's intellectual character and contexts.

Published

A Concise Companion to

Contemporary British and Irish Drama

Edited by Nadine Holdsworth
and Mary Luckhurst

BLACKWELL PUBLISHING
350 Main Street, Malden, MA 02148-5020, USA
9600 Garsington Road, Oxford OX4 2DQ, UK
550 Swanston Street, Carlton, Victoria 3053, Australia

The right of Nadine Holdsworth and Mary Luckhurst to be identified as the authors of the
editorial material in this work has been asserted in accordance with the UK Copyright,
Designs, and Patents Act 1988.

Designations used by companies to distinguish their products are often claimed as trademarks.
All brand names and product names used in this book are trade names, service marks,
trademarks, or registered trademarks of their respective owners. The publisher is not associated
with any product or vendor mentioned in this book.

This publication is designed to provide accurate and authoritative information in regard to the
subject matter covered. It is sold on the understanding that the publisher is not engaged in
rendering professional services. If professional advice or other expert assistance is required, the
services of a competent professional should be sought.

First published 2008 by Blackwell Publishing Ltd

1   2008

Library of Congress Cataloging-in-Publication Data

A concise companion to contemporary British and Irish drama / edited by Nadine Holdsworth
and Mary Luckhurst.
    p. cm—(Blackwell concise companions to literature and culture)
  Includes bibliographical references and index.
  ISBN 978-1-4051-3053-0 (alk. paper)
  1. English drama—20th century—History and criticism.   2. English drama—Irish authors—
History and criticism.   3. Theater—Great Britain—History—20th century.   4. Theater—Ireland—
History—20th century.   I. Holdsworth, Nadine.   II. Luckhurst, Mary.

PR736.C576 2008
822′.9109—dc22
                                                                                          2007001662

A catalogue record for this title is available from the British Library.

Set in 10/12pt Meridien
by Graphicraft Limited, Hong Kong
Printed and bound in Singapore
by Utopia Press Pte Ltd

The publisher's policy is to use permanent paper from mills that operate a sustainable forestry
policy, and which has been manufactured from pulp processed using acid-free and elementary
chlorine-free practices. Furthermore, the publisher ensures that the text paper and cover board
used have met acceptable environmental accreditation standards.

For further information on
Blackwell Publishing, visit our website at
www.blackwellpublishing.com

In memory of Clive Barker,

innovative practitioner
wonderful story-teller
cricket enthusiast
and devotee of detective fiction

a man committed to the exploration and promotion of
the playful, creative, social and political potential of local,
national and international theatres.

Contents

Contents

Illustrations

Notes on Contributors

Helen Freshwater holds an academic fellowship in theatre studies at Birkbeck College, University of London. Her research interests include censorship, the archive, memory, and contemporary physical theatre. She has written essays for *New Theatre Quarterly*, *Poetics Today* and *Performance Research*.

Claire Gleitman is an associate professor of dramatic literature at Ithaca College. She has published numerous articles on contemporary Irish drama in journals such as *Eire/Ireland*, *Canadian Journal of Irish Studies* and *Modern Drama*. She has written for *The Cambridge Companion to Twentieth-Century Irish Drama* and for a collection of essays on Sebastian Barry. She is currently at work on a critical anthology of dramatic literature.

Sarah Gorman is a senior lecturer in drama, theatre and performance studies at Roehampton University. Her current research focuses upon contemporary British, North American and European experimental theatre. Her essays have been published in *Performance Research*, *Contemporary Theatre Review*, *The Drama Review*, *Theatre Journal* and *New Theatre Quarterly*. She is currently writing a book on the New York City Players.

David Higgins is lecturer in English literature at the University of Leeds and the author of *Romantic Genius and the Literary Magazine:*

Biography, Celebrity, Politics (2005). He has published several articles on Romantic-period culture, as well as contributing an essay on Joe Orton to the Blackwell *Companion to Modern British and Irish Drama: 1880–2005* (2006).

Nadine Holdsworth is senior lecturer in theatre and performance studies at the University of Warwick. She has written *Joan Littlewood* (2006) and has edited collections of John McGrath's writings on theatre, *Naked Thoughts That Roam About* (2002) and *Plays for England* (2005). She has published widely on post-war British and Irish theatre, including articles on 7:84, Theatre Workshop, Glasgow Unity, Gary Mitchell, and contemporary Scottish theatre.

Mary Luckhurst is senior lecturer in modern drama and co-director of writing and performance at the University of York. She has edited the Blackwell *Companion to Modern British and Irish Drama: 1880–2005* (2006). She is the author of *Dramaturgy: A Revolution in Theatre* (2006), co-author of *The Drama Handbook* (2002), and co-editor of *Theatre and Celebrity in Britain, 1660–2000* (2005). She has also edited *The Creative Writing Handbook* (1996), *On Directing* (1999) and *On Acting* (2002). In 2006 she was made a national teaching fellow of the Higher Education Academy in recognition of her outstanding contributions to teaching and research in drama. She is a playwright and director and in 2007 directed Caryl Churchill's *Mad Forest* at the York Theatre Royal.

Tom Maguire lectures in drama at the University of Ulster. His research interests are contemporary British and Irish drama, interventionist theatre, and story-telling. He is the author of *Making Theatre in Northern Ireland Through and Beyond the Troubles* (2006).

D. Keith Peacock is a senior lecturer in drama at the University of Hull. His books include *Harold Pinter and the New British Theatre* (1997), *Thatcher's Theatre* (1999) and *Changing Performance: Culture, Aesthetics and Performance in the British Theatre since 1945* (2006).

Dan Rebellato is professor of drama at Royal Holloway, University of London. He is the author of *1956 and All That* (1999) and co-editor with Jen Harvie of a special issue of *Contemporary Theatre Review* on globalization and theatre (2006), and is currently writing a book on *British Drama and Globalization*. He has published widely on contemporary theatre. He is also an award-winning playwright, and his plays, translations and adaptations have been performed in Berlin and London and on BBC radio.

Heike Roms is lecturer in performance studies at the University of Wales, Aberystwyth. She has published widely on contemporary performance practice, in particular on work originating from Wales. She has collaborated with a number of Welsh artists on a variety of performance works and is involved in several artist-run projects and networks in Wales. She is co-editor with Jon McKenzie and C. J. Wan-Ling Wee of *Contesting Performance – Global Genealogies of Research* (2007).

Ken Urban is a playwright and director and teaches at Harvard University. His plays have been produced and developed by Moving Arts, the Lincoln Center, Soho Rep and Annex Theatre, and they are published in *New York Theatre Review, Plays and Playwrights 2002, The Best Women's Stage Monologues 2001* and *The Best Women's Monologues of the Millennium* (2001). He was named a Tennessee Williams scholar at the 2006 Sewanee Writers Conference, where he developed his new play *Sense of an Ending* with Lee Blessing. His essays on theatre have appeared in *Performing Arts Journal, Contemporary Theatre Review, New Theatre Quarterly* and *Svet a Divadlo*.

Geoff Willcocks is senior lecturer and course director for theatre and professional practice at Coventry University. His teaching and research interests include post-war British theatre history and contemporary performance practice. His current research is concerned with representations of the Balkan conflict in British theatre and performance.

Fiona Wilkie is a lecturer in drama, theatre and performance studies at Roehampton University. Her teaching and research interests focus on contemporary performance and interdisciplinary questions of space and place. Her current research is pursuing the problems and possibilities of travel and transience in performance contexts.

Acknowledgements

The editors would like to thank Emma Bennett, Rosemary Bird and Karen Wilson at Blackwell for their care and attention during the process of producing this volume. Once again Fiona Sewell was an outstanding copyeditor. Chris Megson was a helpful reader and Ellie Paremain a handy researcher. We would like to thank Blast Theory, Complicite, Forced Entertainment, Stan's Cafe, and Ken Urban and Hanna Slattne for their help with picture research. Thanks also to Victoria Coulson, who was the Nigella Lawson of York. The editors would like to extend their thanks to the F. R. Leavis Fund and the Department of English at the University of York and to the School of Theatre, Performance and Cultural Policy Studies at the University of Warwick for financial support. Greg Callus will find that his newfound expertise as a theatre historian will be invaluable when he is prime minister. Students on the MA Writing and Performance 2006/7 were especially brilliant: thank you to Tom Cantrell, Shabnam Darbar, Dot Fenwick, Chris Hogg, Doug Kern and Nik Morris. Tom was also an indexer par excellence.

Introduction

Nadine Holdsworth and
Mary Luckhurst

This companion emerged from a realization that the historical scope of the Blackwell *Companion to Modern British and Irish Drama 1880–2005* (2006) meant that it was impossible to do justice to the incredible proliferation of dramatic and theatrical practices that have emerged during the past twenty-five years. Whereas fifty years ago the term 'contemporary British and Irish drama' would have, largely unproblematically, referred to a group of playwrights, companies and their outputs centred on text-based plays performed in traditional theatre spaces, no such assumptions can be made about work produced in the last twenty-five years. If anything characterizes the contemporary theatre scene, it is its eclecticism – in terms of the subjects it addresses, the sites it occupies, its increasing interdisciplinarity and the forms of representation it offers. The prominence of terms such as 'physical theatre', 'site-specific theatre', 'virtual theatre' and 'multimedia performance' testify to the range of practices that have emerged in recent years. These developments have enriched the theatrical domain as they have challenged the primacy of text, promoted the blurring of disciplinary borders and harnessed the potential of new technologies. Several chapters in this volume debate some of the philosophical, thematic and aesthetic questions posed by these practices.

Whilst recognizing the importance of formal diversification, we do not wish to suggest that the traditional play is not alive and well – it certainly is. Indeed, leading and emerging playwrights have been embarking on their own experiments to uncover the forms, language and aesthetic strategies that can best respond to the concerns of the contemporary age. In this volume such creative engagement is represented through discussions of verbatim theatre, aesthetics of 'radical dissonance', Kane's 'ethics of catastrophe', hybrid forms, disrupted narratives and the role of the story-teller and story-telling.

A persistent narrative in this companion is a deliberate shift of focus away from the metropolitan centre and the dominant centrality of work produced at the Royal Court, the National Theatre and the Royal Shakespeare Company that has preoccupied so much of the historiography of recent British theatre. Whilst these production companies are important and represented, chapters in this collection also address work that has been created in Belfast, Cardiff, Edinburgh, Exeter, Sheffield, Stoke-on-Trent, Birmingham, Liverpool and Ulverston. In fact some of the most exciting and innovative work explored in this collection finds a source of creative energy and invention from its origins in and engagement with urban and rural geographical sites, cultural idioms, local histories and heritage that exist way beyond London.

This volume works from the premise that British and Irish playwrights and theatre-makers have an important role to play as ethical witnesses and cultural commentators. Many national and international events of the recent past have produced seismic shifts in the political, economic, social and cultural landscape. These include the demise of the Cold War, symbolically manifest in the collapse of the Berlin Wall, and the resurgence of ethnic nationalism in Europe that resulted in the devastating Balkan conflict and the international reverberations caused by the first and second Iraq Wars. These world-changing events sit alongside national developments such as Scottish and Welsh devolution and the Northern Ireland peace process, all of which raise questions of political legitimacy, national identity and cultural representation. Other concerns preoccupying contemporary dramatists and theatre-makers include the legacy of imperialism and the struggle to interrogate histories, memories and identities; the mounting presence of migration, economic refugees and those seeking asylum; the persistence of atrocious humanitarian abuses; lack of faith in official political processes; the insidious poverty that afflicts communities worldwide and the increasing encroachment of globalization. Discussions of the possibilities and limitations offered by theatrical treatments and interrogations of these events, themes and their consequences are woven through several chapters in this volume.

2

The chapters are divided into four parts in order to identify key thematic concerns and synergies. The first part, 'National Politics and Identities', addresses work that explores such themes as revolution, migration, the immigrant experience, cultural memory, the role of history, Black British urban identity and the forging of new identities in changed political and cultural circumstances. The second part, 'Sites, Cities and Landscapes', explores the various ways in which playwrights and theatre-makers have drawn on the specificities and politics of geographical locations as creative source and subject matter in order to explore ideas around place, belonging, and local, national and global identities. Part III, 'The Body, Text and the Real', draws together chapters that variously address questions of representation, authorship, authority, the potential veracity and political efficacy of text, and the materiality of the body in performance. The final part, 'Science, Ethics and New Technologies', explores how playwrights and theatre-makers have responded to the ethical and aesthetic challenges posed by the rapid advances in nuclear, medical and infor-mation technology, mass media communication and the relentless force of globalization.

We hope that this volume gives a snapshot of the political engage-ment, thematic complexity, theatrical energy and formal experimenta-tion evident in much late twentieth- and early twenty-first-century theatre practice and a flavour of the debates, dialogues and provoca-tions posed by some of Britain and Ireland's leading and emerging playwrights and theatre practitioners.

Part I

National Politics and Identities

Chapter 1

Europe in Flux: Exploring Revolution and Migration in British Plays of the 1990s

Geoff Willcocks

There can be little doubt that 1989 was a pivotal year in European history. The revolutions of the communist Eastern bloc, the break-up of the Soviet Union and the subsequent ending of the Cold War were to confront Europe, particularly the countries of the European Union (EU), with challenges which are proving difficult to resolve. The main challenges were, and still are, concerned with security, economic and political stability, migration, and the process of enlarging the EU to incorporate newly 'independent' nation-states. The plays considered in this chapter provide examples of how British playwrights explored and interpreted the challenges faced by post-communist Europe during the 1990s. The focus of these plays is the events in the countries of the former Eastern bloc and the Balkans.

As this chapter is concerned with the responses of British play-wrights to the events in Europe during the 1990s, brief consideration has to be given to the relationship between Britain and the rest of Europe and specifically the European Union. During the 1980s much of the political debate in Britain concerning Europe had centred upon issues relating to finance – the exchange rate mechanism (ERM), rebates, subsidies, the single currency versus sovereignty; debates driven largely by the so-called Eurosceptics in both Westminster and the business world. The popular understanding of Europe within Britain, fuelled by tabloid newspapers, had, for the most part, been concerned with losing the pound and generating scare stories about European legislation governing minutiae like the straightness of bananas. Moreover, Britain's history as a significant colonial power and its 'special' relationship with the USA have always meant that Britain has tended to see itself as apart from continental Europe, a mindset reinforced by its geographical position as an island off the coast of mainland Europe. These issues are heightened by Britain's continuing post-imperial anxiety with regard to integration with the rest of Europe, representing within the popular and political psyche of Britain another step towards its loss of sovereignty and a diminishment of its position as an independent world leader. The idea of 'Britain', though, is a tricky one and a mainly political concept: generally the Scottish and Welsh tend to identify more with the continent than their old colonial power, England.

The British government's relationship with the rest of Europe is complicated further by the problems that surround defining Europe as a cohesive entity. What are its borders – who is included in and who is excluded from Europe? Does it have shared values? Does it have homogeneous cultural imperatives? While the desire to integrate Europe economically and politically remains strong in certain quarters of the EU, the reality is that the means to achieve this are far from mutually agreed by its constituent nation-states. Moreover, it is important to note that the institution of the EU by no means represents Europe as a whole. A number of European countries still exist outside of the EU, a fact that makes drawing conclusions about pan-European ideals, needs and development based purely upon the stated aspirations of the EU extremely difficult. Although Europe has moved a long way since Henry Kissinger asked whom he should telephone if he wanted to speak to Europe (Leonard 2005: 23), questions of definition still plague the project of European integration, and this is reflected in the plays considered here. For some theatre academics, such as Janelle Reinelt, the task of those British playwrights who have tackled the subject of Europe has been undertaken with almost utopian zeal. In her article 'Performing Europe' Reinelt suggests that the plays which she considers represent an 'interrogation of and intervention in the struggle to invent a New Europe' and that 'theatre may emerge from this early millennial period as a powerful force for democratic struggle in its own unique imaginative and aesthetic modality' (2001: 387).[1] However, while accepting that no playwright would wish to distance themselves from such an ambitious and noble position, this chapter argues that many of the plays produced by British playwrights concerning Europe as it stood during the 1990s reveal a much less optimistic view. The plays that this chapter explores are David Edgar's (b. 1948) *Shape of the Table* (1990) and Caryl Churchill's (b. 1938) *Mad Forest* (1990), Edgar's *Pentecost* (1994) and David Greig's (b. 1969) *Europe* (1994), and finally Sarah Kane's (1971–99) *Blasted* (1995) and Nicolas Kent's (b. 1945) *Srebrenica* (1996). Collectively these plays offer an engaging and at times disturbing account of one of the most significant periods of European history.

The key events that succeeded the revolutions of 1989 and the end of the Cold War are well documented, but their significance lies in the momentous change they brought to the political structure of Europe.[2] The demise of the ideological tensions inherent within the Cold War generated European aspirations for unity, common purpose and mutual understanding. It is significant, therefore, that one of the key political ideas of this period – the notion of a common European home – should be attributed to one of the central architects of this era's political climate, the then Soviet leader Mikhail Gorbachev.[3] It was Gorbachev's hope that the democratization of the Soviet Union and the Eastern bloc would begin to unite Eastern and Western Europe.

Implicit in Gorbachev's desire were the central concepts of unity, cooperation, tolerance, mutual respect and commonality. Unfortunately, the Europe that was to emerge over the next decade was to be one based on precepts far removed from Gorbachev's idyll. While Gorbachev had spoken of an ideal – a Europe without borders – the reality was that borders, both geographical and political, as well as borders of history, ethnicity and identity, became the cause of conflicts the effects of which would be so far reaching that they would significantly contribute to the redefinition of Europe itself. Moreover, with these conflicts came a rapid increase in the numbers of those seeking economic migration and refugee status in Western Europe. Thus, through the changing demography of their major towns and cities, the nation-states of Western Europe were forced to confront the consequences of their promotion of rapid political and economic change.

With the demise of communism the peoples of Eastern, Central and Southeastern Europe were left to answer questions not just about their system of political governance, but also about their cultural and political identity. The thawing of the permafrost of the Cold War, which for over forty years had frozen national borders and even ethnic identities and histories, led to a rapid resurgence in ethnic nationalism. In many ways, perhaps this should not be surprising, as Vaclav Havel, a major playwright himself and the then president of Czechoslovakia, pointed out at a conference on security and cooperation in Europe held in Helsinki during the summer of 1992:

> The sudden burst of freedom has not only untied the straitjacket made by communism, it has also unveiled the centuries-old, often thorny history of nations. People are remembering their past kings and emperors, the states they had formed far back in the past and the borders of those states . . . It is entirely understandable that such a situation becomes a breeding ground for nationalist fanaticism, xenophobia and intolerance. (see Mauthner 1992: 2)

Havel's words proved frighteningly prescient. Throughout much of the 1990s Eastern, Central and Southeastern Europe experienced a period of instability and radical, and occasionally bloody, change. As Havel implies, the borders of these nations, having been previously defined and controlled by the necessities of the Cold War, could now be questioned. Ancient border disputes began to erupt as nascent nation-states began to assert their perceived rightful and historical claims to land and territory.[4] This makes Reinelt's suggestion that 'the idea of Europe has become a liminal concept, fluid and indeterminate' problematic (2001: 365). If the borders of contested parts of Europe were indeed being openly questioned and challenged, it is also true that these new borders were being fiercely defended in the name of ethnic nationalism. Perhaps the starkest example of the horrific confluence of ethnic nationalism and the redefinition of borders in Europe was the bloody conflict that engulfed the Federal Republic of Yugoslavia during the early 1990s. The disturbing reality is that it only took two short years for Europe to move from breaching the Berlin Wall, thoughts of a common European home and the unification of East and West Europe, to the disintegration of Yugoslavia, the destruction of Sarajevo, the massacre at Srebrenica and the events described in the chilling euphemism of 'ethnic cleansing'.[5]

Competing with history

All of the plays considered in this chapter deal in some way with history. A concern with the theatrical representation of history was clearly uppermost in the mind of Michael Billington when he reviewed Howard Brenton and Tariq Ali's *Moscow Gold* (1990), a play concerned with the events of the Soviet Union from 1982 to 1990. In his review, Billington writes: 'You start to wonder how theatre can compete with documentary reality. The short answer is it can't. [. . .] Theatre cannot compete with history: what it can do is illuminate specific moments in time and the burden of decision' (1990: 44). Billington's words, particularly his assertion of 'the burden of decision', imply a specific understanding of history as the story of decision-makers and powerful elites. The reality of any given moment of the past is that it is constructed by a plurality of experiences that generate multiple, not singular, narratives. Two plays that sought, in very different ways, to reconcile the problems of theatrically depicting historical narratives, Edgar's *The Shape of the Table* (1990) and Churchill's *Mad Forest* (1990), concern themselves specifically with the Eastern European revolutions of 1989.

The Shape of the Table (National Theatre, 1990) considers the processes inherent in the political negotiations that took place in the countries of the Eastern bloc following the events of 1989. While concerning itself with the elites implied by Billington, *The Shape of the Table* does not seek to depict the story of one particular country, but rather explores the story of the revolutions in Eastern Europe holistically. As Edgar explains:

> In 1989, I felt there was enough in common between the uprisings in Poland, East Germany, Czechoslovakia, Hungary and Bulgaria to create a representative fictionalised narrative of the fall of Eastern European communism; the play, *The Shape of the Table*, would demonstrate a common process but also dramatise the experience of heady opportunity (on one side) and loss (on the other). (2001b: 2)

While there are undoubtedly inherent problems in extracting the generic processes that are in operation at any given moment in history – for example, the loss of the specific social and political circumstances of each particular nation and the motivations of individual players – for Edgar the task offers significant benefits:

> I think that history tells what *happened*, journalism tells what's *happening* and what I try and do is tell what *happens*. My work is in the present tense, but it is more general, more generic than journalism. I've come round to writing plays about process as a development of an alternative to political theatre in the traditional polemical sense. I suppose a process play is a play that says there is a syndrome of things that

happen in the world and what happens in *The Shape of the Table* is that you take something that happens frequently, you draw out the essence and you fictionalise it; you make it generic.[6]

As the play unfolds the fall of the communist government of Edgar's unnamed country is shown as a fait accompli. Ultimately, representatives from both the new and old order are gathered in one room and tasked with negotiating the future governance of their country. To this end, *The Shape of the Table* revolves almost exclusively around the negotiating table. Indeed, Edgar uses the negotiating table itself, as suggested by the play's title, as a metaphor for the developments and political changes that were occurring throughout Eastern Europe at this time. During the negotiations, the table is revealed as not one single table but many smaller tables that can be tessellated into one whole or divided into smaller or even single units. This metaphor operates on two levels. First, it not only demonstrates the development of political and cultural plurality, but also indicates the aspiration that such plurality should be based not upon mutual exclusivity but upon the ability to act cooperatively for the greater good of all. Secondly, however, the metaphor of the table also reminds the audience that an active desire on all sides is required to make such pluralistic cooperation a reality. Edgar underscores this point at the end of the play when there are reports of a gang of skinheads beating a Vietnamese boy to death and the appearance of graffiti that reads 'Gas all Gypsies Now' (Edgar 1990: 75), elements that prophetically point towards a growing nationalism, ethnic tensions and civil war.

In contrast to *The Shape of the Table*, Churchill's *Mad Forest* (Central School of Speech and Drama, London, 1990), which considers events in Romania during the latter part of 1989, does not represent a single politician or political representative (though the dictator Nicolae Ceaușescu has a powerful implicit presence). Moreover, while Edgar's play offers an examination of the political processes at work in Eastern Europe, *Mad Forest* offers an evocation of the mood and atmosphere prevalent in Romania during the early 1990s. Asked to write a play about the Romanian revolution for the students of the Central School of Speech and Drama, Churchill's approach was to use the actors in the company to help generate the material for the play, as she had previously done for Joint Stock Theatre Company. This approach necessitated a visit to Romania, where the students interviewed a range of people about their experiences during the events of late 1989 and early 1990. As a result, as Sotto-Morettini notes, the play focuses on the 'small vicissitudes of family life [. . .] the "micro-politics" of everyday life' (1994: 105). This process generated a play that reveals large-scale socio-political proceedings through personal, domestic and familial events, centring as it does on two unremarkable families.

Mad Forest is not a process play as typified by Edgar's *The Shape of the Table*; rather it offers its audience a range of voices that speak of an historical event, an experience, which, while collective in nature, is composed of a plethora of individual contributions; and in doing so the play reveals a picture that is fractured and fragmented. This fragmentation is borne out by the play's formal structure, which is segmented into vignettes of action. While most of these sections are realistic in their form, some scenes are surreal – a disturbing feature of the work's construction, which unsettles and unnerves the spectator. For example, a priest is told not to think about politics by an angel, and at the start of act three a dog begs a vampire to make him 'undead'. Even within the more realistic scenes, an atmosphere of fear and uncertainty pervades the work: a husband and wife have to turn the radio up to have an argument for fear that their house is bugged; a family can only speak openly during a power cut; and a woman arranges an illegal abortion, bribing the doctor who only appears to be refusing her request. Even at the end of the play, when the Ceauşescu regime has been removed, the change that Churchill depicts is characterized as painful and uncertain. While Edgar's *The Shape of the Table* articulates the political, philosophical and conceptual processes of the transition that occurred in Eastern Europe, Churchill's *Mad Forest* offers its audience an examination of the immediate consequences of this change. Ultimately, it is a change that leaves the characters of the play traumatized by the event itself, bewildered by its rapidity, fearful of its potential implications and deeply confused about the uncertainty it has generated for the future, a set of concerns that were replicated across Central and Eastern Europe at this time.

Fortress Europe

The state of uncertainty and flux that Europe experienced during the 1990s is the central concern of a number of plays written during this time and shortly after. While Timberlake Wertenbaker's play *Credible Witness* (2001) and David Edgar's work *The Prisoner's Dilemma* (2001a) consider the consequences of European instability during the 1990s,[7] two other plays, Edgar's *Pentecost* (1994) and Greig's *Europe* (1994), explore how Europe has become a site of transition, particularly in terms of the migration of people. Both these plays examine issues that centre upon national identity, borders, language and the question of Europe as a politically and economically united entity.

Following the Eastern bloc revolutions of 1989, one of the significant challenges that faced the EU, which was then comprised almost exclusively of the nations of Western Europe, was that of migration. Migrants fell into two groups, which were by no means mutually exclusive: economic refugees and those displaced by war or political change. The EU's official statistics demonstrated the scale of this challenge. Between 1989 and 1998 close to two million asylum applications were made to Western European nations by citizens of other European countries. In total, including applications from non-European countries, asylum applications made to EU countries between 1986 and 1991 rose by 481 per cent (Gregou 2005: 10). Faced with this dramatic increase in migration the response of many Western European countries, despite the implementation of the Schengen pact, was to impose stricter immigration and border controls.[8] In addition to this, during the mid-1990s the EU was heavily engaged in discussion over the process of enlargement – explicitly which nations should and which should not be included in the EU. It is these issues that occupy central positions in the narratives of both *Europe* and *Pentecost*.

The action of *Pentecost* (Royal Shakespeare Company, Other Place, 1994) takes place in an abandoned church in a Southeastern European country, only referred to as 'our country'. On the wall of the church is a fresco that bears a remarkable similarity to Giotto's *Lamentation* in the Arena Chapel, Padua. Gabriella Pecs, a curator at the National Museum, enlists the help of a visiting English art historian, Professor Oliver Davenport, to help her confirm the provenance of the fresco, which she believes pre-dates Giotto's work. In the opening exchanges of the first scene, as Pecs tells Davenport the history of the church in which the fresco is housed, she reveals to the audience the complex history and 'ownership' of her nation:

Gabriella: All righty, one abandoned church. As well as warehouse, church is used by heroic peasantry to store potatoes [. . .] And before potatoes, Museum of Atheism and Progressive People's Culture. And before museum, prison [. . .] 'Transit Centre'. German Army. [. . .] When we Hungary, it

Catholic, when we are holy Slavic people, Orthodox. When we have our friendly Turkish visitor who drop by for few hundred years, for while is mosque. When Napoleon pass through, is house for horses. (Edgar 1995: 5)

This establishes a degree of confusion and uncertainty as regards the national identity of 'our country'. Edgar constructs a country in which the idea of a national identity is unstable, and integral to this instability is the very fact that the territory, the physical landscape of 'our country', has been a border that over the past few centuries has been repeatedly questioned, claimed and reclaimed by different ethnic groups. This is why the provenance of the fresco is so important for 'our country' as a nation-state and specifically in terms of its national identity as a European state.

If Pecs's research and some educated assumptions are correct, then the fresco in the church was painted close to one hundred years prior to Giotto beginning work on the painting in Padua. As Giotto's painting is considered one of the founding works of the Renaissance, the importance of establishing the provenance of 'our country's' fresco becomes clear as it potentially calls into question the geohistorical location of Southeastern Europe. If Pecs is correct, the genealogy of 'our country' is moved to a more central position within the cultural, philosophical and historical order of that which is considered 'Europeanness'. If this fresco turns out to be what Pecs and Davenport believe it is, then the cultural geography of Europe for the past six hundred years has been wrong. The birthplace of the Renaissance and therefore the cultural development of Europe was not northern Italy, but the southeastern Balkans. However, before the provenance of the fresco can be confirmed the church is invaded by a group of refugees, who take the occupants hostage and insist that the authorities meet their various demands for asylum or the hostages will be killed. This startling *coup de théâtre* initiates the second act of the play.

Through these refugees Edgar is able to evoke the vast ethnic diversity of contemporary Europe. These refugees hail from a very wide range of countries, backgrounds and ethnicities and their presence successfully represents the diversity of the post-Cold War diaspora, including Kurds fleeing Turkey and Iraq, Bosnian Gypsies escaping persecution in Croatia, Palestinians, and refugees from the former Soviet Union. Reinelt has argued that the *concept* of Europe has become 'fluid and indeterminate' (Reinelt 2001: 365), but the reality so accurately depicted by Edgar is that the borders of Europe, specifically

15

between old and 'New Europe', are anything but. By bringing these refugees into 'our country' – the threshold of Europe – Edgar foregrounds the plight of those seeking to enter Western Europe.

The most significant feature of act two is the fact that the cultural centrality of Western Europe is challenged and placed firmly on the periphery, while the marginalized 'other', in this case the refugees, takes centre stage. Theatrically, Edgar explores this in two ways. First, large sections of the act are spoken in a cacophony of European and Near and Middle Eastern languages. Sometimes an English translation is offered, but often the audience, like the characters on stage, are left to interpret what is being said through gesture, actions and the reactions of others, thereby removing the linguistic supremacy of English. Significantly, however, during this act, all the characters, both refugees and hostages, manage to communicate and do make themselves understood, most notably by sharing stories – the universal themes of which are recognized by all present. Secondly, it is revealed that the fresco was painted not by a Western European, Christian painter, but by a Muslim Arab. Both of these elements, while displacing the cultural centrality of Western Europe, also suggest that it is possible, if the desire is strong enough, to develop mutual understanding across borders of culture, history and language. Ironically, this optimism is destroyed when a Special Forces team smash through the wall on which the fresco is painted to recapture the church, killing a number of refugees and Davenport in the process. This violent intervention signals that the political will to defend the borders of Western Europe is undoubtedly stronger than the desire to foster acceptance and understanding across them.

The theme of crossing borders is further considered in Greig's *Europe* (Traverse Theatre, 1994). Set in a defunct railway station, in a generic blue-collar European town, *Europe* examines, through the use of analogy and metaphor, the political and economic condition of migrancy in the 1990s.

The consideration of the movement of people across borders is first presented by some of the geographically inspired names that Greig gives his characters, namely Morocco, Berlin and Sava. Morocco is the gateway between Europe and Africa, Berlin was a city that sat at the heart of a divided Cold War Europe and was itself a divided city, and Sava is the name of the river that acts as most of the northern border of Bosnia-Hercegovina and Croatia, as well as flowing through Slovenia and Serbia. Between them these three names mark out the borders of Europe, both old and new, and act as a reminder within the play of the borders and boundaries that define and problematize the notion of Europe.

At the beginning of scene three Greig's stage directions state that:

> *The station's architecture bears witness to the past century's methods of govern-ment. Hapsburg, Nazi and Stalinist forms have created a hybrid which has neither the romantic dusting of history, nor the gloss of modernity. The predomi-nant mood is of a forgotten place.* (Greig 2002: 7)

Here Greig is keen to foster the idea that the work is set in a location that has, like the church in Edgar's *Pentecost*, a layering of historical impositions. If not an area that has been openly contested then it is at least an area that has been subjected, over the last century, to domina-tion by a number of superior powers. Ultimately, the whole play is pervaded by a sense of helplessness in the face of superior external forces, such as the inexorable march of global capitalism and the divisions that this creates, and the complications of living on the geo-graphical and political periphery of Europe.

Greig explores the notion of Europe and Europeanness partly through the metaphor of trains and travel. The image of the train and the railway system as a whole, on the one hand, binds the play's central characters together and, on the other, facilitates the play's discussion of Europe as a site of change and transformation. At the beginning of the second act, the main concern of Fret, the stationmaster, is the fact that the new timetable does not make sense. For Fret the timetable represents order and stability; it is a temporal map on which the places of Europe are charted relative to each other, not in terms of distance, but in terms of time. Greig uses this metaphor to signal that the cities and places of Europe are not only connected by physical lines of com-munication – roads, railways etc. – but also, and just as significantly, by shared historical connections. The railway system, the 'muscles and arteries' of Europe (53), is held in place by this map, maintaining its smooth operation and continuity, and thus, by implication, ensur-ing the continued function of Europe as a whole. Therefore Greig uses the image of a railway system, which without an adequate time-table will quickly descend into chaos, as a metaphor for a Europe that without moral and political consensus will rapidly fall into conflict, xenophobia and violence.

Within the play the train also represents a vision of Europe that is not a common European home but very much divided, quite literally within the play, between those who are going places and those who

are denied or who deny themselves freedom of movement. This operates at an individual level, but is representative of the economic and
political divisions between what would become known, during the
early years of the twenty-first century, as Old and New Europe.[9]
Greig employs movement as a thematic framing device for the play as
a whole, and through it the personal motivations and situations of
each character can be read within the larger context of Europe during
the mid-1990s. Adele dreams of travel and adventure, but can only
watch passing trains from the roof of the station, whereas for Katia
and Sava travel is an enforced necessity: as refugees it is for them a
means of survival – an escape from bloodshed and imprisonment.
Similarly, for Billy travel is a means of escape, but for him this escape
is economic in that he is leaving his closing factory and home town in
order to find a better life. For Morocco travel is an essential part of his
working life, as he makes an illicit living by the movement of goods,
money and services across borders, or as he calls it 'the magic money
line' (33). Thus Greig, through the theme of movement, manages to
encapsulate much that is indicative of mid-1990s Europe – the migration of refugees, escaping both persecution and economic decline, and
the issues of cross-border trade, tariffs and implicitly a single European currency.

In the final moments of the play, Greig draws together the strands
that he has explored throughout the work. Here the themes of travel,
the plight of refugees, the tensions that exist between national identity
and a nascent European identity, and the dangers of ethnic nationalism are conflated and examined as a whole. Katia and Adele, both
escaping their pasts, travel by train to an undisclosed destination.
While travelling, they recite excitedly the names of European cities,
cities in which, as stateless persons, they will undoubtedly be denied
immigration rights. Simultaneously, Berlin talks of how in an act of
ethnic hatred he firebombed the station, killing Fret and Sava, and
how this act has been widely reported and discussed. Finally, as the
speeches converge, the implications of the brutal realities of imple-
menting the concept of a unified Europe in the face of bitter ethnic
nationalism become chillingly clear:

Berlin: For one day, for one week . . . maybe even for a month.
         Everyone knew the name of our town. And now they know.
         They know that even as they travel to some older . . .
Adele: Salzburg.
Berlin: Or more beautiful . . .

Katia: Sarajevo.
Berlin: Or more important place.
Adele: Just imagine.
Katia: Shh . . .
Berlin: They know that, in our way, we're also Europe. (89–90)

Never again?

I will now turn to two plays that explore the distressing consequences of the tensions articulated by *Pentecost* and *Europe*: Nicholas Kent's *Srebrenica* (Tricycle, 1996) and Sarah Kane's *Blasted* (Royal Court Theatre Upstairs, 1995). Both plays offer salient warnings about ignoring Europe's nationalistic and ethnic tensions and concern themselves intimately with the conflict that followed the break-up of the Federal Republic of Yugoslavia, a horrific conflict that marked the nadir of European transition and change during the 1990s and confronted the EU with one of its sternest challenges.

As Aston notes '*Blasted* captured a feeling of the Bosnian war' (2003: 81), and in a number of interviews given by Kane, she repeatedly returns to the conflict in the former Yugoslavia, especially the Bosnian conflict, as a means of establishing *Blasted*'s political and ethical engagement within contemporary European events (Langridge and Stephenson 1997; Saunders 2002). While much of the initial critical commentary on the play considered the work's content,[10] Kane herself states that the form of the work is an expression of her concerns about Bosnia. The first section of the play can be seen as a piece of social realism, being realistically depicted in the urban, English setting of a hotel room in Leeds. The second section of the play, after the explosion and the unexpected arrival of a soldier, is set in the remains of this room, now part of a war zone, in which the formal properties of time and action have collapsed. In an interview with Stephenson and Langridge, Kane clarifies this:

> The war [within the play] is a direct parallel of the war it portrays – a traditional form is suddenly and violently disrupted by the entrance of an unexpected element that drags the characters and the play into a chaotic pit without logical explanation. In terms of Aristotle's Unities, the time and action are disrupted while unity of place is retained. Which caused a great deal of offence because it implied a direct link between domestic violence in Britain and civil war in the former Yugoslavia.

> *Blasted* raised the question 'What does a common rape in Leeds have to do with mass rape as a war weapon in Bosnia?' And the answer appeared to be 'Quite a lot'. The unity of place suggests a paper-thin wall between the safety and civilisation of peacetime Britain and the chaotic violence of civil war. A wall that can be torn down at any time, without warning. (Langridge and Stephenson 1997: 130–1)

Thus, *Blasted* represents a desire to interrogate social relationships across Europe. Furthermore, Kane does not consider this exploration within the abstract context of society in general, for, as she clearly states above, this is a play about contemporary English society and its relationship to the atrocities being committed in Bosnia. As she highlighted in an interview with Clare Bayley, the connections that *Blasted* makes between England and Bosnia are deliberate and calculated:

> Just because there hasn't been a civil war in England for a very long time doesn't mean that what is happening in Bosnia doesn't affect us [. . .] My intention was to be absolutely truthful about abuse and violence. All of the violence in the play has been carefully plotted and dramatically structured to say what I want about war. The logical conclusion of the attitude that produces an isolated rape in England is the rape camps of Bosnia. And the logical conclusion to the way society expects men to behave is war. (Bayley 1996: 20)

In addition to this, Kane also noted with regard to the hysterical reaction that the play's original production received:

> The representation of violence caused more anger than actual violence. While the corpse of Yugoslavia was rotting on our doorstep, the press chose to get angry not about the corpse, but the cultural event that drew attention to it. That doesn't surprise me. Of course the press wish to deny that what happened in Central Europe has anything to do with us, of course they don't want us to be aware of the extent of the social sickness we're suffering from – the moment they acknowledge it, the ground opens up and swallows them. (Langridge and Stephenson 1997: 131)

Thus, Kane draws a clear line of ethical responsibility from the Bosnian war to the rest of Europe. For her, the Bosnian crisis was not an event being experienced by foreigners in some distant land, but by Europeans, her neighbours. The role of the media in these events, particularly the tabloid press, is ridiculed in the play by one of its central characters – the diseased and abusive Ian, a hack journalist who is only interested in covering salacious local stories. Through his callous disregard for those around him, his rape and sexual abuse of Cate, and indeed the rape and physical abuse that he himself suffers, the mutilation of the soldier's girlfriend and the need for Cate to sell herself for food, Kane creates an image of a dysfunctional world. Coupled with Kane's darkly pessimistic view of European events and the potent warning they hold for all civilized European society, these images invest the play with a disturbing challenge to Western Europe's moral complacency.

In a similar way, ethical accountability for the Balkans was also an important factor in Kent's *Srebrenica*, which reconstructs, using verbatim transcripts, the Rule 61 hearings[11] undertaken at the Hague to investigate the massacre that took place at the UN 'safe area' of the town of Srebrenica in eastern Bosnia in July 1995.[12]

Srebrenica forms part of the Tricycle theatre's tradition of 'tribunal' plays, which collectively Chris Megson has termed 'forensic documentary "replays"' (2004: 5). This evokes the idea that while *Srebrenica* is a factual account, specifically a verbatim re-enactment, it is an edited and theatricalized version of the original trial. This displacement of the original testimonies into a theatrical context allows *Srebrenica* to be seen as evidence within itself and thereby represents an important contribution to the debates generated by the EU's response to the Bosnian conflict.

Originally, *Srebrenica* was played as a prologue to the revival of Norton-Taylor's *Nuremberg* (1996). Clearly, the function it serves by this positioning is to demonstrate a chilling continuity in European history; a point reinforced by Kent when he talks of visiting the Rule 61 hearings at the Hague:

> [and] listening to [that] horrifying evidence I was appalled that so little media coverage was being given to it in this country. I mean, here we are, 50 years after the war that we vowed must never happen again, the Holocaust and the gas chambers, and it's all been going on a 90 minute flight away. (Kingston 1996: 1)

Moreover, Jane Edwardes speaks for many critics and commentators when she observes that the work provides a moral touchstone for Western Europe's involvement in the Balkans:

> We are used to reading news that has been sifted, *Srebrenica* forces the theatregoer to listen very hard. Sitting in an audience in a theatre

enhances one's sense of being part of a society and the responsibilities that that entails. There are no theatrical judgements to be made, but the inescapable conclusion of these disturbing extracts is that history will judge us harshly if Mladic and Karadzic are not brought to trial. (1996: 24)

Srebrenica successfully drew attention to the events in the Hague, not simply by revealing the magnitude and importance of the crimes committed in eastern Bosnia, but also by attempting to generate a sense of responsibility within its audience. This is particularly salient when one considers that one of the founding principles of the EU was that by uniting the countries of Europe the atrocities of war could be avoided.

Although Kent's desire for objective re-enactment is laudable, it does raise the question of whether such a venture is actually required. While, as Billington points out in his review of *Srebrenica*'s performance at the National Theatre the following year, 'theatre can both activate the memory and attack the conscience' (1997: 12), the *Observer*'s Tom Lubbock takes a more critical stance with regard to the reproduction of verbatim testimony as a viable dramatic form:

> If one can judge these edited reconstructions as drama, this is a far more low key affair [as opposed to the Scott Inquiry or Nuremberg]. The criminals do not appear, nor are there any famous faces to impersonate. The witnesses are people we don't know: a UN observer, a colonel, a conscript. Their stories are everything. This makes the form even more puzzling. What exactly is added by those 'authentic' touches – headphones that don't work, the stumbling over words? Why shouldn't the events themselves be dramatised? Is it just the stage's love of trials, the chance to play forensic formality against the massacres described? Or is the stage's self-denial an attempt to honour the legal fiction that only in court can the truth be established? (1996: 11)

While it is possible to feel a certain degree of sympathy for Lubbock's position, it is important to be aware that what is lost through the work's lack of explicit theatricality is compensated for by the play's wider remit with regard to Kent's desire to put actual witness testimonies on stage. What the reconstruction of these events adds, complete with stumbles over words, or headphones that do not work, is the human voice and, more importantly, the human presence. Kent's reconstruction has the effect that it does upon its audience, as proved by the critical response that it received, not just because of the words that the people spoke, but because people speak them. Kent, through this reconstruction, stops this story being reduced to mere maps and statistics, elements that can be readily printed within newspapers or turned into computer-generated graphics on the television news. *Srebrenica* foregrounds the human beings involved and in doing so helps to deny the total construction of the Srebrenica massacre as an organizational catastrophe, helping to maintain the event, at least in part, as a human atrocity.

Collectively, the plays discussed within this chapter represent a theatrical response to a changing Europe. Ultimately, when considered as a whole, these plays tell the story of a period in which the people of Europe strove to come to terms with a world that was altering rapidly; a changing world in which some were compelled to renegotiate not only their borders and land, but also their national identities and their histories. These plays are not utopian works and, while they deal with the difficulties experienced by Europe during the 1990s, nor are they dystopian. Rather they articulate the often complex and problematical questions posed by this period of transition and change – questions of mutual responsibility, interdependency and cooperation, but also questions of territoriality, ethnic nationalism and identity. The EU has undoubtedly made significant attempts to resolve these issues in order to create a Europe that is more politically stable and economically integrated, particularly through the continuing expansion of its membership. However, the fact remains, as these plays attest, that economic and political divisions still exist – between Old and New Europe, between member nations and non-member nations, and even between member nations themselves. While the ideal of political and economic integration still drives the project of a united Europe, the reality is far from ideal.

Notes

1 Reinelt (2001) considers Theatre de Complicite's *Mnemonic* (1999), Edgar's *Pentecost* (1994) and Greig's *Europe* (1994).
2 For example, see: Raymond L. Garthoff (1994). *The Great Transition: American–Soviet Relations and the End of the Cold War*. Washington, DC: Brookings Institution; Walter LaFeber (1993). *America, Russia and the Cold War 1945–1992*. New York: McGraw-Hill; Timothy Garton Ash (1990). *We The People: The Revolution of '89*. Harmondsworth: Penguin; Don Oberdorfer (1991). *The Turn: How the Cold War Came to an End*. London: Jonathan Cape.
3 This notion of a common European home was proposed by Gorbachev in his book *Perestroika*, first published 1987.

4 For more detail about the development of the new Eastern European states post-1989 see: Julie Mostov (1996). 'The Surge of Nations and the Making of New States' in Gerasimos Augustinos (ed.), *The National Idea in Eastern Europe: The Politics of Ethnic and Civic Community*. Lexington: D. C. Heath.

5 For detailed accounts and analysis of the demise of Yugoslavia see: Laura Silber and Alan Little (1996). *The Death of Yugoslavia*. Harmondsworth: Penguin and London: BBC Worldwide; David A. Dyker and Ivan Vejvoda (1996). *Yugoslavia and After: A Study in Fragmentation Despair and Rebirth*. Harlow: Pearson Education; Christopher Bennett (1998). *Yugoslavia's Bloody Collapse: Causes, Course and Consequences*. London: Hurst.

6 David Edgar, unpublished interview with author, 11 May 2004, Birmingham.

7 This is particularly true of Edgar's work, which examines the complexities inherent in the process of negotiating peaceful settlements to bitter and in some cases ancient border disputes. See: Janelle Reinelt and Gerald Hewitt (2003). 'The Prisoner's Dilemma: Game Theory, Conflict Resolution, and the New Europe', *Contemporary Theatre Review* 13:2, 41–55.

8 The Schengen pact, introduced in 1995, saw the relaxing of internal border controls within the EU.

9 The origin of this expression is attributed to US Defence Secretary Donald Rumsfeld during a press conference in Prague, 24 January 2003, in the build-up to the second Gulf War. For further reading, see: Tom Lansford and Blagovest Tashev, eds. (2005). *Old Europe, New Europe and the US: Renegotiating Transatlantic Security in the Post 9/11 Era*. Aldershot: Ashgate.

10 For example, see: Nick Curtis (1995). 'Random Tour in a Chamber of Horrors', *Evening Standard*, 19 January, 46; Michael Billington (1995). 'The Good Fairies Desert the Court's Theatre of the Absurd', *Guardian*, 20 January, 22.

11 The Hague's Rule 61 hearings allows for the presentation of evidence against suspects who have been indicted by the court but who have yet to be apprehended. The purpose of these hearings is to reaffirm the indictment against the suspects and to allow the judges to issue an international arrest warrant.

12 For a full account of the massacre at Srebrenica, see: David Rohde (1997). *Endgame. The Betrayal and Fall of Srebrenica: Europe's Worst Massacre Since World War II*. Boulder, CO: Westview Press.

Primary reading

Brenton, Howard, and Ali, Tariq (1990). *Moscow Gold*. London: Nick Hern.
Churchill, Caryl (1990). *Mad Forest*. London: Nick Hern.
Edgar, David (1990). *The Shape of the Table*. London: Nick Hern.
Edgar, David (1995). *Pentecost*. London: Nick Hern.

Edgar, David (2001a). *The Prisoner's Dilemma*. London: Nick Hern.
Greig, David (2002). *Plays: 1*. London: Methuen.
Kane, Sarah (2001). *Complete Plays*. London: Methuen.
Kent, Nicolas (2005). *Srebrenica*. London: Oberon.
Wertenbaker, Timberlake (2001). *Credible Witness*. London: Faber and Faber.

Further reading

Aston, Elaine (2003). *Feminist Views on the English Stage: Women Playwrights, 1990–2000*. Cambridge: Cambridge University Press.
Bayley, Clare (1996). 'A Very Angry Young Woman', *Independent*, 23 January, 22.
Billington, Michael (1990). 'Can Theatre Compete with the Real Life Drama of Recent Soviet History?', *Guardian*, 28 September, 44.
Billington, Michael (1997). 'Srebrenica; National Theatre, London', *Guardian*, 12 November, 12.
Edgar, David (2001b). 'Making a Drama out of a Crisis', *Guardian* (*Saturday Review Section*), 7 July, 2.
Edwardes, Jane (1996). 'Srebrenica', *Time Out*, 15 October, 24.
Gergou, Sophia (2005). *Local and Regional Authorities and the Immigration Challenge*. Luxembourg: Office for Official Publications of the European Communities.
Kingston, Jeremy (1996). 'Trials of a Court Reporter: All the World's Crime is a Stage for Nicolas Kent', *The Times* (features section), 7 October, 1.
Langridge, Natasha, and Stephenson, Heidi (1997). *Rage and Reason: Women Playwrights on Playwriting*. London: Methuen.
Leonard, Mark (2005). 'Ascent of Europe', *Prospect*, March, 22–5.
Lubbock, Tom (1996). 'Mighty White "Art" is a Minimalist Comedy: Plenty of Gags, but Only One Joke', *Observer*, 20 October, 11.
Luckhurst, Mary (2005). ' "Infamy and Dying Young": Sarah Kane, 1971–1999' in Mary Luckhurst and Jane Moody (eds.), *Theatre and Celebrity in Britain, 1660–2000*. London: Palgrave, 107–24.
Mauthner, Robert (1992). 'CSCE Challenged by Outburst of National freedom', *Financial Times*, 10 July, 2.
Megson, Chris (2004). ' "Thou Shall Not Be Found Out": Documentary Theatre as Political Intervention at the Tricycle Theatre (1994–2003)', unpublished conference paper delivered at 'Political Futures: Alternative Theatre in Britain Today', 17 April, University of Reading.
Reinelt, Janelle (2001). 'Performing Europe: Identity Formation for a "New" Europe', *Theatre Journal* 3:3, 365–87.
Saunders, Graham (2002). *Love Me or Kill Me: Sarah Kane and the Theatre of Extremes*. Manchester: Manchester University Press.
Sotto-Morettini, Donna (1994). 'Revolution and the Fatally Clever Smile: Caryl Churchill's *Mad Forest*', *Journal of Dramatic Theory and Criticism* 9:1, 105–18.

Chapter 2

'I'll See You Yesterday': Brian Friel, Tom Murphy and the Captivating Past

Claire Gleitman

'The time is not come for impartial history', remarked Robert E. Lee in 1868, three years after the end of the American Civil War. 'If the truth were told now, it would not be credited' (Macrae 1952: 222). One might argue that the same has been true for centuries in Ireland, where the question of what constitutes 'impartial history' is a hotly contested one. Indeed, in 1980 Brian Friel (b. 1929), who was then and remains the most celebrated dramatist writing in Ireland, offered an observation about his country's relationship to its past that corresponds strikingly to what Lee noted in 1868: 'The inherited images of 1916, or 1690, control and rule our lives much more profoundly than the historical truth of what happened on those two occasions' (Agnew 1980: 60). Of course, Lee's remark was made just three years after the traumatic conflict that he believed Americans could view only obliquely, whereas Friel refers to events decades and even centuries old that feel vividly current to many Irish citizens (that is, the battle of the Boyne of 1690 and the Easter Rising of 1916[1]). A scene from *Someone Who'll Watch Over Me*, by Friel's younger contemporary Frank McGuinness (b. 1953), neatly encapsulates the cultural condition. This 1992 drama concerns an Englishman, an Irishman and an American who are taken hostage by Lebanese terrorists. In the midst of a debate about Irish–English politics, the Englishman says the following about the potato famine of 1845–50:

The Irish Famine was a dreadful event. I don't dispute its seriousness. But . . . [i]t was a hundred and fifty fucking years ago.

The Irishman counters 'It was yesterday', to which the Englishman replies: 'You are ridiculous, Edward.' Edward's succinct retort is: 'I am Irish' (McGuinness 1992: 30).

The compulsion to remember, or misremember, Ireland's past has been the subject of numerous plays by such authors as Friel, Tom Murphy (b. 1935), Anne Devlin (b. 1951), Sebastian Barry (b. 1955), McGuinness and many others.[2] In this chapter, I will focus upon Friel and Murphy, who came of age in the mid-twentieth century and made their dramatic reputations virtually simultaneously. Friel's first successful play, *Philadelphia, Here I Come!* (1965), was written just four years before Murphy wrote *A Crucial Week in the Life of a Grocer's Assistant*; both plays concern a young man's struggle to decide whether to leave an economically and emotionally stultifying, but still captivating, Ireland. Yet, although they have intersected thematically more than once, the two playwrights are generally contrasted rather than compared, with Friel commonly deemed the lyrical mourner of a vanishing pastoralism and Murphy described as the angrier voice of mid-century Ireland, the 'dramatist-as-Irish-thug' (as Fintan O'Toole describes Murphy's alleged persona) – whom Kenneth Tynan once said he 'would hate to meet in a dark theatre' (O'Toole 1987: 9). But, for all their apparent differences, both authors have shown a persistent interest in the 'making' of history (personal and public), and in the capricious role of memory in determining its shape. In the early 1980s, each produced a play that takes as its subject the frozen backward stare that McGuinness's Englishman indicts as 'ridiculous' but which his Irish counterpart views as an essential component of his identity. As I shall argue, both Friel's *Translations* (1980) and Murphy's *Bailegangaire* (1985) address the question of whether clinging to the past life of a culture hinders its progress into the future. In doing so, they offer incisive explorations of the manner in which history, or truncated versions of history, may take individuals and nations captive, holding them in thrall like Walter Benjamin's famous Angel of History, who stares backwards in horror at a catastrophic past while being hurtled forward against its will into an inconceivable future.[3]

In many respects, Friel's *Translations* may be viewed as the natural outgrowth of work he had been doing for two decades; in its seemingly elegiac lament for a dying rural existence it looks back to *Philadelphia* and forward to *Dancing at Lughnasa* (1998). Murphy's *Bailegangaire* is more of a departure, for reasons I shall discuss later. Yet both plays were intimately affected by the cultural moment out of which they grew, when an ardent debate was taking place about how to reenvision Ireland's past. In the early 1980s, Ireland's conflict with Britain and its own population of Northern Irish Protestants was feverishly intense, prompting the then fledgling Field Day Theatre Company (founded by Friel himself along with many of the most renowned artists and intellectuals in Ireland) to write the following about why the theatre was created:

> All the directors felt that the political crisis . . . made the necessity of a reappraisal of Ireland's political and cultural situation explicit and urgent. . . . They believed that Field Day could and should contribute to the solution of the present crisis by producing analyses of the established opinions, myths and stereotypes which had become both a symptom and a cause of the current situation. (Field Day 1986: vii)

As the above manifesto makes evident, Field Day was not merely a theatrical venture but a self-consciously political one. Its founders chose to establish Field Day in the contested territory of Northern Ireland and in the city of Derry, whose very name is a matter of furious dispute. The fact that Derry's Protestant inhabitants insist upon calling the city 'Londonderry', the name that the British imposed upon it, while Catholics cling to 'Derry' (which derives from its original Gaelic name, Doire), and those who regard themselves as politically neutral opt for 'Slash City' (suggesting the compromise 'Londonderry/Derry') tells us much about the deep political and historical significances that may lie within a name. It is this issue precisely that Friel takes up in *Translations*, which was Field Day's premiere production. The story of *Translations'* ecstatic reception in Derry is well known;[4] and yet, though it played a crucial role in reanimating conversations in Ireland about the nation's relationship to its history, language and identity, some aspects of the play sparked hostile debate, namely its treatment of historical 'fact' and the extent to which its portrait of pre-colonized Ireland is, in the words of one critic, 'grossly oversimplified' (Connolly 1987: 43).[5] In short, critics have asked: is *Translations* a reappraisal, or is it simply reinscribing 'established . . . myths'? Is it an incisive analysis of bygone yesterdays, or merely a nostalgic dirge that mourns their passing?

Translations' subject is the 1833 drawing by the British Army Engineer Corps of the first Ordnance Survey map of Ireland, an exercise of imperial authority that involved the Anglicization of many Irish place-names. This act of 'translation' has a devastating impact on the Gaelic population of Baile Beag, the Donegal village in which the action is set. The encounter between the Irish-speaking locals and the English military involves a series of misunderstandings and mistranslations that convey much about the deep political and emotional implications residing, *pace* Juliet Capulet, in a name. *Translations* begins prior to the intrusion of the colonists, and its opening moments reveal an ostensibly thriving Irish village marked by signs of optimism and reju- venation. The first line belongs to Manus, the son of the local school- master, who says: 'We're doing very well.' That the villagers are, in some respects, doing well is reinforced by what follows. A mute girl named Sarah is taught by Manus to utter her name, prompting him to declare: 'Nothing'll stop us now! Nothing in the wide world!' (Friel 1981: 12). Soon thereafter, we learn that Manus's father Hugh is absent because he is attending a newborn's christening, and the character Maire enters to announce that they have just enjoyed the 'best harvest in living memory' (15). All these signs of promise will be extinguished by act III: Sarah will relapse into silence; Manus, with whom she is in love, will repeat his words lifelessly and with a telling alteration ('There's nothing to stop *you* now' [56, emphasis added]), before abandoning her for a world that seems bleak rather than wide; the recently christened baby will have died; and the British authorities will be threatening to level the entire parish. This simple outline may seem to validate the claims of Friel's harshest critics, such as Sean Connolly, who claims that *Translations* is a nostalgic dramatization of Ireland's fall from its Edenic origins, a fall brought about by superficially ren- dered, brutish colonizers (Connolly 1987). Yet a more careful analysis will reveal a richer if vexing interplay in *Translations* between nostalgia and irony, as the play both laments the loss of a vital ancient culture and critiques that culture's own, festering malaise.

The crowning irony in *Translations*, as has been noted often, resides in its central device. In this play celebrating the richness of the Gaelic tongue, not a word of Irish is spoken (place-names excepted). The lines of the Irish peasants, though written in English, are meant to be understood as Irish, as one first deduces from a remark early in act I. Berating herself for her ignorance of English, Maire recalls that there *is* one English sentence that she has mastered, however clumsily:

'In Norfolk we besport ourselves around the maypoll' ... God have mercy on my Aunt Mary – she taught me that when I was about four, whatever it means. (15–16)

29

Later, when the English sappers arrive and Manus's brother Owen must translate for them, we deduce that *their* English is *really* English. Friel handles his device so skilfully that there is no difficulty in discerning when the English is English and when it is Gaelic. His characters' failure to communicate is touching and even tragic; it becomes comical when we resist suspending disbelief and consider that they are, in fact, speaking the same language. The contemporary analogy is arrived at easily: twentieth-century citizens of Northern Ireland who spoke the same tongue still could not 'interpret between privacies' (67), in Hugh's words, because of the swamp of conflicting ideologies and distrust that divided them. Thus the division is shown to be less linguistic than psychological and cultural, a point to which I shall return.

Further irony inheres in the fact that Friel was compelled to write his play in English unless he meant to settle for a tiny audience of Irish nationals rather than the huge international one that *Translations* enjoyed. The knowledge that Gaelic is a nearly dead tongue kept alive only by the vigilant efforts of patriots lends poignancy to the play. It also renders absurd the remarks of the pedant Hugh, who boasts that English is a language best suited 'for . . . commerce' while Gaelic and the classical tongues make 'a happier conjugation' (25). As Lionel Pilkington has observed, Hugh's 'formulation of this view consists of an etymological pedagogy that demonstrates the opposite'; it is English that is rooted in Greek and Latin and it is English etymologies that Hugh forever insists his students trace (Pilkington 1990: 286). Thus the play reminds us of the ascendancy of the colonizer's language even as its central character insists on the merits of his native Gaelic.

Yet Hugh is not naïve; he perceives keenly that the colonialists' endeavour will have as its ultimate issue the annihilation of his language and his world. To dramatize the course of that annihilation, Friel sets the play in a hedge-school where Hugh presides as master. Ireland's hedge-schools were a remnant of the draconian Penal Laws, which sought to inhibit Catholic emancipation and forbade, among other things, the education of Catholics. In defiance, many Catholics carried on their schooling in clandestine locations like barns or alongside hedges. But by 1833 the Penal Laws had been relaxed and the hedge-schools were about to be overtaken by National Schools instituted by the British, in which Catholics would be educated according to a modern curriculum and only English was permitted. As the play makes evident, the hedge-school is an increasingly marginalized location; the word 'hedge' itself connotes a marginal entity and the school is a vestige of an earlier need that barely survives on the cusp of the implementation of the new system. Friel may tempt us to idealize the intellectual vibrancy of Hugh's school, where the older Irish peasants ponder word origins and speak Latin and Greek with ease, in contrast to the rather implausibly boorish British Captain Lancey, who has no fondness for words of any kind and mistakes Latin for Gaelic.[6] Yet the opening stage directions are littered with adjectives that hint at the obsolete nature of the hedge-school world – 'disused', 'remains', 'once', 'without' – and those items with the potential for usefulness (the cart-wheel, the farming tools, the churn) are 'broken and forgotten' (11). Further, as was typical of hedge-schools, Hugh's classroom emphasizes classical literature and languages; he drills his students in the rudiments of dead cultures that are as useless to them in the changing world as is their own Gaelic. Situating himself in a dramatic tradition stretching from Anton Chekhov to Tennessee Williams, Friel contrasts the effete lyricism of an old world with the efficient muscularity of a new one. In so doing, he compresses centuries of Irish history into one poetically rendered moment, in which an old way of life shows itself to be ill-equipped to withstand the pressures of modernity.

Throughout *Translations*, Friel makes clear that Baile Beag is threatened by its own internal deficiencies as well as by pressures from without. While there is undeniable charm in the character Jimmy Jack, for whom Greek gods are as real as anyone in Baile Beag, his preference for a heroic ancient world over the troubled one in which he lives leads him to a progressive retreat backwards and inward, so that by the end of the play he seems genuinely to believe that he is betrothed to Athena. Further, Jimmy Jack – who lives in filth and never bathes – is surrounded by other characters who are maimed in some fashion: Manus is lame; Sarah is mute; Hugh is a drunk. Even the seemingly tough-minded Maire explodes with fury when Doalty and Bridget fret about the 'sweet smell' that may portend a potato blight: 'Sweet God, did the potatoes ever fail in Baile Beag? . . . There was never blight here . . . But we're always sniffing about for it . . . looking for disaster' (21). Yet Maire's scorn is misplaced; in 1833, the potato famine was a mere 12 years away, and its tentacles would certainly reach Donegal.

Thus, Friel peppers his play with subtle reminders of its historical horizons. Maire, whom Manus hopes to marry, is exasperated by his plan to follow in his father's footsteps ('Teach classics to the cows?

Agh' [29]) and declares her own intention to learn English to facilitate her emigration to America. The hedge-school curriculum is irrelevant to the material concerns with which Maire must contend, and she invokes the words of the 'Liberator', Daniel O'Connell – who agitated on behalf of Catholic emancipation – to bolster her claim that she requires English to survive in a changing world: 'The old language is a barrier to modern progress' (25). Meanwhile, a reference to the Donnelly twins suggests another response to encroaching change: these delinquent schoolboys, who (to Hugh's dismay) cease attending his school and never appear on stage, constitute a menacing absent presence as they register disapproval of the troops' actions first by minor pranks and finally by the murder of Lieutenant Yolland. In the Donnelly twins are the seeds of the Irish Republican Army (IRA), which blossomed from the resistance activities of just such rural agitators. Although the Donnelly twins eventually win support from some of the locals as the oppressive intentions of the British forces become clear to them, Friel seems more intent on showing what is problematic about violent resistance than he does on endorsing it, as I shall argue later on.

As it happens, the internal phenomena threatening the indigenous peasant culture help to guarantee the victory of British mercantile imperialism, which appears in the form of the officious Lancey and the awkward Lieutenant George Yolland. While Lancey carries out his task with aloof pragmatism, Yolland rapidly succumbs to the charms of the culture that it is his job to uproot. A dreamy romantic enraptured by anything Irish, Yolland speaks in act II about his failure to please a dictatorial father who was born on 'the very day the Bastille fell' (40). (Friel's evident indifference to the fact that this would make Yolland's father 44 in 1833 – meaning he would have been about 15 when his 'late twenties/early thirties' son was born – is of a piece with Friel's unwillingness to allow poetic meaning to yield to historic 'fact', even in a history play.) Imbued with the revolutionary spirit of 1789, the older man was in sync with a new world defined by progress. Yolland, by contrast, is pathetically out of step. Timid and sentimental, he feels he has found his natural home in Ireland and longs to stay there 'always'. But it is the Ireland on the wane that has ensorcelled him, the land of saints and scholars where learned men swap 'stories about Apollo and Cuchulainn . . . as if they lived down the road' (40). This is the Ireland Yeats pronounced 'dead and gone' in 1913 and which may never have existed outside of the wishful constructions of artists disenchanted by a grim modernity. In Friel's play, Romantic Ireland is granted fitful life in the form of the doddering

Hugh and Jimmy Jack. Yolland falls for them as does the audience, but his dewy-eyed myopia alerts us to what we might otherwise overlook: these loveable linguists can barely clothe or sustain themselves, and at least one of them is clearly a drunk.

Owen, Hugh's prodigal son, is in many ways as blind as Yolland, though at first he seems less naïve. A translator for the sappers, he is every inch 'the go-between', as he describes himself at the close of act I while introducing Maire, his brother's intended, to the British Yolland (33). Upon arrival back in Baile Beag, he delightedly notes that 'everything's just as it was! Nothing's changed!' (27). His remarks resonate on several levels: the lack of change may be a sign of stagnation, but to the extent to which Baile Beag's consistency is a virtue it is Owen's job to transform it. Undaunted by this, he smoothly takes the lead in the hedge-school game of conjugation and etymology despite his years away, while engaging in relaxed banter with the British officials whom he calls his 'friends'. But it soon becomes evident that Owen's effort to reside in two conflicting worlds renders him an outcast in both. To Manus, Owen's job as the army's menial is abhorrent in part because it depends upon denying who he is. When the sappers mishear his name and take to calling him Roland, Owen does not bother to correct them: 'What the hell. It's only a name' (33). Later, alone with Yolland, Owen mentions the error and the men engage in some poteen-induced hilarity about name variations:

Yolland: What'll we write –
Owen: – in the Name-Book?
Yolland: R-o-w-e-n!
Owen: Or what about Ol –
Yolland: Ol – what?
Owen: Oland! (45)

In this moment of camaraderie Owen proposes a fusion of the names which is also a fusion of the near homophones Owen and Yolland, thus reaching for a potential union between the cultures and the men. But the fusion, enabled by the great quantity of 'Lying Anna's poteen' they have consumed, has the chilling effect of heightening their confidence in their task: 'Welcome to Eden!' they declare proudly to Manus, 'We name a thing and – bang! – it leaps into existence' (45).

Yet the play's larger burden is to suggest the profound personal and cultural significance in a name, so that its obliteration may result in its referent leaping *out* of existence and in the eradication of the

'Eden' that Yolland reveres. To contest Yolland's fear that 'Something is being eroded' by their orthographical work, Owen tells a tale about the naming of a crossroads, known as Tobair Vree, to bring home to Yolland the capricious, even trivial nature of place-names and their origins. Yet the tale suggests the opposite. While the tides of time, change and imperfect memory may virtually wash away the past, a name may go on evoking that past for those who, like Owen, recall its referent – who recall, in this instance, that Tobair Vree was named for an old man who drowned in a well that he hoped would cure a disfiguring growth. When Owen relinquishes his own name for the sake of careerist expediency, he forfeits his grip on an identity rooted in a personal and cultural past, and his act is a self-abasing compromise with the powers that be.

But in a fashion that again underscores the interplay of nostalgia and irony in *Translations*, the Tobair Vree story cuts two ways. The old man called Brian drowned in the well because he 'got it into his head' that its water would cure his growth; he persisted in this belief though he bathed his face in that well every day for seven months with no appreciable change in the growth, until he finally toppled in and drowned in what was meant to cure him. To cling to a delusion despite repeated evidence of its falsity is as self-destructive to Brian as is the Baile Beag villagers' resistance to change and modernity, which will impose itself upon them as surely as it will upon Benjamin's Angel, however much they may all (Maire excepted) stare determinedly backwards.

Ironically, it is Hugh, the central embodiment of the old Gaelic world, who insists on the inevitability of change while also insisting on the value of what is being eroded. When we first see Owen and Yolland doing their work, Friel notes that their job is 'to take each of the Gaelic names – every hill, stream, rock, even every patch of ground which possessed its own distinctive Irish name – and Anglicize it' (34). This emphasis upon the 'distinctive Irish name' of each object suggests that the names being replaced are intrinsically and organically linked to their referents, so that the renaming exercise is not merely an act of colonial arrogance but a violation of the natural order of things. Elsewhere, though, the play suggests that language is not an inherent constituent of the natural world but something *always* arbitrary and artificial. As Hugh notes, 'words are . . . not immortal. And it can happen . . . that a civilization can be imprisoned in a linguistic contour which no longer matches the landscape of . . . fact' (43).[7] The ornate Gaelic vocabulary, he suggests elsewhere, functions as compensation for the meanness of Irish lives. 'You'll find, sir', he tells Yolland:

> that certain cultures expend on their vocabularies. . . . acquisitive ener-
> gies entirely lacking in their material lives . . . It is our response to mud
> cabins and a diet of potatoes; our only method of replying to . . . inev-
> itabilities . . . Can you give me the loan of half-a-crown? (42)

Even in this remark, however, Hugh's use of the word 'inevitability' is juxtaposed against his request from his son for 'half-a-crown' suggesting that the old man's 'learned helplessness' (to borrow a term from contemporary psychology) contributes to the poverty that he views as an unalterable fact of Irish peasant life.

Though Hugh fails to see the role such habits play in the peasantry's inability to withstand external threats, his recognition of the ephemeral nature of languages and cultures – suggested also in his reference to Ovid's lines, 'No matter how long the sun may linger on his long and weary journey / At length evening comes with its sacred song' – adds layers to the play's portrait of the demise of the Gaelic world (41). While names are precious as reservoirs of the past and markers of personal identity, Hugh suggests that the natural flux of language ensures that they will change perforce, and such linguistic changes are part and parcel of the currents of time.

Indeed, the play's most poignant indication of the emotional resonance of names is simultaneously a hint of the impossibility of the permanent endurance of anything at all. Act II concludes with a love scene between Yolland and Maire in which we appear to witness a moment of real translation, a reaching across linguistic barriers facilitated by words. Though at first the lovers are stymied by their inability to speak the same tongue, it soon occurs to Yolland to make use of the place-names that he has learned while doing his work. His notion makes possible a love dialogue that seemingly transcends language, the kind of exchange that Masha and Tuzenbach achieve in Chekhov's *Three Sisters* by an exchange of 'Tram tra ras':

Yolland: Carraig na Ri. Loch na nEan.
Maire: Loch an Iubhair. Machaire Buidhe . . .
Yolland: Tor.
Maire: Lag. (52)

Words, detached from their referents, become incantatory; their sounds and rhythms seem to carry the lovers to a realm beyond language.

Yet there is trenchant irony here, as the place-names that allow the lovers to bridge the gap dividing them are also the names Yolland is under orders to destroy. Further, at the heart of the dialogue is a profound misunderstanding hinging on the word 'always'. While Yolland wishes to stay in the Ireland with which he is fervently in love, it is Maire's equally fervent wish to leave. Thus he expresses his desire 'to live here – always' while she asks him to take her 'away' with him, 'anywhere at all' (52). As the characters unknowingly give voice to conflicting desires, each asks the other in his or her own tongue: 'What is that word – "always"?', a word that the incisive Hugh will later pronounce 'silly', 'not a word to start with' (67). At its poetic heart, *Translations* is a play about the agonizingly transitory nature of all things, about the fiction of 'always'.

Still, while act I presented the historical currents driving change in Baile Beag, act II is in some ways a temporary evasion of them. Owen and Yolland and then Maire and Yolland form fragile bonds across the linguistic and cultural abyss; in the latter case this occurs in what Friel designates as 'a vaguely "outside" area' (49), an undefined space in performance (in contrast to the schoolroom, which Friel wishes to see rendered realistically, complete with a back wall, a stairway and various everyday props) that momentarily enables an escape from class, geography and history. In act III we return to the schoolroom, and history, like the walls in the schoolroom, closes in on the characters in the realistic space. Yolland is presumably murdered, after bidding farewell to Maire with a linguistic error that sums up his retrograde vision: 'he tried to speak in Irish', Maire tells us, 'he said, "I'll see you yesterday" – he meant to say, "I'll see you tomorrow"' (77). Lancey threatens to set fire to the village if Yolland is not found, and the community splinters. Manus, devastated by Maire's unfaithfulness, leaves Baile Beag, and Owen tries belatedly to make amends first by proposing that they 'go back' to the original place-names and then by departing to join forces with the Donnelly twins. Sarah, whom Seamus Heaney and others have viewed as a figure for Cathleen ní Houlihan, reverts to silence, and the play concludes with the drunken ramblings of Hugh and Jimmy Jack as they drift deeply into the classical past (Heaney 1980: 1199).

Yet each man expresses some clarity in a revealing moment at the end of the play. Jimmy, having announced his intention to marry Athena, admits to Maire that his plan has a pitfall; Zeus might object to the 'mixed' marriage: 'Do you know the Greek word *endogamein*? It means to marry within the tribe. And the word *exogamein* means to marry outside the tribe. And you don't cross those borders casually – both sides get very angry' (68). Jimmy's remark contains the play's most explicit warning about the danger of crossing borders, which are protected by the god Terminus whom Yolland invoked earlier (42). While *Translations* is a play about language, the gap polarizing the natives and the invaders is rooted in a much more fundamental historical disjunction. The British are dedicated to a notion of progress that fails to take into account the autonomy of the cultures they uproot, while the Irish cling to an image of themselves that is outdated and illusory. As Hugh remarks in his final words to Owen: 'it is not the literal past, the "facts" of history that shape us, but images of the past embodied in language . . . [W]e must never cease renewing those images; because once we do, we fossilize' (66). Owen, uttering what resembles the battle-cry of generations of republicans, vows: 'I know where I live' (66). But this knowledge is woefully belated, and Owen's transfer of allegiance from the British to the Donnelly twins (whose precise political aims Friel keeps as shadowy in the play as he does their bodies) seems more abrupt than thought through. Where Owen lives is changing, and his newfound dedication to a cherished image of an inviolate Ireland is an evasion of the facts of life that plague the Irish peasantry – the economic hardships and natural threats that constrict their lives as surely as does the imperialist presence.

Hugh's warning to the now radicalized Owen is one that echoes through the Irish drama and returns us to the problem of the frozen backward stare: 'Take care, Owen. To remember everything is a form of madness' (67). To remember everything may mean remaining stuck in the past, longing to restore an original purity that may never have existed and that in any case is 'dead and gone'. Yet Owen leaves the stage in search of the Donnelly twins and does not hear or heed Hugh's warning. He also fails to hear Hugh's lengthy reminiscence about his own flirtation with violent resistance, when he and Jimmy Jack left their homes to join the 1798 Wolfe Tone rebellion, whose goal was to secure independence for Ireland but which ended in disastrous defeat. As Hugh recounts the misadventure, he and Jimmy Jack left jauntily, imagining themselves as 'heroic' (67). But after marching for 23 miles, they felt themselves growing 'homesick for Athens, just like Ulysses', and returned home, heeding the call of what Hugh describes as 'the need for our own' (67). In a manner reminiscent of the drama of Sean O'Casey, Friel pits abstract 'heroics' against the home and hearth, the infant lying in wait in the cradle, or what Hugh calls 'older, quieter things' (67). Hugh's implicit recommendation that the Irish embrace their homes rather than heading off to fight may seem naïve, as those homes are on the brink of being burned to the ground. Yet Hugh points to a habit of mind that may contribute to the problem, though it surely did not cause it. What he advocates, finally, is an accommodation with the changing world that may be read as complacency, except that it is enriched by his refusal to embrace the certainty that undergirds partial conceptions of history and politics: 'My friend, confusion is not an ignoble condition' (67).

This is not to suggest, of course, that *Translations* condones the British action. The act of map-making was economically as well as imperialistically motivated; the British hoped to impose taxes on the Irish more easily while also extinguishing their culture, as Friel makes evident early in the play when Lancey connects the cartographic exercise with taxation (though Owen glosses over the implications of Lancey's words with his deft 'translation' [31]). The English are desecrators when they rob Ireland of its names, and their action is 'an eviction of sorts' (43) that results in the destruction of an ancient way of life. It was incumbent on the Irish, as Hugh and Maire both insist, to adapt to the modern age; yet it is a brutal form of tyranny to impose change on another culture and to presume to determine the course of that change, and that brutality spawned a rage in Ireland that would retain its intensity a century and a half later. As darkness falls on *Translations* and the old Gaelic world, Hugh turns to the classical models that are familiar to him in an attempt to articulate the tragedy that is engulfing Ireland: 'there was an ancient city which . . . Juno loved above all the lands . . . Yet . . . a race was spring-ing from Trojan blood to overthrow some days these Tyrian towers' (68). By invoking the *Aeneid*'s depiction of the fall of the ancient city of Carthage, which was destroyed by imperialist Rome, Friel places the play's action in the context of a recurring event in human history while also lamenting the ongoing dispossession that is its result. As Nicholas Grene has argued, the analogy serves to suggest 'the arbit-rariness of the configurations of power in which one culture flourishes at the expense of another's ruin' (Grene 1999: 47). In its final mo-ment, *Translations* underscores the passing not only of Gaelic Ireland but of Hugh himself, who criticized his son's overzealous remem-bering and now succumbs to memory loss, as he strains to recall lines from the *Aeneid* that he once knew 'backways'. Thus the play counterpoints its critique of obsessive memory with a tragic sense of loss, as the old repositories of memory fade into silence and are engulfed by what Tennessee Williams (whom both Friel and Murphy have invoked as an important influence) dubbed the game of 'seven card stud':[8] that is, the practical, brute and forward-looking forces of modernity.

Although Tom Murphy's *Bailegangaire* concerns itself with personal rather than historical memory, its analysis of Ireland's relationship to its past parallels *Translations'* perspective and extends it into the 'seven card stud' present, where two of *Bailegangaire's* three characters are doing their best to forge lives for themselves as their octogenarian grandmother, known as Mommo, remains haunted by a nightmarish past from which she seems obstinately determined not to awaken. While *Translations* is set in mid-nineteenth-century Ireland at a time when Gaelic was still spoken, it is *Bailegangaire* that is full of snatches of Gaelic. In this respect and others, it poses great challenges for its audience, which must contend with its linguistic demands and its Byzantine twists and turns, as well as for the necessarily very old actress who plays the part of Mommo, as Siobhán McKenna did in 1985 at the Druid Theatre Company, in what proved to be her final role. In some respects *Bailegangaire* is a more hopeful play than many of Murphy's earlier works, and it takes place not in his usual urban domain but in a rural kitchen, the customary setting of many Irish 'peasant plays'.[9] Unlike those more reassuring models, however, *Bailegangaire* is characterized by an unwaveringly anti-romantic stance that may help to account, along with its linguistic complexity, for its failure to enjoy international recognition on a par with *Translation*, whose political critique is more easily overlooked. Nevertheless, *Bailegangaire's* rich beauty as well as its penetrating depiction of Ireland's fixation upon its past surely merit its being placed alongside *Translations* as one of the most breathtaking achievements of the Irish theatre.

Bailegangaire is set in the west of Ireland, near Galway, in what Murphy describes as 'the traditional three-roomed thatched house' (Murphy 1993: 91). This location is perfectly suited to a play that functions on two levels: it relates a saga about both the present and the past. A thatched cottage in the west of Ireland is an immediately recognizable icon of the pastoral paradise cherished by the Celtic revivalists of the earlier twentieth century, such as W. B. Yeats and Lady Gregory, who looked to rural Ireland as a more vital and romantic alternative to dreary urban modernity. But, as one of Murphy's characters notes acerbically, 'there's rats in that thatch' (133). In 1984, the time of *Bailegangaire's* action, a thatched cottage is an anachronism, a fact made all the more evident when we learn that the house is down the road from a Japanese electronics factory that is on the verge of closure. In the present-tense action of the play, two sisters on the brink of middle age struggle with a familiar domestic predicament: they must decide how to care for their irascible and aggressive grand-mother, who is falling into senility. Meanwhile, cars pass to and fro on their way to the plant, and the sisters are dimly aware of energetic goings-on that will change the life of the town in ways they can barely fathom. Indeed, 'a small computerized gadget' obtained from the plant is carried onstage at the start of act II and the sisters study it uncom-prehendingly: its function is as obscure to them as are the activities of the Japanese, whom one of the sisters insists (in an impotent gesture of defiance) upon calling Chinese.

At first glance, the situation for these women seems grim. The elder of the two, Mary, has just returned from England, where she worked as a nurse. Like many Irish immigrants, Mary found that London offered economic stability but little in the way of personal sustenance, and so she made her way back to the thatched cottage where she was raised in search of something she might call home. Her younger sister, Dolly, has a home, and a very modern one at that. As Dolly points out with not very convincing zeal: 'I've rubber-backed lino in all the bedrooms now . . . and the *lounge*, my dear, is carpeted' (107). In reality, Dolly's home is a horrifying place where she endures repeated beatings from a wayfaring husband, seeking escape by pur-suing sexual assignations with strangers. At the moment she is carry-ing the fruits of one of those anonymous sexual acts: an unborn baby that she hopes to fob off on her childless elder sister.

Thus, *Bailegangaire* suggests that the brave new tomorrow of indus-trialized Ireland – the one that Lancey and his confederates were so eager to bring into being – is in fact barren: the one mark of fertility currently inhabiting Dolly's belly is an unwanted burden and the various accoutrements of modern life do little to sustain the characters, as Dolly eventually admits: 'I hate my own new liquorice-all-sorts-coloured house' (150). Yet Murphy's project is not to contrast a spiritu-ally impoverished present with a nostalgic portrait of a rural paradise lost, any more than Friel's was in *Translations*. Rather, pre-industrial-ized rural existence as he depicts it is plagued by famine and death, and havens like those evoked in Yeats's 'Lake Isle of Innisfree' (where 'midnight's all a glimmer, and noon a purple glow'[10]) are available for rent by charmed tourists because their former inhabitants have fled them to escape wretched lives of poverty and despair. In short, *Bailegangaire*'s thatched cottage invokes the idealized yesterday of Irish legend to explode its fictions; this idyll, we come to recognize, is a fiction that has spawned an obsessive and even crippling preoccupation with the past. Meanwhile, the present doles out destitution to a popu-lace that does not know how to make its way into the future except by limping along with the broken-down crutch of a partial mythology.

The centrepiece of the play and the focal point of its interplay between past and present is a fragmentary tale that the senile Mommo alternately tries and tries not to tell. That tale concerns 'how the place called Bochtán [meaning "a poor place"] . . . came by its new appella-tion, Bailegangaire, the place without laughter' (92). This is a saga that Mommo has been recounting for years: her granddaughters know it so well that when she falters they can jump-start her narrative by reciting lines of it for her. But they do not know the story's ending, because Mommo never tells it. The story takes place in 1950 on the day of a market to which a couple – known in Mommo's telling as 'the strangers', though we soon surmise that they are Mommo herself and her now dead husband – travel in the hopes of selling their wares. But the market is sluggish and few goods sell. Hence, they must make the long journey homeward to their three orphaned grand-children, anticipating a bleak Christmas. When bad weather stalls their journey, they stop at a pub in Bochtán. What ensues is a laugh-ing competition between two mighty competitors. As *Bailegangaire*'s setting summons the mythology of the idealized Irish peasantry while subverting its usual assumptions, the laughing contest owes a debt to ancient Celtic and Norse rituals of flyting and bardic poetic competi-tions, yet in decidedly mock-heroic fashion. Mommo's exuberant nar-rative is replete with stock epithets: 'the bold Costello' (135); grand foreshadowing gestures, 'for there was to be many's the inquisition . . . on all that transpired in John Mah'ny's that night' (119–20); and boasting challenges, 'I'm a better laugher than your Costello' (127). The act of telling the story, which Mommo relays in a colourful blend of Gaelic, Gaelicized English, and pure pungent bellows of sound, evokes the vigorous Irish *seanchai* (that is, bard or story-teller) tradi-tion while also signalling an undertone of exhausted despair. In the spirit of the Ancient Mariner or more than that of Mouth in Beckett's *Not I* (1972), Mommo is driven to tell her tale repeatedly while refus-ing to relinquish the third-person pronoun to acknowledge it as her personal tragedy and the source of her abiding pain.

Bailegangaire is ultimately brought to a close when the embedded story is allowed to merge with the present tense of the enveloping action, resulting in a re-enactment of a central episode in the family's

Claire Gleitman

life. This occurs because of a change of heart that takes place in Mary, who devotes the first half of the play to begging Mommo to cease her relentless story-telling but later finds herself driven by a desire to see her 'finish it', so that they might 'move on to a place where, perhaps, we could make some kind of new start' (153). Thus, Mary shifts from irritated to eager audience and, later, to active participant, as she fills in bits and pieces of the saga, even adopting Mommo's verbal idiosyncrasies when Mommo's energy flags.

As Mary endeavours to bring Mommo to 'the last piece that [she] never tell[s]' (157), we learn that during their hours at the Bochtán pub Mommo's husband (prompted perhaps by the frustration engendered by his failure at the market) chose to challenge the village's most renowned laugher to a duel whose victor would be he who laughed last. To spur on the laughter, Mommo supplied the combatants with a topic that was sure to keep them 'laughing near forever', namely, 'Misfortunes' (158). Laying aside her own anxiety about the grandchildren waiting alone in the darkening evening, Mommo started the men on the subject of 'potatoes, the damnedable crop was in it that year', stimulating howls of laughter from the commiserating peasants (163). The men contributed their own supply of calamities, and Mommo brought them to higher pitches of hysteria as she catalogued the names of her four dead sons – some lost because of cruel tricks of fate and others because of her unbending severity. Gradually, the contest built to a crescendo as the company roared with laughter at the material circumstances that foster frustrated lives: the 'scabby an' small' spuds; the rotted hay; and the children who refuse to stay alive into adulthood:

> All of them present, their heads threwn back abandoned in festivities of guffaws: the wretched and neglected, dilapidated an' forlorn . . . , ridiculing an' defying of their lot on earth below – glintin's their defiance . . . an' rejection, inviting of what else might come or *care* to come! – driving bellows of refusal at the sky. . . . The nicest night ever. (164–5)

Though Mommo's litany of lost sons ostensibly links her with Maurya, of Synge's *Riders to the Sea* (1904), she and her company will have none of Maurya's stoic resignation; there is not a hint of the sensibility that allows Maurya to declare, after her last son dies, that 'no man at all can be living forever and we must be satisfied'.[11] Profoundly *dissatisfied*, Murphy's villagers hurled defiant 'bellows of refusal' upwards at an inscrutable and indifferent God.

42

But the contest came to a terrible end, since (as is well known) humans rarely get away with laughing at the gods. The Bochtán village hero – who was in fact a rabbit poacher – confessed that he too sold nothing at the market and died of a heart attack, apparently brought on by an excess of laughter. The bewildered villagers, robbed of their hero, collapsed in a brawl, but the strangers escaped and made their way home, where a misfortune of harrowing proportions awaited them. In the play's closing moments it is revealed that Tom – the tiniest grandson, Mary and Dolly's little brother, whom Mommo insists throughout the play is 'in Galway' – perished in a fire while Mommo was busy spurring her husband on in a laughing contest that granted fleeting, cathartic release as well as a momentary connection with her usually remote husband. The result was that she lost the only males remaining in her life: her grandson and then her husband days later, for reasons unspecified but we surmise because of guilt and grief. This, we discover, is what the tale has concealed all these years: that the constitutive moment in the family history was one of ghastly failure that killed a child and shattered the lives of its members.

Once Mary learns the full story of what delayed her grandparents on that fateful day, much about her familial history and her *own* history becomes clear to her. Recalling Tom's burning, she recalls her own, childish effort to help: 'Then Mary covered . . . the wounds . . . from the bag of flour in the corner. She'd be better now, and quicker now, at knowing what to do' (169). Murphy's ellipses hint at the emotional turmoil contained in this recognition; Mary chose to become a nurse in part to make amends for what she felt as a failure back then, although she was only a child of seven.

As both Mary and Mommo give shape to the past, Mommo seems at last to step into the present, calling Mary by her name for the very first time. In *Bailegangaire*'s closing moments, the sisters huddle on either side of their tempestuous grandmother in her large bed and Mary speaks the play's final lines:

> It's a strange old place . . . in whatever wisdom He has to have made it this way. But in whatever wisdom there is, in the year 1984, it was decided to give that – fambly . . . of strangers another chance, and a brand new baby to gladden their home. (170)

By concluding his play with an act of naming, as well as a reclaiming by Mary of the previously blighted 'home', Murphy recalls *Translations* and reverses its dramatic structure. Thus, he suggests the possibility that Ireland might at last move beyond its condition of namelessness and dislocation – a condition brought about by centuries of oppression, poverty and famine, as well as by its own inability to move forward into a radically altered present. The necessary avenue to what Mary envisions as 'another chance', it seems, is to relinquish one's status as a captive to a truncated 'history', and instead to tell the story of the past out of which the present grows not as glorifying mythopoesis but with a willingness to uncover the failures that Mommo previously veiled in consoling fiction. The result, indicated by Mary's appropriation of Mommo's story-telling diction and her incorporation of Dolly's baby into her vision of 'home', is an embrace of past and present that may allow the women to inhabit a future infused with hope. At the very least, the conclusion of the story offers the possibility that the future might be more than an endless recapitulation of the past, as formerly manifested by Mommo's unremitting, repetitive story-telling.

The difficulty Mommo has in completing her saga suggests the larger problem of accessing Irish history in all its troubled complexity, a problem that reverberates through Ireland's drama. What appears to arrest the attention of contemporary Irish dramatists is not merely the weight of their turbulent history, but the manner in which 'history' takes shape in such a way as to serve the ideological and psychological imperatives of those who remember it. Thus a Protestant Irishman in another play by Frank McGuinness, *Observe the Sons of Ulster Marching Towards the Somme*, after recounting a burlesqued version of the Easter Rising to an audience of approving Protestants, declares: 'To hell with the truth as long as it rhymes' (McGuinness 1986: 65). What matters is not the story's veracity but the degree to which it confirms what the teller already believes and wishes to go on believing. Although remembering everything may be a form of madness, as Hugh asserts, Mommo's brand of madness is the result of remembering selectively, if also obsessively; she is enthralled by a past at which she cannot stop staring and yet cannot fully face except through fragments of mythologized narrative. By remaining frozen in time in the moment preceding the catastrophe, incapable of articulating it or of moving beyond it, Mommo and her granddaughters crystallize in exaggerated form the condition that plagues their culture more broadly. Throughout *Bailegangaire* Mary and Dolly replay their old arguments regarding who betrayed whom more egregiously and whose obligation it is to make amends now. Caught in such circular squabbles, they avoid confronting the immediate and urgent issues, personal and economic, that are preventing them from moving on with their lives. In this regard, the sisters parallel the British and Irish captives in *Someone Who'll Watch Over Me*, who remain locked in their age-old quarrels while in the background a Third World that that they barely attempt to understand lurks as a potent, if invisible, force to be reckoned with – much like the Japanese in *Bailegangaire*, who are as unfathomable to Mary and Dolly as are the Arabs to McGuinness's hostages.

As the sisters squabble, Mommo goes on telling what she insists on transforming into a comforting bedtime story for children safe at home, rather than a story about children abandoned, driven away and killed because of her ferocity, which was itself engendered by the fierce, hard-scrabble conditions of Irish peasant life. Once Mommo is brought to revisit the past fully and truthfully, it becomes possible for Mary to see the present clearly and hence to imagine a different future – for herself, for her female relatives, and for a baby yet to be born. Thus Murphy imagines a way out of the impasse that he, Brian Friel and so many contemporary Irish dramatists stage, as they wrestle with the problem of how to remember the past and remember it fully, while also unloosing oneself from its ironclad grip.

Notes

1 The battle of the Boyne is one of the most notorious (or celebrated, depending on one's political position) events in Irish history, when the Protestant King William of Orange defeated the forces of Catholic James II at the River Boyne in what is now Northern Ireland. To Protestants, this is a day of celebration; to Catholics, it is precisely the opposite, as it ushered in centuries of British oppression. The Easter Rising began on 24 April 1916, when a group of roughly a thousand Irish men and women attempted to seize Dublin with the intention of reclaiming Ireland as an independent republic. For further reading, see William Irwin Thompson (1967). *The Imagination of an Insurrection*. New York: Harper & Row; and Declan Kiberd (1995). *Inventing Ireland: The Literature of the Modern Nation*. Cambridge, MA: Harvard University Press.

2 See, for example, Friel (1989). *Making History*. London: Faber and Faber; Murphy (1977). *Famine*. Dublin: Gallery Press; Devlin (1986). *Ourselves Alone*. London: Faber and Faber; Barry (1995). *The Steward of Christendom*. *Plays: 1*, ed. Fintan O'Toole. London: Methuen; and McGuinness (1986).

3 Walter Benjamin (1969). 'Theses on the Philosophy of History' in *Illuminations*, ed. Hannah Arendt. New York: Schocken, 257–8.

Claire Gleitman

4   See Marilynn J. Richtarik (1995). *Acting Between the Lines: The Field Day Theatre Company and Irish Cultural Politics, 1980–1984*. Oxford: Oxford University Press, for more information about Field Day as well as about the premiere of *Translations*.

5   See, for example, in addition to Connolly, Edna Longley (1994). *The Living Stream: Literature and Revisionism in Ireland*. Oxford: Bloodaxe. For responses to such charges, see Elizabeth Butler Cullingford's (1997) examination of the 'Stage Englishman' figure, 'Gender, Sexuality, and Englishness in Modern Irish Drama and Film' in Anthony Bradley and Maryann Gialanella Valiulis (eds.), *Gender and Sexuality in Modern Ireland*. Amherst: University of Massachusetts Press, 159–85; and Declan Kiberd (1995). 'Friel Translating' in *Inventing Ireland*, 614–23.

6   As J. M. Andrews has pointed out, the Royal Engineers were the best-educated branch of the British Army and would have known Latin from Gaelic. See J. M. Andrews and Kevin Barry (1983). '*Translations* and *A Paper Landscape*: Between Fiction and History', *Crane Bag* 7:2, 118–24.

7   Here and elsewhere, Friel has Hugh quote almost verbatim from *After Babel* by George Steiner, who argues that all communication is in essence an act of translation. Hugh articulates this idea most explicitly when he questions Maire's belief that learning English might enable her to 'interpret between privacies' (67). See Steiner (1975). *After Babel: Aspects of Language and Translation*. Oxford: Oxford University Press.

8   Tennessee Williams (1947). *A Streetcar Named Desire*. New York: New Directions, 179.

9   The term 'peasant play' refers to a tradition of Irish drama that is associated with the Abbey Theatre and that has become much reviled for the dogged realism and easy sentiment that is commonly associated with it. For a tongue-in-cheek consideration of the genre, see Brian Friel (1972). 'Plays Peasant and Unpeasant', *Times Literary Supplement*, 17 March, 305–6.

10 W. B. Yeats (1983). *The Collected Poems of W. B. Yeats*, ed. Richard J. Finneran. New York: Collier Books, 39.

11 J. M. Synge (1979). *Playboy of the Western World and Riders to the Sea*. London: Unwin, 93.

Primary reading

Delaney, Paul, ed. (2000). *Brian Friel in Conversation*. Ann Arbor, MI: University of Michigan Press.
Friel, Brian (1981). *Translations*. London: Faber and Faber.
McGuinness, Frank (1986). *Observe the Sons of Ulster Marching Towards the Somme*. London: Faber and Faber.
Murphy, Tom (1993). *Plays: Two, Bailegangaire*. London: Methuen.

Further reading

Agnew, Paddy (1980). 'Talking to Ourselves: Brian Friel Talks to Paddy Agnew', *Magill* (December), 59–61.

Connolly, Sean (1987). 'Dreaming History: Brian Friel's *Translations*', *Theatre Ireland* 13, 42–4.

Deane, Seamus (1985). *Celtic Revivals: Essays in Modern Irish Literature*. London: Faber and Faber.

Field Day Theatre Company (1986). *Ireland's Field Day*. Notre Dame: University of Notre Dame Press.

Grene, Nicholas (1999). *The Politics of Irish Drama: Plays in Context from Boucicault to Friel*. Cambridge: Cambridge University Press.

Harrington, John, and Mitchell, Elizabeth J. Mitchell, eds. (1999). *Politics and Performance in Contemporary Northern Ireland*. Amherst: University of Massachusetts Press.

Heaney, Seamus (1980). Review of *Translations* by Brian Friel, *Times Literary Supplement*, 24 October, 1199.

Jordan, Eamonn (2003). *Theatre Stuff: Critical Essays on Contemporary Irish Theatre*. Dublin: Carysfort Press.

Kearney, Richard, ed. (1985). *The Irish Mind: Exploring Intellectual Traditions*. Dublin: Wolfhound Press.

Macrae, David (1952). *The Americans at Home*. New York: Dutton.

McGuinness, Frank (1986). *Observe the Sons of Ulster Marching Towards the Somme*. London: Faber and Faber.

McGuinness, Frank (1992). *Someone Who'll Watch Over Me*. London: Faber and Faber.

Morash, Christopher (2004). *A History of Irish Theatre 1601–2000*. Cambridge: Cambridge University Press.

Murray, Christopher (1997). *Twentieth-Century Irish Drama: Mirror up to Nation*. Manchester: Manchester University Press.

Murray, Christopher (2000). *Brian Friel: Essays, Diaries, Interviews, 1964–1998*. London: Faber and Faber.

O'Toole, Fintan (1987). *The Politics of Magic: The Work and Times of Tom Murphy*. Dublin: Raven Arts Press.

Pilkington, Lionel (1990). 'Language and Politics in Brian Friel's *Translations*', *Irish University Review* 20, 282–98.

Richards, Shaun, ed. (2004). *The Cambridge Companion to Twentieth-Century Irish Drama*. Cambridge: Cambridge University Press.

Roche, Anthony (1995). *Contemporary Irish Drama: From Beckett to McGuinness*. New York: St Martin's Press.

Chapter 3

Black British Drama and the Politics of Identity

D. Keith Peacock

In this chapter I examine black British drama as a post-colonial phenomenon that, since the 1970s, has exhibited and explored the changing self-awareness and cultural status of Afro-Caribbean immigrants to Britain.[1] Black dramatists have gradually gained access to the white-dominated means of representation to offer a presence and a voice for those who, because of their race, ethnic origin and history, have been considered by the white majority and, indeed, often by themselves to be outside mainstream culture. In their plays they have contested modes of representation and, in Stuart Hall's words, as in 'other forms of visual representation of the Afro-Caribbean (and Asian) "blacks" of the diasporas of the West – the new post-colonial subjects [place] . . . the black subject at their centre, putting the issue of cultural identity in question' (Hall 1990: 222). Indeed, during the 1980s and 1990s black British drama was characterized by the interrogation of the politics of identity.

Until now the exploration of issues of cultural and individual identity in black British drama has primarily involved considerations of origin, migration, displacement, diaspora, arrival and otherness that have produced new narratives of identity, gender, sexuality and nationality. In the 1990s Stuart Hall, amongst others, introduced the concept of cultural hybridity, which privileged culture above race in the consideration of the diasporic experience. According to Hall, cultural identities are always hybrid; 'come from somewhere, have histories. But, like everything which is historical, they undergo constant transformation' (1990: 225). Hybridization – the mixing of cultural identities to create not black-British (multicultural) but an altogether more complex identity – has been most apparent in third-generation, teenage Afro-Caribbeans, who are represented in some of the plays discussed in this chapter. Interestingly, elements of this group have, often to their parents' horror, established an urban presence by developing a hybrid subculture influenced by the gang and gun cultures of Jamaica and Afro-American urban societies portrayed by rap singers. Externally, this identity is signified by baseball caps, hoods, baggy trousers and Adidas trainers and by a Jamaican argot or rap talk. Homi K. bhabha, however, draws attention to Paul Gilroy's reference to the positive, hybrid features of contemporary black music, 'its dialogic, performative "community" . . . – rap, dub, scratching – as a way of constituting an open sense of black collectivity in the shifting, changing beat of the present' (Bhabha 1994: 178). The subculture associated with rap music can nevertheless be seen by some people as a threat; for instance, Joseph Harker (2002) describes how 'Rap culture has hijacked our identity' and maintains that 'we must reclaim from the street thugs what it means to be black.'

Central to the black British drama of the 1970s, 1980s and 1990s was the experience and effect on black cultural identity of the post-Second World War West Indian diaspora, neatly illustrated by Nikos Papastergiadis:

> 'I am here, because you were there!' declared a black man in response to racist assaults on his right to stay in Britain. . . . Neither the memories nor the abuse have forced him to abandon the hope of making a new community for himself and the others around him. But how to build a new community when the ground is foreign? What will hold 'the people' together when their needs and dreams are always in the making? (Papastergiadis 2000: 196)

The West Indian diaspora has been of concern even for second-generation black British dramatists. Reference to origin and migration is fundamental, for example, in Winsome Pinnock's (b. London 1961) *A Hero's Welcome* (Royal Court Theatre Upstairs, 1989). The play is set in Jamaica, where the characters feel trapped and see immigration to England as a means of individual betterment. The reality of immigration is revealed through the character of Len, who lived in England during the Second World War, and the play interrogates the immigrant's diasporic sense of self, their displacement and otherness.

On his return to Jamaica after the war Len was welcomed as a war hero. He is happy to accept the personal status and relates how, as a British soldier, he was wounded in the leg by a German soldier whom he then shot. He attempts to make a life on the island by educating himself from books. The majority of the island inhabitants are poor and feel trapped; some, including Len's attractive wife, Minda, her friends, Sis and Ishbel, and her young lover, Stanley, dream of escape, of breaking the boundaries. 'Some a these people think that this island is the centre of the universe,' Minda tells Stanley. 'Imagine. They don't think that there's anything beyond that horizon. I want more than that. Stanley. Much more' (Pinnock 1993: 34). Minda and Stanley are trapped by poverty, Sis by family, and Ishbel by pregnancy.

Escape is promised by recruitment posters bearing the invitation 'Come find a Job in England' and 'The Motherland needs You' (44) that appear around the island. Stanley is inspired to find the money for the fare and to take Minda with him to the fantasyland of 'cars as long as rivers, houses that touch the sky. And the people are so rich that gold and silver falls out of their pockets as they walk along the streets an' they don't even bother to run back an' pick it up' (45). When Minda asks Len to take her to England he refuses and she decides to escape with Stanley. Sis, who left school early to help support herself and her mother, dreams of bettering herself but does not want to leave the island to do it. Len provides her with books to educate herself so that she can help improve the island 'an' build a better world' (36). However, the trap is released for her when her mother is given a live-in job by a businessman's widow, and she realizes that the only way she can improve the situation at home is to go abroad to be educated. Ishbel would also like to leave the island but is left pregnant by Stanley and sent away to have the baby at her aunt's in another part of the island.

Pinnock's play explores the narratives of arrival of Afro-Caribbean immigrants in Britain in 1948. Len reveals that the story of his war-time experience is a fiction and admits that 'I never involved in the war you know. I mean, I never fought. The nearest I got to a gun was pushing bullets through a machine factory in Liverpool' (54). His 'war-wound' limp was caused by a piece of machinery falling on his foot. He also demolishes the immigrant's dream of acceptance and a better life by describing how, travelling to England, he was seasick and was met by a grey-blue sky. Worst of all, in the factory, the owner did not want to give the black workers equal pay, the white workers would not work alongside them, and even went on strike to get rid of them.

In *Leave Taking* (Liverpool Playhouse Studio, 1987) Pinnock had already explored the immigrant's construction of a new identity from a female point of view, placing her characters in an alien environment to expose issues relating to displacement, diaspora, arrival and otherness. The play focuses on four female characters, with one male character acting as a link between them. The psychological effects of diaspora and arrival are revealed through the older, female, first-generation immigrants, Enid and Mai, and the male Broderick, all of whom measure their present existence in England against their past lives of poverty in Jamaica. They reveal the problems experienced by immigrants, who are between cultures, in coming to terms with and finding an identity in their new society. Although he retains an echo of his origin in his Jamaican English, Broderick has attempted to prove his Britishness by always standing up for the British national anthem. Despite this, he has not been accepted into British society and is threatened with deportation as an alien. Enid wanted to assimilate by what she perceives to be 'fitting in' and 'sticking to the rules' and has abandoned Jamaican English, although, out of duty, she grudgingly retains economic contact with her mother. An unseen character, Gullyman, also tried to assimilate by adopting an external signifier of Britishness and speaking Standard English. To Broderick's disgust he also 'forgot everybody, all him friends, him people back home, just cut everybody off' (Pinnock 1989: 153). At first Gullyman was financially successful, but he lost his money and, with no community to support him, is now living on the streets as a beggar. Mai is an Obeah woman who makes her living, like Ram, as a spiritual counsellor to other immigrants, including Enid, who, while she has tried to assimilate, feels the need for support from a familiar belief system. Mai maintains her Jamaican English but has adapted her rituals to fit into a British context. When asked by Enid to help with her relationship to her daughters, Mai replies 'If this was back home I woulda' say bring me two a' you best fowl as a sorta sacrifice. Over here I don't think the blood a' two meagre chickens going to make you better' (175). As part of her treatment, Mai offers Enid medicine and tells her to make the sign of the cross on her forehead when she takes it. As Gabrielle Griffin points out, 'the mixture of medicine and religious act Mai prescribes presents a hybridized form of intervention expressive of the protagonist's *entre-deux* condition' (Griffin 2003: 41). As part of her ritual Mai has also adapted traditional props to fit her new environment. At the commencement of the consultation she dons a 'large Afro wig', which is associated with the American and European Black Pride movement of the 1960s rather than with the traditional West Indian Obeah ritual. Like the barrister's wig, this serves to transform her from her everyday self and signals the beginning of the ritual. Mai no longer uses the ritual of immersion in water because her landlady complains that she does not like strangers using her bath. In fact, Mai's methodology, as she teaches Del, is primarily psychological and comes from observation rather than ritual: 'You see everything you need to know in their eyes' (186). Outside the ritual, Mai also keeps chickens in the backyard to remind her of life in Jamaica. Her accommodation with British culture is not an abandonment of her past but a useful adjunct that not only helps first-generation immigrants but provides employment for the second generation.

Otherness is represented by Enid's two daughters, Del and Viv, who were born in England. Enid has tried to mould them according to her vision of assimilation into British society. The process has involved dislocating them from the colonial culture that she abandoned to come to England and has interfered with their realization of identity in a racist society. Through Del and Viv's dilemma, Pinnock implies that there is a fundamental relationship between race and culture. Although they have been brought up in England, being black debars them from full acceptance as English and, despite never having been to Jamaica, both girls feel estranged from English society. Viv has responded to her mother's vision of betterment and assimilation by means of academic achievement, though this has proved more pertinent to the West Indies than to 1980s Britain. However, the sense of otherness and estrangement expressed in Viv's 'I need another language to express myself. (*Slight pause.*) Swahili perhaps' (172) inspires in her a desire to visit Jamaica. Enid's claim that her daughters' upbringing has not equipped them for the life of poverty in Jamaica from which she fled is used to discourage them from discovering their cultural roots. Dissatisfied with the identity imposed on her by her mother, Viv undertakes a minor rebellion by missing an examination, but has nowhere to turn to for cultural affirmation of her identity. Pinnock does not resolve her dilemma and, because of her mother's unwillingness to allow her to learn about her racial and cultural roots, Viv's search must continue.

Del rebels against her mother's plans for her by losing herself in partying. Ironically, she discovers a sense of self-worth and purpose in, unintentionally, becoming pregnant outside marriage, something that Enid left the West Indies to avoid. 'Now, for once in my life I can't run away. For the sake a' my kid I got to stand and face up to who I am. For once in my life I feel like I got a future' (189), she tells Enid. Del, like her mother, turns to Mai for support. Mai recognizes in Del an affinity with Jamaican culture and trains her to succeed herself as an Obeah woman. Mai's culturally hybrid Obeah allows Del access to its rituals and contributes to the sense of self that permits her reconciliation with her mother. At the end of the play Del accuses her mother of making her and Viv weak by suppressing her 'real self', which she left 'behind somewhere in the past', leaving only an 'empty shell' (189). The play's epigraph might be 'only connect', for now that Del has been reconnected with her past she has become strong and is able to offer her mother the comfort and support that she and her sister were denied.

The play suggests that assimilation into the new culture is not the answer for either first- or second-generation immigrants. Pinnock appears to be agreeing with the assertion of the earlier black British dramatist Mustapha Matura that, in the creation of a black British identity, 'it's more important where we're coming from' (Anon. 1981: 10) than where we are. Emotional survival by finding a meaning in life, involves, as in Mai's case, not the rejection of one's heritage but its adaptation to the new environment.

The past and history are discussed in relation to individual identity in Roy Williams's (b. London 1968) *The Gift* (Birmingham Repertory Theatre, 2000) and Kwame Kwei-Armah's (previously Ian Roberts; b. Hillingdon 1967) *Fix Up* (National Theatre, 2004), in the former's *Little Sweet Thing* (New Wolsey Theatre, Ipswich, 2005), and the latter's *Elmina's Kitchen* (Royal National Theatre, 2003, and Garrick Theatre, London, 2005), where the focus is on third-generation teenagers and their place within a hybrid urban culture. The plays' exploration of the effect on individual young people of the emergence of a nihilistic black-British subculture of violence, which has also been adopted by young urban whites, reflects a significant contemporary concern. Among the findings of a report commissioned by the Home Office on *Shooting, Gangs and Violent Incidents in Manchester: Developing a Crime Reduction Strategy* in 2002 were that 'victims of gun violence in South Manchester are mainly young, black or mixed race males, who themselves have criminal records'; that 'about sixty per cent of shootings are thought to be gang related'; and that 'gang-related criminal behaviour includes drug-related offences, but only as one element of a patchwork of violent and non-violent crime'. Perhaps most disturbingly, the report also concluded that 'gang membership is not just about criminality, for some young males it incorporates a credible lifestyle choice' (Bullock and Tilley 2002: iv). In a telling article in *Black Britain*, Deborah Gabriel quotes the opinion of a black criminologist, Martin Glynn, that 'a bad man in the community can develop a massive reputation on the basis of his criminal activities, increasing the motivation to commit crime' (Gabriel 2005). Crime is therefore, in part, seen to be related to identity. Keno Ogbo, project coordinator of the 'Inside Out' project funded by the Home Office, claims that crime in black communities is prevalent 'where there are [*sic*] a lack of role models in the community' (Gabriel 2005). This is compounded by poverty, economic deprivation, poor housing and the failure of the education system. Success is measured by teenagers in material terms – 'the guy that they look up to has the car and the girls, we know he's doing this and that but he's our man and he understands where we're coming from' (Gabriel 2005). Gun crime was thought to be so prevalent amongst black youths that, after her 22-year-old son, Damian Cope, was shot and killed in July 2002 his mother, Lucy, set up the nationwide organization 'Mothers Against Guns'. Its aim was to lobby politicians to introduce stiffer penalties for those convicted of gun-related crime.

Kwame Kwei-Armah's *Elmina's Kitchen* explores the source of identity, financial attraction and physical threat to young black men of the urban drug and gun culture described above. The central character, Deli (Delroy), who owns the café, Elmina's Kitchen, attempts but fails to protect his son from involvement in crime. While it is set in contemporary London, the play also refers to immigration, displacement and diaspora. The play's specific cultural location in relation to past and present is established precisely at its opening by means of a rich variety of visual and aural semiotics described in the stage directions. These signifiers move from origins to hybridity. The first appears in the prologue, performed in a spotlight on the dark stage and therefore outside the play's contemporary reality. A costumed African plays a gurkel, 'a one string African guitar famed for possessing the power to draw out spirits' (Kwei-Armah 2003: 3). The character also appears, detached from the action, at points later in the play. The costumed African represents the past and, in flicking handfuls of powder around the playing area, may be exorcizing the evil spirits of the present and siting the performance as a ritual that will draw attention to, and perhaps contribute to, the eradication of present evils. A further association of past and present follows in the form of a musical accompaniment that combines traditional African music and American blues in a slow lament. When the lights go up, a realistic contemporary set represents the West Indian food take-away, Elmina's Kitchen, on Hackney's 'Murder Mile'. The take-way is 'one notch above tacky' (3) and represents an earlier black West Indian culture rather than a contemporary English one. It is dominated by a huge picture of Deli's late West Indian mother, Elmina. Next to the picture is a poster inscribed with values from that previous culture, ranging from 'Life is costly, care for it' to 'Life is an opportunity, benefit from it' and 'Life is a promise, fulfil it'(3). Apparently, these values are ignored by the black community in contemporary England, for there is another sign which reads, 'NO DRUGS ARE PERMITTED ON THESE PREMISES, RESPECT' (3). As the play illustrates, 'respect' conveys to the young something different from respect for others or for social rules. The final aural signifier, before the action commences, is that of the song, *Sufferer*, played on the television by the Jamaican 'ragga' singer 'Bounty Killer', whose lyrics condemn Kingston's criminal gunmen. Thus, even before its action begins, the play's cultural context and conflicts are powerfully established.

The conflict within the play is not interracial but intracultural. There are no white characters, and reference is repeatedly made from the opening of the play to *British* blacks and to *Jamaican* 'Yardies' who are taking over the crime in the community. When Deli's father, Clifton, blames whites for all the problems faced by blacks he is sharply rebuked by his son. The Jamaican, Trinidadian and Grenadian accents of a number of the play's characters signify the diaspora. This is particularly apparent in Digger's accent, which swings at will from 'his native Grenadian to hard-core Jamaican to authentic black London' (4). In this community black youths are involved in protection rackets and drug selling. The violence associated with the latter is, however, extended and intensified with the arrival of the Yardies. 'Respect', as understood by Deli's 19-year-old son, Ashley, means neither moral nor social respect but fear of violence. He asks his father, who has avoided a fight during a disagreement with a local Chinese shopkeeper, 'How am I supposed to walk the street an look my bredren in the eye when mans all grip up my dad by his throat and you didn't deal wid it?' (10). Ashley claims that Deli's brother, Dougie, who is about to be released from prison, would not be so passive. However, when Dougie is released, another criminal shoots him. Ashley believes that being a gangster will gain him respect and that his possession of a BMW and a gun will provide him with a public identity. Using Standard English, which points to the difference between his authentic self and his adopted identity, Ashley rejects both education and a job delivering take-away food for his father. 'College does not fit into the plan I have for my life. You want to keep selling your little plantain burgers, good luck to you, may you always be happy. Me, I'm a man' (63). Despite himself being a 'bad man', Deli retorts that 'the true sign of intelligence is how man deals with the problems of his environment' (64) and warns Ashley that 'where you are trying to head, it's a dead ting, a dark place, it don't go nowhere' (65).

Digger is not prepared to employ Ashley as a gangster and explains that being a bad man entails more than driving around in a BMW:

> And you wanna be a man? Go back to school, youth, and learn. You can't just walk into dis bad man t'ing, you gotta learn the whole science of it. You step into that arena and you better be able to dance wid death til it make you dizzy. You need to have thought about, have play wid and have learnt all of the possible terrible and tortuous ways that death could arrive. And then ask yourself are you ready to do that and more to someone that you know. (30)

The play suggests that, although Hackney has its home-grown black 'bad men', they are not as dangerous as the immigrant Jamaican Yardies who have taken violence to another, more extreme level as a means of dominating local crime. Digger initially differentiates himself from the Yardies, one of whom, Rodent, he describes as 'the Yardie bwoy that rape all them people dem pickney when he was collecting. Motherfucker gave the trade a bad name' (9). By the end of the play, however, Digger is working for the Yardies, collecting protection money even from Deli, whom he has previously protected. Digger threatens to kill Deli, who, in order to save his son from prosecution for setting fire to a business whose owner would not pay protection money, has informed on him. Digger challenges Ashley to shoot his father, saying that killing an informer will enhance his reputation and identity as a bad man. However, when it appears that Ashley is about to do so, Digger realizes that the boy is beyond redemption and shoots him dead. As Digger's final line suggests, the killing will continue – 'Yes. Ah so dis war run' (94).

Kwei-Armah depicts a community in which violence is out of control because its young men have no positive aspirations and have not been taught social responsibility. Nikos Papastergiadis's question of 'how to build a new community when the ground is foreign? What will hold "the people" together when their needs and dreams are always in the making?' has particular poignancy here (Papastergiadis 2000: 196). But Tony Thompson, in the *Observer* (2003), quotes Lyndon Gibson of the urban National Youth Project: 'It's no longer a black or white issue. These guns are in the hands of the whole community.' Assistant chief constable Nick Tofiluk of the West Midlands Police agrees that 'The use of firearms is not an Afro-Caribbean issue alone. White and Asian networks exist that possess firearms and are involved in the supply of illicit drugs both to the Afro-Caribbean networks and in competition with existing networks' (ibid.). This concern is apparent in Roy Williams's *Little Sweet Thing*, in which the questions of origin, diaspora, arrival and otherness referred to in *Elmina's Kitchen* are irrelevant. The question of identity in a contemporary hybrid English urban culture, argues Williams, is now one for both black and white teenagers.

The environment of the play is one of low aspiration and incipient violence. It begins with the release from prison of a gangster, Kev, who has decided to reform but, because he left school without any qualifications, is only able to find work as a shelf-filler in an Indian supermarket. His friend, the mixed-race Jamal, has stepped into his shoes as the local 'bad man', works for the local gangster, and drives around in a flashy car. A white friend, Ryan, whom he has protected since childhood and who now works for Jamal, tries to raise his status by cheating Jamal and becoming his superior. Jamal is ordered to kill him but is unable to do so. Nevertheless, in retaliation for the threatened assassination, Ryan kills Jamal and, accidentally, Kev's sister, Tash. Violence breeds violence and this act provokes Kev in turn to kill Ryan.

What could have been a dark study of gang warfare is, however, lightened by the vital, witty and intelligent teenage girl, Tash, who, as her teacher tells her, has everything to live for. Significantly, the audience is never provided with the details of Jamal's or Kev's criminal activities, which, presumably, involve drug dealing. The aim appears to be, not to romanticize the gangster lifestyle, but to present the inevitable consequences for black and white urban teenagers for whom crime appears to offer an identity.

The play's culture is not Afro-Caribbean but hybrid. There are no West Indian names such as the Hope, Gravel and Lester of Williams's *Starstruck* (1998) or the Delroy and Clifton of Kwei-Armah's *Elmina's Kitchen*. Of the characters' names in *Little Sweet Thing* only one, Jamal, indicates a racial background other than English. Natasha, Zoe, Miss Jules, Kev, Ryan and Angela are simply names favoured by a contemporary urban English community.

The negative features of this hybrid English culture, of which the teenagers are a part, are described by the 25-year-old teacher, Miss Jules, who, herself, chose to reject the black urban subculture.

> I don't understand how you kids live. How you refuse to ask yourself hard questions about your own lives, what you want from them, your responsibilities. Respect for others, have manners, self-control. No, you're all being force-fed some retarded subculture from good old US of A. (Williams 2005: 73)

This nihilistic black subculture, modelled on that of the USA, offers the attractions of money and power and appears to command respect, but also promotes black-on-black murder. This is conveyed by a hooded teenager who appears at the beginning of the play and challenges Kev, who has just been released from prison, to play basketball. The Hood later appears to Tash, whom he threatens to rape if she does not give him her mobile phone. He leaves with the warning 'tell yer brother, I'm waiting' (53). He later reappears to Tash and the white girl, Zoe, who wants to become a sexy 'bad girl'. The Hood represents the inevitability of the black teenagers' surrender to the subculture of sex, drugs, violence and crime. He appears finally to Kev at the end of the play when Ryan's involvement in crime and his killing of Kev's sister, Tash, appear to leave Kev with no choice but to strangle Ryan. When Ryan is dead the Hood enters and throws Kev the basketball, indicating that he has now surrendered to the inevitable because he subscribed to the myth that the true mark of a black teenager was his worth, not in education or aspiration, but on the street.

In both plays positive cultural values and opportunities are represented by an adult: in *Elmina's Kitchen* by the reformed Afro-Caribbean father, Deli, and in *Little Sweet Thing* by a surrogate mother in the form of the black female teacher. The latter introduces the question of identity early in the play when she tells the teenage schoolchildren in detention to write an essay on 'Who you are, what do you want' (9). The feisty black 15-year-old, Tash, appears to be confident in her inauthentic identity of 'bad girl' who gains 'respect' by frightening other girls. Secretly she wants to be like her white friend, Zoe. Although Zoe is a boring swot who acts her age and likes the boy band Westlife, her identity is at least authentic. Both, however, are concerned with what others will think of them and while Tash wants to be like her, Zoe is tired of Tash's taunts and sets out to be a stereotypical bad girl who sleeps with any man she fancies.

The play suggests that the problems facing its urban teenagers are ones not of racial discrimination but of identity and aspiration. The teenagers have a number of choices of identity. They can work to realize their potential talents, contribute to society, and maintain good relationships with others. On the other hand, they can submit to low aspiration by staying in their community, taking a dead-end job such as shelf-filling, or adopt the criminal, violent and exploitative features of the black urban subculture which appear superficially attractive and easily attainable. The consequences of these choices are made clear at the close of the play. Tash, who is evidently intelligent and apparently self-confident, identifies herself externally with black urban subculture, although internally she wants to use her intelligence and be a free spirit. However, her environment in the form of that violent subculture ultimately claims her life. Zoe, the white girl, abandons her authentic identity to become 'a ho' to black gangsters. The white teenager, Ryan, dies having tried to be a 'bad bwoi' and in so doing killed Jamal and Tash. Kev fails to shake off his gangster past and ends up a murderer. Only by fleeing their environment do the mixed-race Angela and the white boy Nathan establish an individual identity, as does the teacher, Miss Jules. Nathan, if he can achieve self-discipline, will possibly become a professional footballer, and Angela will go to Manchester University. The ending of the play with Ryan's onstage murder by Kev is shocking, violent and nihilistic, as is the gangster culture, and reveals how difficult it is for teenagers, black or white, to escape moral, spiritual or mortal destruction by such an environment.

While, in *Little Sweet Thing*, as in many of his plays, Roy Williams ignores the diaspora and focuses on the definition of individual identity by young people, both black and white, debbie tucker green in her plays does not foreground issues of race, individual or cultural identity. Instead, she offers, as a black British woman, a perspective on the emotional lives and psychology of her characters. She refuses to speak of her own ancestry, although her family appear to have come from Jamaica, and is unwilling to reveal her date and place of birth, considering that her origins are irrelevant to an understanding of her work. Nevertheless, tucker green emphasizes that 'I'm a black woman . . . I write black characters. That is part of my landscape' (Gardner, 2005). As C. L. R. James suggests, a black person who has grown up in a western society but does not feel completely a part of it 'will give a new vision, a deeper and stronger insight into both western civilization and white people in it' (Mercer 1994: 1). Indeed, tucker green herself recognizes that her desire and ability to offer a different perspective are consequent on her ethnic origin and cultural location:

> Obviously I'm a black woman, so I know the conversations I've had with my friends. With Zimbabwe, we were like 'You know what, if it was them, they'd makes sure it was on the news, they would sure it was flagged up 24/7 if it was white people'. So that's from my standpoint, but obviously my standpoint is different to somebody else's standpoint, maybe a white person's standpoint. (McLaughlin 2005)

A black woman's perspective on international concerns appears in *Trade* (Swan Theatre, Stratford-upon-Avon, 2005), which employs a collage of voices, performed by three black actresses, to explore female sex tourism from the points of view of the First and Third Worlds. The play is not simply about exploitation and financial transactions but about women's perceptions of themselves and other women in the context of economics. In *Stoning Mary* (Royal Court, 2005) tucker green employs racial difference not to make a point about identity or racism, but for its theatrical and political impact on a white British audience. The play combines three stories associated with various parts of Africa: a Wife and Husband argue over an Aids prescription that can save only one of their lives; a child soldier's parents fight over the memory of their son and dread his return; a woman visits her younger sister, who is to be stoned to death for murder. To force the audience to reflect on its attitude to Aids, civil war and the brutal punishment of women in sub-Saharan Africa, the black African characters are portrayed by white actors. The aim is to create a Brechtian *Verfremdungseffekt* (alienation effect) through which the audience experience the characters and their concerns from a viewpoint other than that prescribed by the British media. The intention is not to distance the audience but, by altering their perspective and thereby forcing them to read the situations portrayed in terms of their own environment, to generate empathy. The alienation effect is enhanced theatrically by giving a number of characters alter egos, which are performed simultaneously and describe the characters' thoughts.

Wife Ego: Think
Wife: you look better'n I do

Wife Ego:	say
Wife:	'Y'lookin better'n –'
Wife Ego:	lies
Husband:	'No I don't.' (tucker green 2005: 8)

As the above suggests, unlike most plays written by black British male dramatists, the form of tucker green's plays is not realism. Also, identity is not portrayed as cultural, with its potential for change, but generic – Mother, Father, Wife, Husband, Son and Daughter – although there are occasionally social roles such as Corrections Officer in *Stoning Mary*, and the Hoteliers and an American Tourist in *Trade*. Only in tucker green's first play, *Dirty Butterfly* (Soho Theatre, 2003) are the characters given names – Amelia, Jason and Jo – to emphasize that they are portraying personal, rather than socially or culturally predicated responses. Amelia and Jason are black and Jo is white. Race is, however, irrelevant to the concerns of the play, which are power, guilt and voyeurism. Of more importance is the revelation of individual psychology conveyed by the characters' reaction to each other and, on Jo's part, also towards her abusive male partner whom we never see. This play, like those previously discussed, refers to identity, but a personal rather than cultural identity. Both Amelia's and Jason's responses to Jo's abuse reveal something about themselves.

tucker green makes the audience complicit in the action of the play by requiring the performance to be in the round, and conveying immediacy by not establishing a realistic location for the first scene. The characters address each other in a rhythmically poetic rather than literal manner and each member of the audience must construct his or her own narrative. tucker green does not believe in the concept of a 'grand narrative'. Speaking of *Stoning Mary*, she says 'younger people might feel differently about the play to older people, black different to white, Asian different to black' (2005). The poetic, rhythmic speech which characterizes tucker green's plays conveys subjective responses to situations and events and sometimes, as in *Born Bad* (Hampstead Theatre, 2003), introduces a variety of responses and perceptions of a single experience. This is not, therefore, the materially verifiable social reality of most black British drama but one stimulated by the dramatist and constructed subjectively by each member of the audience. The style, as tucker green admits, owes much to Ntozake Shange's theatrical choreopoem, *For Colored Girls Who Have Considered Suicide When the Rainbow is Enuf* (Berkeley, California, 1974) and Caryl

Churchill's *Far Away* (Royal Court Theatre Upstairs, 2000). In addition it can be seen in Sarah Kane's *Crave* (Traverse Theatre, 1998), in which characters A, B and C speak independently and do not interact, in Harold Pinter's *Landscape* and *Silence* (Aldwych, 1969), and in Samuel Beckett's *Play*.

The structure of *Dirty Butterfly* also demands that the actors themselves shape their own narrative in the first scene, for 'throughout this section options can be taken regarding who is talking to who and when, with varying implications for the characters. The form of the piece has been left open for these choices to be made' (tucker green 2003: 2). A possible overall narrative for this scene appears to be that Amelia and Jason live together. Next door Jo is being physically abused each night by her male partner and is so frightened of waking him and incurring his displeasure that she dare not get out of bed to go to the toilet. She is, however, complicit in his abuse in that she will not leave her partner and blames herself for the beatings. Jason lies in bed and uses a glass to listen to the abuse through the wall. He finds it sexually arousing and masturbates. He too, therefore, is complicit for his own purposes, in that he will not try to stop the abuse: 'maybe I coulda phoned like I should, but I forgot I didn't have you number. And maybe I regret I never called round like I could but I forgot I don't even know you' (34). Amelia sleeps downstairs on the sofa so that she does not hear the abuse and claims that '*we* don't need to know' (24). There is no binary opposition between the characters but instead a poetic interweaving of their emotional lives. Each morning Jo awakes with a feeling of butterflies in her stomach, thinking that this will be the last day of her life. The butterflies are 'gone ballistic', 'gone wrong' (4), having been made dirty by her sexual and physical abuse.

As in *Top Girls* Caryl Churchill moves from the surrealism of the first act into the realism of the second and third, so in *Dirty Butterfly* the poetic structure of the main section of the play is replaced by the shocking realism of the epilogue. Here Amelia cannot avoid Jo's predicament and is literally brought face to face with its nature when she is obliged to wipe up Jo's blood, the result of sexual abuse, from the floor of the café, which is 'extremely shiny, clinically clean' (38), before the arrival of her employers. The play ends with the impression that nothing will change and the abuse will go on.

The black drama discussed above has progressed from 'an awareness of the black experience as a *Diaspora* experience' (Hall 1992: 258), and illustration of its effects, to the exploration of cultural and identity politics and the strategies that black West Indian immigrants and their children have employed to assert their presence and define their identity in what proved to be a hostile and racist culture. This question of identity in English society during the 1970s and 1980s cannot be confined to the black community, as Kobena Mercer has suggested, and was just as pertinent to the white English majority. Immigration, devolution, and post-imperial crisis have all changed the face of Britain, and currently questions of 'race', nation and ethnicity have brought us to the point where 'the possibility and necessity of creating a new culture – that is, new identities – is slowly being recognized as *the* democratic task of our time' (Gramsci 1971: 276; Mercer 1994: 3). In the drama written by second-generation dramatists since the end of the twentieth century, the focus has shifted to the exploration of the politics of identity in the here and now, whose starting point is not the West Indies, but London, and sometimes encompasses white characters. It is a recognition, as Hall suggests, that cultural identities are hybrid and 'undergo constant transformation' (1990: 225). At the beginning of the new millennium, in the work of debbie tucker green, there is also a hybrid approach that does not privilege racial difference but explores, from a black woman's perspective, gender, social and domestic relationships. It is still too early to judge whether tucker green's work represents a wider cultural hybridity in which identity politics, considerations of origin, migration, displacement, diaspora, arrival and otherness will no longer be foregrounded, and the designation '*black* British drama' will become redundant.

Notes

1 This chapter does not extend to British Asian drama. See, for example: Bhatti, Gurpreet Kaur (2004). *Behzti*. London: Oberon; Gupta, Tanika (1997). *Skeleton*. London: Faber and Faber; Khan-Din, Ayub (1997). *East is East*. London: Nick Hern. See also: George, Kadija, ed. (1993). *Black and Asian Women Writers*. London: Aurora Press; Godiwala, Dimple, ed. (2006). *Alternatives Within the Mainstream: British Black and Asian Theatres*. Cambridge: Cambridge Scholars Press; Griffin, Gabriele (2003). *Contemporary Black and Asian Women Playwrights in Britain*. Cambridge: Cambridge University Press; Harvie, Jen (2005). *Staging the UK*. Manchester: Manchester University Press; Verma, Jatinder (1996). 'Towards a Black Aesthetic' in A. Ruth Tompsett (ed.), *Black Theatre in Britain* (*Performing Arts International* 1:ii, Amsterdam: Harwood Academic, 9–21.

Primary reading

Beckett, Samuel (1968). *Play* in *Play and Two Short Pieces for Radio*. London: Faber and Faber.

Kwei-Armah, Kwame (2003). *Elmina's Kitchen*. London: Methuen.

Pinnock, Winsome (1989). *Leave Taking* in Kate Harwood (ed.), *First Run*. London: Nick Hern, 139–89.

Pinnock, Winsome (1993). *A Hero's Welcome* in Kadija George (ed.), *Six Plays by Black and Asian Women Writers*. London: Aurora Metro Press, 21–55.

Pinter, Harold (1997). *Landscape* and *Silence* in *Plays Three*. London: Faber and Faber, 165–88, 189–209.

Shange, Ntozake (1992). *For Colored Girls Who Have Considered Suicide When the Rainbow is Enuf* in *Plays One*. London: Methuen, 1–64.

tucker green, debbie (2003). *Dirty Butterfly*. London: Nick Hern.

tucker green, debbie (2005). *Stoning Mary*. London: Nick Hern.

Williams, Roy (2005). *Little Sweet Thing*. London: Methuen.

Further reading

Anon. (1981). 'Finding a Name'. *Platform* 3.

Bhabha, Homi K. (1994). *The Location of Culture*. London: Routledge.

Bhabha, Homi K. (1996). 'Culture's In-Between' in Stuart Hall and Paul du Gay (eds.), *Questions of Cultural Identity*. London: Sage, 53–60.

Bullock, Karen, and Tilley, Nick (2002). *Shootings, Gangs and Violent Incidents in Mancester: Developing a Crime Reduction Strategy*. London: Home Office.

Chrisman, Laura, and Williams, Patrick. eds. (1994). *Colonial Discourse and Post-Colonial Theory*. New York: University of Columbia.

Gabriel, Deborah (2005). 'Black Men and Crime: Understanding the Issues and Finding Solutions', *Black Britain*, www.blackbritain.co.uk/feature/details.aspx?i=6&c=Crime&h=From+2005%3a+Black+men+and+crime%3a+understanding+the+issues+and+finding+solutions.

Gardner, Lyn (2005). 'I Was Messing About', *Guardian Unlimited*, 30 March, http://arts.guardian.co.uk/critic/feature/0,,1448031,00.html.

Gilroy, Paul (1987). *There Ain't No Black in the Union Jack*. London: Unwin Hyman.

Gilroy, Paul (1993a). *Small Acts*. London and New York: Serpent's Tail.

Gilroy, Paul (1993b). *The Black Atlantic: Modernity and Double Consciousness*. London: Verso.

Gilroy, Paul (2000). *Against Race: Imagining Political Culture Beyond the Colour Line*. Cambridge, MA: Belknap Press.

Gilroy, Paul (2004). *After Empire: Melancholia or Convivial Culture*. London: Routledge.

Gramsci, Antonio (1971 [1930]). *Selections from the Prison Notebooks*. London: Lawrence and Wishart.

Griffin, Gabriele (2003). *Contemporary Black and Asian Women Playwrights in Britain*. Cambridge: Cambridge University Press.

Hall, Stuart (1990). 'Cultural Identity and Diaspora' in Jonathan Rutherford (ed.), *Identity: Community Culture, Difference*. London: Lawrence and Wishart, 222–37.

Hall, Stuart (1992). 'New Ethnicities' in James Donald and Ali Rattansi (eds.), *'Race', Culture and Difference*. London: Sage, 252–9.

Harker, Joseph (2002). 'Rap Culture has Hijacked Our Identity', *Guardian Unlimited*, 6 March, http://education.guardain.co.uk/schools/story/0,662616,00.html.

McLaughlin, Emily (2005). Interview with debbie tucker green in Royal Court Young Writers Programme, www.royalcourtthetare.com/files/downloads/StoningMary.pdf.

Mercer, Kobena (1994). *Welcome to the Jungle*. London: Routledge.

Papastergiadis, Nikos (2000). *The Turbulence of Migration*. Cambridge: Polity.

Thompson, Tony (2003). 'Gun Crime Spreads "Like a Cancer" across Britain', *Observer*, 5 October.

Young, Robert J. (1995). *Colonial Desire: Hybridity in Theory, Culture and Race*. London: Routledge.

Chapter 4

Northern Irish Drama: Speaking the Peace

Tom Maguire

Theatre and the Peace Process

On 31 August 1994, the Army Council of the Provisional Irish Republican Army (PIRA) announced a complete cessation of military activities, in which it was followed within a matter of months by the Combined Loyalist Military Command. It seemed that the conflict in Northern Ireland was finally coming to a resolution. On Good Friday 1997, the signing of the Belfast Agreement between nationalist, republican and unionist parties, with the support of the British and Irish governments, offered hope for a new political dispensation. This was endorsed overwhelmingly in referenda in both states in Ireland a year later. Politicians and the paramilitaries, it would seem, had usurped the role of the artist, claimed by playwright Stewart Parker (1941–88), of providing for their society a 'working model of wholeness'(Parker 1986: 19).[1]

This model, however, has depended upon agreeing the right words to end the disputes of the past and to call into being a new politics within a reformed state, a process that remains incomplete. Dialogue, discussions and negotiations have replaced much of the political violence, but politicians have struggled to build and maintain a consensus around how and by whom the state should be governed. It was not until 28 July 2005 that PIRA announced the end of its armed struggle, with its final act of decommissioning being undertaken two months later. Meanwhile, the devolved government of the Northern Ireland Assembly and its power-sharing executive had collapsed in November 2002, with a return to direct rule from Westminster. Therefore, there has continued to be a role for theatre-makers in the process of reimagining Northern Ireland, challenging the clichés of the Troubles play and the stereotypes to which it has contributed.[2]

Although exceptional in breaching the boundaries of institutionalized theatre practice in the relationship between its material and the site chosen to present it, Tinderbox's *Convictions* (2001), staged as a site-specific performance in Belfast's Crumlin Road Courthouse, none the less epitomizes a number of strategies which have been adopted by theatre practitioners in reimagining Northern Ireland. Its narratives engaged directly with the legacy of the past; its various parts offered platforms to a range of voices which have been routinely excluded from dominant representations of Northern Ireland; and, in both its site and performance forms, it was innovative in its modes of representation. I will deal with each of these strands within the play and the wider context of theatre production below.

Composed of a series of separate one-act performances within different areas of the former courthouse where many of the major trials of the Troubles had been staged, *Convictions* incorporated a new generation of playwrights, with work by Owen McCafferty (b. 1961), Nicola McCartney (b. 1972), Daragh Carville (b. 1969), Damian Gorman (b. 1961) and Gary Mitchell (b. 1965); together with the established writers Martin Lynch (b. 1950) and Marie Jones (b. 1955).[3] Each play took its title from the particular room in which it was set and each had a different director casting the 10-strong company in multiple roles across the production as a whole, with the audience promenading from one room to the next. Its direct attempt to explore how it might be possible to speak about the past has characterized a number of post-ceasefire productions such as Joseph Crilly's *On McQuillan's Hill* (1999), Michael Duke's *Revenge* (2004), Sean Caffrey's *Out Come the Bastards* (1999) and Dave Duggan's *AH6905* (2005).

The production's mosaic of voices, what Jen Harvie has termed its 'pervasive dialogism' (2005: 54), foregrounded a range of alternatives to dominant narratives of life in Northern Ireland, a second strand within contemporary play production. For example, Gary Mitchell has done much to portray the lives of working-class loyalists, apparently left behind as political dialogue has replaced political violence.[4] In other plays, such as Owen McCafferty's *Shoot the Crow* (1997), Richard Dormer's *Hurricane* (2001) and Maria Connolly's *Massive* (2002),

67

Alan Mckee and Conor Grimes in *Convictions* by Tinderbox Theatre Company
Photo: Darren James

the conflict is not the direct focus, and alternative experiences of living in Northern Ireland have been allowed to emerge.[5]

A third strategy has been the development of new forms of representation. In *Convictions*, a number of the performances were presented within forms of direct audience address through which the characters and action are constituted by the performance of narration, a kind of story-telling theatre in which diegesis becomes more important than mimesis. While narration between characters within the dramatic world is a standard dramatic convention, in this form of performance, actors and/or characters are able to move outside the world of the play to narrate to the audience directly as a principal means of engaging them in the action of the drama.

The roots of this form in Northern Ireland can be traced within the work of Charabanc Theatre Company in the 1980s. The company's performances were influenced by the alternative theatre movement in Britain through the experience and knowledge of Pam Brighton, who, having worked with 7:84, Monstrous Regiment and Hull Truck, went on to direct Charabanc's first three plays. They drew too on their own experiences of story-telling within the working-class communities in which the company members had grown up. Additionally, the form was expedient in allowing the company to stage work with limited budgets.[6] The form has been used too by Brian Friel in *The Freedom of the City* (1973) and most notably *Faith Healer* (1979), which is comprised of separate monologues from each of its three characters played directly to the audience.

In plays like Marie Jones's *A Night in November* (1994), Conall Morrison's *Hard To Believe* (1995), Robert Welch's *Protestants* (2004), MacDara Vallely's *Peacefire* (2004) and Dave Duggan's *AH6905* the central narrative is controlled by a single character who represents the other characters by a mix of embodiment and narration. The presentational style of these monodramas has been developed into plays with a number of actors, such as Jones's *Stones in His Pockets* (1998) and Lynch, Grimes and McKee's *The History of the Troubles Accordin' to My Da* (2001). These plays retain the break with the conventions of realism in their use of direct narration to the audience and in their emphasis on the speaker, shifting away from the concerns of *histoire* to a concern with *discours*.[7] Thus, what becomes central is the act of speaking and the situation in which it takes place.

In the rest of this chapter, I wish to explore how this concern with speaking has been addressed through three specific productions: Nicola McCartney's *Heritage* (1998), Daragh Carville's *Language Roulette* (1996) and Owen McCafferty's *Mojo Mickybo* (1998) respectively.

Nicola McCartney's *Heritage*

Nicola McCartney resists easy categorization as a playwright. Born and brought up in Belfast to parents from different religious backgrounds, the focus of her professional life has been split primarily between Scotland and Ireland. She studied at the University of Glasgow, trained as a director with Charabanc in Northern Ireland and then set up her own theatre company, lookOUT, in Scotland in 1992, and has worked subsequently as a writer and director. As well as contributing to *Convictions*, McCartney has written *The Millies* (2002) for Replay Productions, Belfast, and *All Legendary Obstacles* (2003) for the Abbey, with a prodigious and varied output in Scotland for companies such as lookOUT, 7:84 (Scotland), the Traverse and Catherine Wheels Theatre Company. She won the Best Play Award at the

Edinburgh Festival for *Easy* (lookOUT) in 1995; was shortlisted for the Susan Smith Blackburn Prize for *The Hanging Tree* (lookOUT, 1998); and won the Best Children's Play Award at the TMA Theatre Awards in 2002 for *Lifeboat* (Catherine Wheels).

Heritage was first staged by the Traverse Theatre Company in October 1998, and was revived by the company in 2001. Premiered in the optimistic aftermath of the endorsement of the Belfast Agreement, with new political institutions emerging, the play interrogates the choices faced by people within Northern Ireland in constructing the state in which they will live. However, McCartney reconfigured the representation to avoid the recurrent and obvious motifs of the conflict by displacing the setting in *Heritage* to rural Canada between the years of 1914 and 1920. This period covers the key dates in Ireland's political history from the onset of the First World War through 1916, the year of the Easter Rising and the battle of the Somme – events key in the history of republican and loyalist histories respectively – to the Irish War of Independence. The distancing offered by the location of the action in Saskatchewan at the time of the emergence of a separate Canadian national consciousness allowed McCartney to interrogate the hold of the past on the present at precisely the time that people in Northern Ireland were engaged in the project of rebuilding the state and their civil society. Both historical moments offer themselves as points of crisis and transition.

The central narrative focuses on the coming to adulthood of Sarah, the daughter of the Protestant Ulster-Scots McCrea family, originally from County Antrim.[8] The McCreas cling firmly to the traditions of Orangeism that they have carried from home and are suspicious of agitation for an independent Canada and the growing Fenian movement, which is gathering support amongst some of their fellow immigrants from Ireland. Although the McCreas initially welcome the friendship offered by their progressive Irish neighbour Peter Donoghue, when his son Michael begins an affair with Sarah, and a series of tit-for-tat sectarian attacks are mounted by local gangs, they try to force her to break with him. Despite Michael's increasing involvement with the local Fenians, the couple continue to see each other, until eventually, Michael is killed while setting fire to the McCreas' barn. Faced with the loss of her lover, Sarah leaves home to make her own life.

Represented by this bare structure, the play apparently repeats the recurrent device which Christopher Murray has called 'The Romeo and Juliet typos' (1997: 192–4). Joe Cleary suggests that in such figurations, the relationship of the lovers 'seems to be operating as an allegory for some kind of national romance: in the erotic embrace of the lovers, traditionally antagonistic communities come to recognize each other as political allies' (1999: 514). This device, however, relies on a simplification of the various religio-political and class divisions within the conflict and, in the requirement that one or both of the lovers should die, demonstrates the impossibility of overcoming these divisions on a personal or political level. Reading the play in this way, Michael's demise becomes the result of his acceptance of the myths of militant Irish nationalism which he has learnt at the knee of his grandmother, Emer.[9] Emer insists that Michael learn this history, despite the resistance of Peter to 'romantic nonsense about the Old Country and coffin ships and martyred rebels' (McCartney 2001: 112).

Part of this 'romantic nonsense' in which Michael is schooled is the Celtic myth of Deirdre of the Sorrows, a tale in which two young lovers, Deirdre and Naoise, have to flee Ireland if they are to be able to live together. The shared recitation of the tale becomes an explicit motif for the growing relationship between the two young lovers in the play. Eventually, in the play as in the myth, it is the need to fulfil the demands of the young man's martial honour that leads to a separation between the lovers and culminates in his death. Juxtaposing the myth with the needless death of Michael in a pointless action against his neighbours is McCartney's most direct commentary on Northern Ireland's political violence.

Importantly, however, the play's focus is split between the plot line of the young lovers and Sarah's relationships with her own family as she develops into womanhood. She is not defined exclusively in terms of her relationship with Michael, but is given an independent life within the plot and a stage existence which is marked by her direct engagement with the audience. The love story is not core to her identity, or to all of the events of the play. The action is framed, crucially, as her memory told from the point in time of the morning after she has left her family following the fire in which Michael has died. Her recollections flit between events which she describes and others in which she acts. She speaks lyrical passages direct to the audience which connect her to the Canadian landscape. This is a landscape in which the diversity of the trees, which are listed in a long, lyrical section at the beginning of the play, offers an allegory for how the land might support diverse identities that might be transplanted from their Irish past and transformed in this new setting. It is a setting in which she revels and through which she roams freely:

Below me
Vastness of the plain
Dotted with matchbox houses
Fields sleepin under white snow meltin
Spattered little brown patches where the plough went in late
Criss-cross sewn together with snake-rail fences
Muddy grey below stretches wide under muddy grey above
Forever. (8)

For Sarah, then, the issue is one of her identity at a liminal point in her own existence. She must cross over from the world which she has been bequeathed by her parents with its nineteenth-century customs and limitations into the new land of Canada in a new century with its challenges and opportunities, where what she is and will become is not yet settled. In this sense, Michael dies because he confuses his inherited history with an understanding of how the world is now. The process of narrating the events that have brought Sarah to this point is a way of making sense of her past, her heritage. To do so, she bends it to her words, taking control of it by finding ways of capturing in language the experiences that have brought her to this place and time. It is not therefore an outright disavowal of the traditions of Orangeism with which she has been brought up. One of the most captivating speeches in the play is her description of the Twelfth of July Parade and the beating of the Lambeg Drum, the pride of the Orange Lodge:

One head made of ass's skin could shatter a window
And boom and boom and boom boom boom!
Shudders and shakes you to the liver
High G on the D flute
Thrill of the pain it gives you in the heart
Brother John marchin, puffin, whistlin
Isn't he doin well?
Go on, John! (42)

Her words are a means of putting the past in an order, as a place from which she has travelled and must now leave behind. Her heritage becomes only one part of the wider context, alongside her present and her future, not a memory to which she must forever pay obeisance. She has still her own vision to discover and her own potential to fulfil. Her final decision is not to return to the home of her parents but to walk on into the dawn of a new day and a new independent existence.

In rejecting this past, she is, however, rejecting also the Irish nationalist vision which brought Michael to his death. *Heritage* is not an example of what John Wilson Foster has described as an Ulster Protestant self-distaste whose indirect expression 'might be the embrace of "Irish" culture at the expense of the lesser "Ulster" culture' (2001: 13).[10] The play does demonstrate Sarah's openness to this Irish culture through listening to Emer. Indeed, ending the first act with an exuberant dance between Michael and Sarah in the Donoghue kitchen allows the audience an insight into the liberation from the pressures of home that she enjoys there. However, each side of the binaries of dominant nationalist identity is demonstrated as containing and constraining Sarah's personal identity as a woman. In this new world, a woman must make her political decisions based on her own self-interest, not on the demands of the past.[11] This connects with wider debates about the relationship of gender politics to the politics of national identity in Northern Ireland. Pelan argues, for example, that

> The traditional polarisation of Irish politics and historiography into Irish/ English, nationalist/unionist and revisionist/post-colonial, has meant that women, historically, have not only been forced to choose between such binaries in terms of their personal politics, but have been represented as being contained within these political categories. (1999: 244)

For Sarah, her heritage, with its requirement that she be defined by an affiliation to an external identity as an Orangewoman, has proven to be unserviceable in this new country and new age. Here, she takes on personal responsibility for forging her identity.

Daragh Carville's *Language Roulette*

If words are the tools by which Sarah McCrea fashions her sense of self in *Heritage*, their use in Daragh Carville's *Language Roulette* is less straightforward. The play's title comes from a game which expatriate English-speakers play in Paris:

Joseph: The idea is to go into a public place, where there are crowds, like in the métro, and you choose somebody you don't like the look of, and then you – abuse them. [. . .] it has to be in English. It's called Language Roulette because there is a chance your victim will be able to understand. And if he does – you get your head kicked in! (93–4)

As a first professional play, *Language Roulette* has enjoyed remarkable success.[12] After an initial production by Tinderbox at the Old Museum Arts Centre, Belfast, it was revived in 1997, touring Ireland and transferring to London's Bush Theatre and the Traverse, Edinburgh. Carville has since written *Dumped* (Tinderbox, 1997), *Observatory* (Peacock Theatre, 1999), *The Holyland* (National Youth Theatre, 2001) and *Family Plot* (Tinderbox, 2005). He received the Stewart Parker Playwright Award in 1997 and the Meyer-Whitworth Prize in 1998.

The play is set in 1994, the year of the first paramilitary ceasefires,[13] with the action moving between a shared house in Belfast and a local pub, involving a group of six twenty-somethings connected by their relationship to Colm. Colm, Joseph and Tim were formerly at school and university together. Colm has arranged to meet up with Joseph, who has recently returned to Belfast from working abroad. Ollie is a few years younger and Colm's lodger. He and his friend Sarah (both of whom function as minor characters outside the main group) inveigle their way into the reunion at a local pub. There Colm's ex-wife Anna and Tim join them. Colm, Anna, Tim and Joseph had once been a tightly knit group and the evening will reveal what bonded them, what split them apart and how they might be able to relate to each other now.

In the opening scene of the play, Colm is making a futile attempt to tidy the house in anticipation of Joseph's arrival. Ollie and Sarah play mindless word-games, deliberately misunderstanding each other as part of a ritual exchange to pass the time. This introduces the central focus of the play: the deployment of words to avoid or at least defer the revelation of the truth. Like Pinter, Carville has an ear for the ways in which speech fails (sometimes intentionally) to communicate in its banality and repetitions. Characters mishear each other, or mistake each other's meanings, or twist and turn words deliberately to their own ends. He points to this as both a social and existential issue, since he gives the central characters a shared background in having once staged *Waiting for Godot* together as students. They all make bad puns, exchange banter, tease each other, play drinking games based on names, challenge each other to play Truth or Dare, exchange recollections of the past, sing songs and catchphrases from television programmes and advertisements from the past. The main characters now use words as their stock-in-trade: Colm teaches in a primary school; once a playwright, Joseph uses his skills as a linguist to work his way between European countries; Anna writes for the local newspaper; and Tim is a small-time actor. The past that stands between them is an affair between Anna and Joseph while she was married to

Peter O'Meara and Peter Ballance in *Language Roulette* by Daragh Carville
Photo: Phil Smyth

Colm and the baby she conceived and then aborted; and Joseph's inaction when Tim was beaten up. However, no matter how they try to avoid the past, the truth eventually breaks through with the help of drink and drugs strategically administered by Tim.

Tim is the motor-force behind the disintegration of these linguistic devices to conceal or ignore the truth. He has set himself up as the person to cut through the lies:

Tim: [. . .] I'm the fucking truth-teller. (*To Anna.*) I lied for you and Joe back then. (*To Colm.*) I lied to keep you in the dark. I lied to protect them. Mummy and daddy here. But when I saw what it was to have your best friends stand by you, when I saw what it was to have your best friend stand by while you get beaten to shit, I changed my mind. I became the fucking truth-teller. I told the truth about all of us and that put an end to our incestuous little family, didn't it? (153)

He introduces the game-playing in the pub and through this, he drives the others to confront their past. His manipulation is relentless, his words weapons wielded to wound, the sharp side of the verbal interplay characteristic of Belfast speech and marketed to outsiders as 'craic'. Ultimately, however, Tim's search for truth achieves nothing, since it refuses forgiveness and disallows reconciliation. His raking up of the past destroys the attempt of Colm and Joseph to forget what has gone between them and leaves the three old school friends alone in the final moment of the play with nothing more to say to each other. What it does not remove, however, is the sense that they are all bound by this past and must find a way to live together despite it. While Carville, then, has tried to avoid directly engaging with the institutional politics of Northern Ireland, his play engages on the level of the individual precisely those issues with which political leaders continue to struggle.

Owen McCafferty's *Mojo Mickybo*

In Owen McCafferty's *Mojo Mickybo*, the verbal dexterity which is characteristic of the dialogue in *Language Roulette* is the most striking dimension of its performance form. The play was first staged by Belfast's Kabosh theatre company[14] at the Andrews Lane Studio in Dublin in October 1998 as part of the Dublin Theatre Festival, winning two Dublin Fringe/Sunday Times Awards and a Granada Television Play award for Best Drama in 1999. Written for a cast of two male actors who play all of the 17 roles, it presents the experience of two young boys in Belfast in the summer of 1970 through a combination of mimetic and diegetic devices.

Its achievement is to create for the audience a sense of childhood exuberance and the innocence of a relationship between the two boys as their friendship develops over the course of one summer. The boys play out their relationship as a film fantasy, ignorant of the sectarian divisions emerging around them, which, at that time, had not yet been made manifest in the division of neighbourhoods across the city by barriers erected to keep communities apart. It is only when Mickybo's father is shot dead that the divisions fracturing the rest of Belfast manage to split the friendship apart, since through this they discover that they are from different sides of the divide. This division stays with them even as they grow into adulthood. Like *Heritage*, then, this is also a tale of a relationship 'across the barricades', albeit from a different perspective to the traditional romance.

McCafferty's work is imbued with a very distinctive instinct for dialogue which he developed initially as a short-story writer, before turning to plays in 1992. His plays have been produced by Kabosh, Belfast's Lyric Theatre and Druid in Galway, with his work eventually winning recognition in London.[15] Such success is all the more remarkable given McCafferty's distinctive use of words within the plays. He has evolved an idiosyncratic form of speech which weaves Belfast vernacular and elements of popular culture into a dense, economical and rhythmic form which resembles and yet defies ordinary speech. In this new language form, charactonyms reveal the essence of the individual, as in Barny Rip The Balls, Fuckface and Gank the Wank. The sheer pleasure in the sonority of words which this form generates is demonstrated, for example, when, leaving the cinema after watching *Butch Cassidy and the Sundance Kid*, the two boys taunt the manager about the illicit affair he is having with the box-office woman:

Mickybo: bye bye uncle sidney (*Exaggerated kissing.*)
Mojo: uncle sidney lumbers big seven bellies (*Firing guns.*)
Mickybo: mcmanus luiga riva
Mojo: s o s dannybobo
Mickybo: don del a vista (18)

As in *Language Roulette*, the references to popular culture indicate the extent to which many people lived lives just like their counterparts elsewhere in the United Kingdom and across the island.

McCafferty's work draws on the same story-telling performance mode as a number of the pieces within *Convictions*. McCafferty embraces this staged story-telling in two ways: within the dramatic world and as a performance form. Within the narrative, characters use stories for a variety of reasons. The boys initiate their relationship through a competitive exchange of tall tales about their crotchety, child-hating neighbour. As their relationship develops, imagining shared stories becomes part of the ways in which they express their friendship, particularly in the figuration of themselves and their everyday lives as Butch Cassidy and the Sundance Kid, and of a particular bus trip in which the local seaside resort of Newcastle becomes Bolivia. They also use story-telling as a threat, only maintaining their silence about his affair if the cinema manager admits them despite the fact that they are under age.

They are not the only story-tellers, however. Mickybo's mother greets the friends each time they call with a different fantastic improvisation behind which she conceals her own enveloping despair:

Mickybo's Ma: . . . there was this strange noise came out of the radio it sounded like the king had eaten something very large that didn't agree with him and was choking on his own boke – then a voice said we come in peace earth people – then the voice said don't lose your heads earth people if you lose your head you lose your money – things may be gettin a bit hairy but we're here to save you all especially wee mickybo mickybo's ma an the man that she loves header and all that he is – we're shippin you out to a planet where there's no dishes the stew makes itself the sky rains beer and the hills are made of bubblies – so we're alright wee honeybun – we don't need to live in the hut that you and mojo built over the timbers – cause the spacemen are coming to save us (31)

Stories can be used, therefore, as in *Language Roulette*, as a way of avoiding the truth. When Mojo's father arranges a meeting with his lover in a local café where she works, it becomes a secret about the boy's treat of three ice creams that he and Mojo must keep to themselves. Likewise, when Mojo's mother splits up with her husband, Mojo is fed the story that he is going on his holidays to his aunt's house. McCafferty's proficiency is in creating economically such stories, which are taken at face value by the boys, while at the same time deploying dramatic irony as the audience pieces together the back-story which the words conceal.

Story-telling is crucial to the performance of the piece too. The play's action is framed by a narrator who, it turns out, is the adult Mojo recalling the past, just as in McGuinness's *Observe the Sons of Ulster Marching Towards the Somme* (1985) and Friel's *Dancing at Lughnasa* (1990). Mojo speaks directly to the audience, providing linking sections and explanations. This device is extended into the overall style of the performance, which requires a presentational style of acting that acknowledges the presence of the audience and allows the performer to breach the divisions between the actual and fictional worlds. The form also gives prominence to the performer's physicality as he is required to shift between different characters, and connects it to developments in physical theatre performance forms elsewhere.[16] Kabosh were already engaged in an exploration of a physical language that would rescue performance from the confines of naturalism when they took the script on. It is a paradoxical feature of this form that the playwright foregrounds the physical virtuosity of the actor. This is evident where the two actors switch rapidly between multiple roles even within the same moment. Thus, when Mojo and Mickybo fight Gank and Fuckface, they have to play all four characters:

> *Mickybo hits Fuckface and they tussle with each other. Mojo shadowboxes and watches the fight.* [. . .]
> *Gank and Mojo aren't keen. They make half-hearted attempts to go for each other. Fuckface is on top of Mickybo holding him down.* (41)

This is achieved by having one actor play Mickybo and Fuckface, while Gank and Mojo are played by the other. In playing two characters who are involved in the action at the same time, the actor must extend the normal conventions which relate the speaker and his situation to the rest of the dramatic world within a scene through physical and verbal markers of deixis. Here, the careful delineation and shift of focus from one implied speaking perspective to the other requires deft control in the punctuation of the actors' movements. Through this, the actor plays each character within a specific sequence through which the perspective and actions of each character are switched in rapid alternation to give the effect of simultaneity. The actor can achieve such switches without changing his position on the stage as long as he can clearly delineate and differentiate physically the perspective of the characters involved. This technique, which is grounded in the physical dexterity of the actor, emphasizes the partiality of the dramatic representation. Its very performativity demonstrates the contingency of experience while at the same time validating the authority of a number of subject positions.

The Limits of Personal Narratives

It might appear then that through such productions the contemporary theatre in Northern Ireland is serving as a forum in which stories are told which challenge the hitherto dominant, monolithic constructions of identity. The experiences of individuals become validated by being performed and acknowledged by the wider community and attention is drawn to the ways in which speaking constructs versions of reality, as both a warning and an invitation to use the power of language. It remains problematic, none the less, that each of the dramas discussed here remains on the level of the personal. They lack the scale to take in a wider perspective of the contemporary reality or the preceding years of violence which might address significant structural issues.[17] Instead, by emphasizing only the personal aspects of the political, these dramas repeat the dominant narratives of the British and Irish states and their successive governments: 'these narratives placed the burden of conflict resolution on the Northern Irish themselves by blaming the continuing violence on the refusal of the two communities to make a sincere effort to resolve their differences' (Cornell 1999: 71). Peace, just like the conflict which preceded it, is seen both as an issue internal to Northern Ireland, and one to be settled by individuals at a neighbourly level stepping out of their opposing but hopelessly interlocked tribes.[18] In seeking to present the singularity of experiences which have been masked by the totalizing accounts of the past, playwrights have avoided representing any more general story. While Richard Norton-Taylor's *Bloody Sunday: Scenes from the Saville Inquiry* (2005) received national attention as part of a series of tribunal plays at the Tricycle Theatre in London, even it could focus only on the individual experiences of one specific incident.[19] Thus the story of the state's involvement in the conflict and the peace remains almost entirely untold. When it is presented theatrically, the work is dismissed as propagandist and biased.[20] While playwrights have celebrated the diversity of individual voices, just as in the past, when speaking the peace only some stories are spoken while others remain untold.

Notes

1 Parker is one of the only playwrights from Northern Ireland to articulate at length an explicit vision for the role of theatre in society.

2 For a definition of the Troubles play, see Mark Patrick (1989). 'Trouble with the Troubles', *Theatre Ireland* 20, 19–21.

3 For a further discussion of the politics of the choice of playing space, see Michael McKinnie (2003). 'The State of This Place: *Convictions*, the Courthouse, and the Geography of Performance in Belfast', *Modern Drama* XLVI:4, 580–97.

4 This portrayal has not always been welcomed by the loyalist community. Mitchell is the only professional playwright in Northern Ireland who

has been directly subjected to violent intimidation by loyalist paramilitaries apparently in response to his dramatic output. See Louise Jury
(2005). 'Defiant Playwright Mitchell Hits Back', *Belfast Telegraph*, 30 December, 7.

5   The necessity of seeing beyond dominant representations of identity has
been an underlying principle too in a number of interventions in community theatre such as Martin Lynch's *The Stone Chair* (1989), JustUs
and DubbelJoint's *Just a Prisoner's Wife* (1995) and *Binlids* (1997), and the
work of Derry Frontline. See, for example, David Grant (1993). *Playing
the Wild Card: Community Drama and Smaller-Scale Professional Theatre.*
Belfast: Community Relations Council; and Dan Baron Cohen (2001).
*Theatre of Self-Determination: The Plays of Derry Frontline: Culture and Educa-
tion.* Derry: Guildhall Press.

6   For a discussion of the work of the company see, for example, Helen
Lojek (1999). 'Playing Politics with Belfast's Charabanc Theatre Com-
pany' in John P. Harrington and Elizabeth J. Mitchell (eds.), *Politics
and Performance in Contemporary Northern Ireland.* Amherst: University of
Massachusetts Press, 82–102; and Imelda Foley (2003). *The Girls in the
Big Picture: Gender in Contemporary Ulster Theatre.* Belfast: Blackstaff Press.

7   Keir Elam summarizes Benveniste's distinction between *histoire*, 'the
"objective" mode dedicated to the narration of events in the past,
which eliminates the speaking subject and his addressee . . . and *discours*,
the "subjective" mode geared to the present, which indicates the inter-
locutors and their speaking situation. *Histoire* abstracts the *énoncé* – the
utterance produced – from its context, while *discours* gives prominence to
the *énonciation*, the act of producing the utterance within a given context' (Elam [1988]. *The Semiotics of Theatre and Drama.* London: Routledge,
144).

8   Sarah's father Hugh articulates, however, the instability of the identity
which they have brought with them from Ulster in explaining to Sarah
that 'We're Scots Irish Canadian British subjects' (47).

9   Emer Donaghue typifies the tradition of 'unmotherly mothers' within
Northern Irish novels, who operate as seductive influences drawing
others into the violence: 'Deprived now of what is supposedly their
only real reason for existence they become cranky. Aged, asexual, un-
feminine, they can become purveyors of violence against their previous
natural instincts' (Rolston 1996: 409).

10 This criticism is aimed directly at Marie Jones for her *A Night in November*,
in which the central character sheds his Ulster Protestant identity for an
Irish one. Such deprecation of loyalism has a long stage history. See
Laura E. Lyons (2000). 'Of Orangemen and Green Theatres: The Ulster
Literary Theatre's Regional Nationalism' in Stephen Watt, Eileen Morgan
and Shakir Mustafa (eds.), *A Century of Irish Drama: Widening the Stage.*
Bloomington, IN: Indiana University Press, 34–56. This essay traces the

emergence of the stage Orangeman in the productions of the Ulster literary theatre in the early part of the twentieth century, specifically in the work of Gerald McNamara.

11 The parallels between Canada historically and contemporary Northern Ireland are resonant again in this respect. Canada enfranchised women in 1918, while the Women's Coalition was formed in Northern Ireland to ensure that women would be directly represented in the negotiations within the peace process.

12 Originally from Armagh, Carville studied drama and film at the University of Kent, going on to work with fellow Kent graduate Tim Loane, co-founder of Tinderbox.

13 These broke down with the bombing by PIRA of Canary Wharf in February 1995.

14 *Mojo Mickybo* was produced by Kabosh, as was McCafferty's earlier *Freefalling* (1996). Kabosh's artistic director, Karl Wallace, is, like McCafferty, a graduate of the University of Ulster.

15 *Mojo Mickybo* has had a number of revivals including at the Lyric Hammersmith in 2003. In 1999, McCafferty was a writer on attachment at the Royal National Theatre, and his *Closing Time* was staged there in 2002, with *Scenes from the Big Picture* opening in the following year. This production won the John Whiting Award, the Meyer Whitworth Award and the Evening Standard Charles Wintour Award for New Playwriting. More recently, his *Shoot the Crow*, originally staged by Druid in 1997, was revived in 2005 at the Trafalgar Studios. In February 2005, his version of *Days of Wine and Roses* opened at the Donmar Warehouse. A full-length film based on a screenplay by McCafferty and Terry Loane was shot as *Mickeybo and Me* in 2005, directed by Loane for Working Title Films.

16 For example, the influences of Lecoq-trained theatre-makers is evident in Ireland in the work of companies like Barrabas and Blue Raincoat. Dario Fo has also exploited the relationship between his physicality and narrative which he discovered within the historical performance forms of the medieval jongleurs.

17 See, for example, Joseph Ruane and Jennifer Todd (1996). *The Dynamics of Conflict in Northern Ireland*. Cambridge: Cambridge University Press, which provides a structural analysis of the conflict.

18 A cynic might suggest that in some part this explains why audiences outside of Northern Ireland have been so receptive to these plays.

19 Based directly on testimonies to the official inquiry into the killing by the British Army of 13 civilians following a march for civil rights in Derry in 1972, the play was one in a sequence of tribunal plays mounted by the Tricycle in London before touring to Belfast, Derry and Dublin. However, like the inquiry on which it is based, the play does not engage in detail with British government policy or the involvement of senior figures from the government and the security services.

20 Thus, for example, when in 1999 JustUs and DubbelJoint mounted *Forced Upon Us*, a play hugely critical of the Royal Ulster Constabulary, the Arts Council of Northern Ireland responded to criticism by withdrawing £20,000 of funding in the week before the production was due to open, apparently on the 'artistic' grounds that the play was propagandist.

Primary reading

Caffrey, Sean (2003). *Out Come the Bastards*. Belfast: Lagan Press.
Carville, Daragh (1998). *Language Roulette*, in John Fairleigh (ed.), *Far From the Land: Contemporary Irish Plays*. London: Methuen, 63–158.
Carville, Daragh (1999). *Observatory*. London: Methuen.
Carville, Daragh (2001). *The Holyland*. London: Methuen.
Carville, Daragh, Gorman, Damian, Jones, Marie et al. (2000). *Convictions*. Belfast: Tinderbox.
Friel, Brian (1990). *Dancing at Lughnasa*. London: Faber and Faber.
Friel, Brian (1999). *Plays 1*. London: Faber and Faber.
Jones, Marie (2000). *Stones in His Pockets/A Night in November*. London: Nick Hern.
McCafferty, Owen (2002). *Three Plays: Mojo Mickybo, The Waiting List, I Won't Dance – Don't Ask Me*. London: Nick Hern.
McCafferty, Owen (2003). *Shoot the Crow*. London: Nick Hern.
McCafferty, Owen (2005). *Days of Wine and Roses*. London: Nick Hern.
McCartney, Nicola (2001). *Heritage*. London: Faber and Faber.
McGuinness, Frank (1996). *Plays 1*. London: Faber and Faber.
Morrison, Conall (1998). *Hard to Believe*, in John Fairleigh (ed.), *Far From the Land: Contemporary Irish Plays*. London: Methuen, 310–41.
Norton-Taylor, Richard (2005). *Bloody Sunday: Scenes from the Saville Inquiry*. London: Oberon.

Further reading

Byrne, Ophelia (2001). *State of Play: The Theatre and Cultural Identity in Twentieth Century Ulster*. Belfast: Linenhall Hall Library.
Cleary, Joe (1999). 'Domestic Troubles: Tragedy and the Northern Ireland Conflict', *South Atlantic Quarterly* 98:3, 501–37.
Cornell, Jennifer (1999). 'Recontextualising the Conflict: Northern Ireland, Television Drama, and the Politics of Validation' in John P. Harrington and Elizabeth. J. Mitchell (eds.), *Politics and Performance in Contemporary Northern Ireland*. Amherst: University of Massachusetts Press, 197–218.
Grant, David (2001). 'Theatre – Plays and Playwrights' in Mark Carruthers and Stephen Douds (eds.), *Stepping Stones: The Arts in Ulster 1971–2001*. Belfast: Blackstaff Press, 27–51.

Harvie, Jen (2005). *Staging the UK*. Manchester: Manchester University Press.

Maguire, Tom (2006). *Making Theatre in Northern Ireland Through and Beyond the Troubles*. Exeter: University of Exeter Press.

Murray, Christopher (1997). *Twentieth Century Irish Drama: Mirror up to Nation*. Manchester: Manchester University Press.

Parker, Stewart (1986). *Dramatis Personae*. Belfast: John Malone Memorial Committee.

Pelan, Rebecca (1999). 'In a Class of their Own: Women in Theatre in Contemporary Ireland' in Helen Gilbert (ed.), *(Post)Colonial Stages: Critical and Creative Views on Drama, Theatre and Performance*. Hebden Bridge: Dangaroo Press, 243–52.

Pilkington, Lionel (2001). *Theatre and the State in Twentieth Century Ireland*. London: Routledge.

Roche, Anthony (1989). 'The Return of the Story-Tellers', *Theatre Ireland* 17, 21–3.

Rolston, Bill (1996). 'Mothers, Whores and Villains: Images of Women in Novels of the Northern Ireland Conflict' in Bill Rolston and David Miller (eds.), *War and Words: The Northern Ireland Media Reader*. Belfast: Beyond the Pale, 403–18.

Wilson Foster, John (2001). 'Making Representation: The Literary Imagery of Ulster Protestants: Some Historical Notes' in Desmond Bell (ed.), *Dissenting Voices/Imagined Communities* (Belfast Film Festival pamphlet). *Proceedings of Belfast Film Festival*, 12–14.

Part II

Sites, Cities and Landscapes

Chapter 5

The Production of 'Site': Site-Specific Theatre

Fiona Wilkie

Current Contexts

On 25 February 2006, the new National Theatre of Scotland (NTS) was launched with a series of performances in primarily non-theatre locations across 10 different Scottish cities. These pieces were collected under the title of *HOME* and occupied such spaces as a disused shop in Stornoway, a tower block near Glasgow and a glass factory in Caithness. As an event, *HOME* was intended to signal from the very beginning of the new organization a deliberately non-centred approach. In direct contrast with the London-based National Theatre (whose 'nation' is now less easy to define), the National Theatre of Scotland is not a building but a mobile idea, a label that can be attached to theatre projects across Scotland and beyond. Following *HOME*, the opening season included two further site-specific events made in collaboration with Scottish companies experienced in the form: *Falling* (2006), a promenade performance around Glasgow city centre in association with the company Poorboy, and *Roam* (2006), Grid Iron's large-scale work for Edinburgh Airport. It is clear that the artistic team of the NTS, led by the former Paines Plough artistic director Vicky Featherstone, finds something of value in site-specific theatre for the devolved and fluid model that it seeks to establish. In this case the value, I suggest, lies not in the opportunity to interrogate spatial relationships that has attracted many other site-specific practitioners, such as those discussed below. Rather, site-specificity offers a convenient marker of a set of ideas with which the NTS wants to be associated: experiment, accessibility, the connection between art and everyday life, and a shift away from the primacy of the metropolitan theatre building.

The potency of site-specific theatre at the beginning of the twenty-first century is further evidenced by the recent moves of some of the organizations that the NTS might seem to be critiquing. As I write, some of the UK's key arts institutions (including the National Theatre and the Barbican Centre) are engaging explicitly with site-specific events as part of their mainstream programmes. The experimental company Shunt has appeared in the National Theatre programme for the past two seasons with performances in the vaults under London Bridge station.[1] And as part of its 'Young Genius' season (autumn 2005) the Barbican brought *Underground* by the Brighton-based dreamthinkspeak to the old abattoir in Clerkenwell. This kind of institutional interest arguably builds on the frequent adoption of site-specific modes in the commissioning by city authorities of celebratory 'City of Culture' events.

The European City of Culture scheme has been an official way of validating and funding those activities of representation and mediation that a town authority will undertake in any case; it began in 1985 (with Athens), and the first city in Britain or Ireland to take part was Glasgow in 1990. Dublin followed in 1991, Cork in 2005, and Liverpool will follow in 2008. The Glasgow celebrations memorably included a prominent commission for the theatre-maker Bill Bryden, whose resulting performance in the Glasgow docks – *The Ship* (1990) – has been described as one of Scotland's biggest ever theatrical events.[2] Cork, too, positioned site-specificity high on its agenda; its celebrations included a festival entitled *Relocation* (or, perhaps, re: location), which included four invited site-specific performances from companies based in Ireland (Corcadorca), Scotland (Grid Iron), France (Compagnie Jo Bithume) and Poland (Teatr Biuro Podrozy). Though the impulses behind these two examples seem to differ in terms of perspective (of the inhabitant or the international visitor) and level of social engagement, both reveal a belief that performance might somehow endow a city's quotidian or civic spaces with renewed significance.

There is, perhaps, a danger in all of these examples of the site-specific being 'uncritically adopted as another genre category by mainstream art institutions and discourses' (Kwon 2002: 1). Certainly the prominent theatre critic Michael Billington recognizes the potential for site-specificity to be nothing more than a gimmick when he argues that 'the search for "found spaces" is in danger of turning into a bourgeois game for those bored with conventional theatres'.[3] But there are also, I think, possibilities suggested by this move. For example, mainstream practices are useful in drawing critical attention to the institution as a site of production of cultural knowledges. Further, though they might not offer the subtlety of inquiry into spatial and theatrical meanings found in many alternative practices, these mainstream examples do at least bring into the popular domain debates about the theatre's relationship to other areas of everyday life, including public and political life.

The increased visibility of site-specific practice points, in part, to a wider need to reconsider our relationships to the spaces we inhabit. In recent years, many of the most pressing issues of socio-cultural debate have been characterized by questions of place. These include globalization, immigration, ecology, territory, the construction of a new Europe, the shifting relationships of Britain to the US, and the changing understandings of warfare now that conflicts are no longer organized according to national borders. An apparent 'placelessness' (Relph 1976; Hill and Paris 2006) is often identified as a defining feature of postmodernity, though this paradoxically reminds us that 'a sense of place is also arguably vital (in its absence as well as its presence) to the postmodern condition' (Hodder and Shanks 1995: 245). Disciplines such as cultural geography and urban studies have developed as a means of critically addressing these social contexts, while site-specificity represents for the theatre an important means of doing the same. Simply put, site-specific theatre privileges place. It suggests that the act of dividing the activity labelled 'theatre' from the building labelled 'theatre' holds possibilities for responding to and interrogating a range of current spatial concerns, and for investigating the spatial dimension of contemporary identities (personal, communal, national and international).

The beginnings and considerable expansion of site-specificity as a mode of theatrical encounter can be located directly in the period covered by this volume. That is to say that it was not until the 1980s that British companies and critics began consistently to apply the term 'site-specific' to theatre. Further, the range of variously 'site-specific', 'site-related' and 'site-oriented' theatre practices emerging in the 1990s and beyond – including the mainstream practices introduced above – is testimony to the growing significance of the form.[4] Though acknowledging the wide range of practices that use the 'site-specific' label, my discussion will argue for two broad shifts in emphasis across the past two decades. A shift in form can be noted from performance that *inhabits* a place to performance that *moves through* spaces. A further, and at times parallel, shift occurs in the nature of the site-specific inquiry, which seems to move from a concern with the political and cultural meanings of particular locations to a focus on broader questions of what *site* as a category might mean. In making this argument, I want to step back from the mainstream examples offered at the beginning of this chapter to trace the companies, artists and concerns that have shaped British site-specific theatre since the 1980s.

A number of critical vocabularies have been useful to practitioners and commentators in understanding the work, including those of minimalist art, political democracy, architecture, archaeology, civic organization and psycho-geography.[5] However, following Kaye (2000: 3), the frame that I find most productive for considering the range of these practices together is provided by the concept of 'site' itself. I propose that by asking how *site*, rather than *space* or *place*, has been approached, constructed and understood in site-specific theatre, we might move some way towards evaluating the contribution of such work and imagining the possibilities it offers for future exploration.

Early Work and Concerns

The label 'site-specific' is borrowed by the theatre (and, later, by dance) from the visual arts, where it is understood as a direct condition of 1960s minimalism.[6] Here, in an attempt to disrupt the apparent autonomy of the modernist art object, the space of encounter between the work and the viewer is deemed of prime importance. That is, the minimalist sculpture does not pretend to contain a fixed, closed meaning but only acquires meaning in the precise space and time in which it is encountered.[7] For Nick Kaye, this is therefore a theatrical encounter (2000: 3). Already, then, the theatre borrows an understanding of *site* that is not simply a synonym for *place* but that includes the presence of an audience. One possible consequence of this is that to be site-specific is also to be audience-specific. Another important result of the minimalist legacy for theatre is that questions of *what* exactly constitutes the work and *where* its borders can be drawn are brought to the fore. The use of non-theatre venues (sometimes, problematically, referred to as 'found spaces') contributes –

implicitly or explicitly – to an inquiry into what the theatre *is* and might be.

Some key figures in a number of the early British site-specific theatre companies first trained in visual art before moving into work in theatre, and therefore brought something of this visual arts sensibility to bear on their shaping of site-specific theatre. David Wheeler of IOU (founded 1976, West Yorkshire) and Julian Maynard Smith of Station House Opera (founded 1980, London) are two such figures; both draw on a developed sense of sculptural rather than narrative-based properties in devising their site-specific shows.[8] In works such as *The House* (1982), IOU aimed to 'enhance the possibilities' of the chosen site (in this case, a derelict house and its surroundings), 'animating' it through musicians and glimpsed live actions but also by building onto it so that the shape of the site is fundamentally altered.[9] Much of the early work of Station House Opera, too, operates through importing materials – most famously breeze blocks – into the performance site and using these to manipulate the encounter between performers, audience and space.

But, though the imperatives of minimalist sculpture have helped to shape an awareness of site for these practitioners, other models and legacies need to be acknowledged. The work of IOU, for example, might be fitted into a narrative of street theatre (Mason 1992: 136–43), whereby it is read as simply extending the logic of location through which street theatre operates: popular, accessible, experimenting with scale, informed by visual art practices, and often politically charged. Indeed, IOU have created a repertoire of static and 'walkabout' street performances, whose aesthetics actively inform their site projects. In the case of Station House Opera, the structures and conditions of building-based theatre have been important; the company's work in theatres cannot be separated easily from its outdoor projects. Though the performances produced by Station House Opera can often usefully be described as site-specific, this label has not been privileged by the company itself. Rather, I suggest that the company's work maintains an interest in the kinds of space – architectural, theatrical, interpersonal, surreal – that performance can be used to create. This is evident in the works involving people, objects and furniture being harnessed and flown around the performance space, such as *Drunken Madness* (1981) and *Cuckoo* (1987). It is also central to the company's breeze-block performances, including *The Bastille Dances* (1989) and *The Salisbury Proverbs* (1997).[10] More recently this ongoing interest has been developed into an active theatrical investigation in works such as *Roadmetal, Sweetbread* (1998) and *Live From Paradise* (2004). Here, Station House Opera has begun to stage an explicitly spatial question: can performance generate an alternative site, different from and yet uncannily similar to the physical space shared by the performers and spectators, and, if so, what might happen there?

I will return to this question later, arguing that it is part of a larger move towards rethinking site in contemporary performance. To get to that point, however, it is important to consider how the *site* of site-specificity was constructed and interrogated in the prominent work of the 1980s and 1990s. I propose to do this in two stages. The first of these uses the influential Welsh company Brith Gof as a model of complex and layered site-specific theatre, focusing particularly on the large-scale production *Haearn* (1992). The second attempts to draw together some of the significant concerns and approaches of theatre-makers and commissioning practices of this period.

The De-industrial Site: Brith Gof

One of the terms most clearly associated with the theatre work of Brith Gof[11] is de-industrialization. This seems conveniently to lead to a social context (Welsh life in the wake of the demise of its major industries), a political agenda (positioned explicitly against Conservative government policy[12]) and a set of performance spaces (disused large industrial buildings). However, if the work remained at this level there would be little to say about it beyond a recognition of the value of theatre in drawing attention to the human damage caused by Thatcher's reign. Brith Gof's ethical commitment to Wales has also, importantly, been about trying to articulate useful contemporary cultural identities within which performance might play a significant role. Such an aim explores the relationship that is frequently asserted between identity and a 'sense of place'. As the sociologist Kevin Hetherington has suggested, 'identity, as well as being about identification and organization, is also about spatiality. In part, this means that identity involves an identification with particular places, whether local or national' (1998: 105). In a similar vein, Edward Casey writes of the power of place 'to tell us who and what we are in terms of *where we are* (as well as where we are *not*)' (1993: xv). The cosy way in which these associations have tended to be popularly understood is challenged by contemporary forms of displacement and migration, and indeed on a smaller scale by the desire felt by many politically left-wing site-specific theatre practitioners to celebrate the local while interrogating conservative forces of parochialism. But that does not mean that the spatial dimension of identity is not still powerful; indeed, the persistent connection between place and identity has in many cases been one of the relationships signalled by the term 'site'. We can find this use of the term, for instance, in Hetherington, who continues the passage quoted above to argue that 'certain spaces act as sites for the performance of identity' (105). The site of Brith Gof's performances might then be understood not just as a geographical location, but as a place in which cultural identities and social relationships can be productively examined.

A further kind of examination occurs in Brith Gof's work. In addition to the context of political intervention at a time of widespread de-industrialization, much of the work of the company pursues an inquiry into notions of what *theatre* might be. Co-founder and artistic director Mike Pearson has asserted that 'I want to find different arenas for performance – places of work, play and worship – where the laws and bye-laws, the decorum and learned contracts of theatre can be suspended. I want to make performances that fold together place, performance and public' (1998: 40). The complex engagement between place, performance and public is something that has also fascinated Clifford McLucas, Pearson's co-artistic director at Brith Gof from 1989. McLucas developed a conceptual model of 'the host, the ghost and the witness' through which he sought to represent the possibilities and responsibilities of each of the three key 'participants' in the site-specific theatre event.[13] In this model, the non-theatre venue is imagined as 'hosting' the performance, which in turn is cast in the role of a ghost that haunts the site temporarily, perhaps disrupting its atmosphere but always able to be seen through. The ethically loaded role of the witness is assigned to the audience. For McLucas, the work is a 'hybrid' of all three parts of this model, 'and you can mobilize the three in all kinds of ways' (interview with author, 6 October 2001).

The possibilities for such mobilization were, to a large extent, informed by the disciplinary backgrounds of the two artistic directors of Brith Gof. In the case of McLucas, his training as an architect led to his conception of the texts, themes, spatial arrangements and temporal structures of the company's site-specific theatre as a series of interlocking architectures, his interest then developing to the 'possibilities inherent in the "in between" places' produced by these architectures (McLucas in Kaye 2000: 130). The equivalent model for Pearson is

Fiona Wilkie

not, perhaps, the physical theatre legacy of his early work with RAT
Theatre and Cardiff Laboratory Theatre, but archaeology (which he
studied as an undergraduate). This offers a sense of layers and exca-
vation, of the performance as palimpsest, and of the traces that both
performance and site might leave.[14]
A series of large-scale works made by the company in the late
1980s and early 1990s is described by McLucas as 'hand-in-glove'
(interview 2001), where the site suggests a productive metaphor that
is taken up and developed in the performance. The first of these
works, *Gododdin* (1988), is an example often discussed in critical writing (Pearson and Shanks 2001: 101–12; Harvie 2005: 46–53), in part
because its marriage of an ancient Welsh poem of war to a contemporary space of (largely) male economic defeat (in its first performance,
a disused Cardiff car factory) affords a broad examination of gendered
national identities. Further, the production's later moves[15] to a series
of different, and differently culturally inscribed, non-theatre sites
elsewhere in Europe mean that it contributes to a wider discussion of
the nature of specificity: what are the implications of a performance
that tours (or, rather, relocates) and still bears the label 'site-specific'?
The explorations begun in *Gododdin* continued in *Pax* (1991), arguably culminating in *Haearn* (1992; the Welsh title translates as 'iron').
This production was mounted in a British Coal workshop in the Welsh
valleys that had been disused for many years; the metaphor emerging
from the site and taken up by the performance in the hand-in-glove
relationship mentioned by McLucas concerns the dehumanizing process of production. The space is filled with spoken and sung narratives,
live and projected human actions, and a grid of dozens of regular
platforms that serve to fold together different forms of production –
mechanical, medical, literary, biological, mythical, electronic and theatrical – in a site that had not seen production of any kind for around
fifteen years. Within this structure, the performance text intertwines
the Greek myths of Hephaestus and Prometheus with the early nineteenth-century retelling of the latter in the novel *Frankenstein*, accounts
of Mary Shelley's own experience as a producer of writings and of
children, and personal stories of the industrial revolution. The uniform
layout of the vast factory interior seems to diffuse any sense of a
foreground and background, centre stage and margin, with the effect
that the black-and-white projected film of steel workers, for example,
does not appear as a backdrop to Mary Shelley's recollections of the
death of a child ('I was a mother, and am so no longer'[16]) any more
than the emphatically Welsh female voice of Frankenstein's creature

94

('And what was I? Of my creation and creator I was absolutely ignorant') is a soundtrack to the rhythmic manipulations of a performer's limbs, strung within a frame on top of a platform; these exist alongside each other in an economy of equal value.[17]

Haearn's theatrical elements appear to be part of the assembly line of the 'production' as a whole, though the urge for a final product is resisted. In an echo of the first-hand accounts of the industrial revolution that it incorporates ('half-naked demons pouring with sweat and besmeared with soot were hurrying to and fro . . . rolling or hammering or squeezing their glowing metal as if it were wax or dough'), the performance displays a concern with the materials of its site (fire, water, iron, leather, flesh), though it organizes these through the technologies of theatrical production (light, smoke, amplified sound, framed physical action). The overall effect is of an environment so complex and multi-temporal that it might constitute a sealed world of its own. However, the company was always acutely aware of the potential porosity of its site, the social and cultural contexts that could be referenced through the work. As McLucas recalled,

> we did *Haearn* in a small town called Tredegar, which is one of those towns in the south Wales valleys that were absolutely decimated during the 80s. . . . When we did this piece, which was about the industrial revolution and in a sense about the creation of the working classes, it resonated in all kinds of immediate and poetic ways with its audiences, but the one thing that really cranked the energy level up was that a fortnight before the first show Michael Heseltine closed all of the pits in South Wales. (interview with author, 6 October 2001)

I suggested above that Brith Gof's work constitutes a theatrical as well as a social inquiry. In this sense, it is worth noting that what developed through the company's large-scale performances and into the later projects of both its key figures[18] was a concern not just with the nature of theatrical *space* but with the nature of theatrical *time*. *Haearn*'s mechanical division of the duration of the event into 13 equally weighted sections was a technique later refined in *Tri Bywyd* ('Three Lives'; 1995), whose dramatic structure, weaving together three timespaces, 'was of thirty-nine sections of two minutes' duration, punctuated by three re-enactments of death' (Pearson and Shanks 2001: 161). Space, we are reminded, is constructed and experienced through time. In theatrical terms, this recognition has often involved rethinking the duration and scale of the performance event.

New Spaces, New Scales: Mid-1990s and Beyond

The shift in scale towards which the Brith Gof artistic directors were drawn following *Haearn* finds echoes in the work of other practitioners working in site-related modes at the time. The large-scale grand event, the small-scale fleeting encounter and the many performance models in between these poles represent formal and aesthetic but also political choices. The choice available is to some extent inflected by the kinds of site produced by post-industrial patterns of working, living and travelling. Such spaces have been of interest, for example, to the prominent Sheffield-based company Forced Entertainment (founded 1984), for whom the investigation of contemporary landscapes has been of interest not only in its explicitly site-specific works – *Dreams' Winter* (1994); *Nights in This City* (1995) – but also in its work in theatre, particularly *The Travels* (2002), and for other media, such as *Nightwalks* (1998) and *Paradise* (1998).[19] The work of Blast Theory, for instance *Desert Rain* (1999), might be located within a similar framework.[20]

An alternative approach to seeking new ways of inhabiting and performing space was adopted in the 1990s by Welfare State International (founded, without the suffix 'international', in 1968), one of the first theatre companies to use the term 'site-specific'. Following, first, many years of touring, making spectacular celebratory events for sites across the UK and beyond, and, secondly, a seven-year residency in Barrow-in-Furness, in the northwest of England, Welfare State began to set down roots in Barrow's near neighbour Ulverston, working through the 1990s on acquiring a permanent building-base in the town. The result – Lanternhouse – finally opened in 1999. David Wiles suggests that 'the company's move to Ulverston reflects a widely felt desire at the end of the twentieth century to recover a portion of "absolute space" in a world where "abstract space" is the norm' (2003: 62). That may be the case, but the focus of the work is now less likely to be on a particular geographical place than on an idea of mythical or spiritual spaces. Certainly the move makes concrete the company's commitment to the local (even as it redefined itself as 'international'), which has been a rejection of the desire to make a universal statement through art. Welfare State's former artistic director John Fox aligns this recent period in the company history with what he has described as 'the flight from spectacle' (2002: 128–43), turning away from the large-scale moving displays of pyrotechnics, huge sculptures, musicians and carnivalesque costumes that had become the company's stock-in-trade. Instead, the focus more recently – particularly in the rites-of-passage ceremonies developed by the company – has been on the relationships between public and private spaces and between artistic spaces and those of everyday lives.[21]

This is not to argue that the large-scale spectacular event has disappeared from the contemporary spectrum of site-specific theatre, but rather that the imperatives to create such work have changed. Many of the more recent examples of the site-specific spectacle have been instigated not by the artists themselves but by those organizations responsible for the economic prosperity and, therefore, cultural 'branding' of particular towns and cities.[22] Perhaps the prime example of this kind of work can be found in the European City of Culture events mentioned above.

Continuing the now familiar discourses of this and similar schemes, it is possible to consider the countless official millennium celebrations as part of one large 'country of culture' festival. The many local events begin to function metonymically, standing in for an aligned vision of a national 'sense of place' (and time).[23] As the year 2000 approached, many agendas in Britain (those, for example, of the government, regional councils and the media) began to focus on issues of performance and especially site-specific performance, though of course these weren't the terms that were used to frame the discussions. Questions of *how* and, crucially, *where* the millennium should be performed – to ourselves and to others – were no less prominent for thousands of small-event planners around the country than for those debating the economics, politics and possibilities of flagship projects such as the Millennium Dome[24] and the London Eye. Exactly *what* was being performed here also merits inquiry: an image of a centralized (Great) Britain, perhaps, or a new picture created out of devolution; a set of (official or marginalized) pasts, a celebration of the present or a prognosis for the future; a list of achievements or a means of entering into dialogue with (versions of) history. In each case, problems of representation are brought to the fore; the level and ferocity of debate surrounding the Dome demonstrate the public's investment in theatrical dilemmas concerning the implications of choosing one mode of representation over another and the ways in which this might be 'read'. And across the country, large-scale, site-specific performance events (such as the *York Millennium Mystery Plays* directed by RSC associate director Greg Doran at York Minster) were produced as ways of asserting civic and national pride, drawing on positive histories and contemporary narratives to create powerful statements of shared identity.

We are alerted to the potentially problematic role in which the practitioner is cast in celebratory City of Culture or millennium events – validating the space or implicitly standing for a set of values inherited from the city or country authorities – by the alternative site-specific responses that are available outside of the official frame. I am referring here to those projects that are not commissioned by social authorities to have an explicitly celebratory agenda. It is significant, for example, that Pearson/Brookes' impetus for interrogating Cardiff as a lived and performed site in a series of works (including *Carrying Lyn* [2001], *Polis* [2001], *Raindogs* [2002] and *Who Are You Looking At?* [2004]) came in part from Cardiff's failed bid for the 2008 European City of Culture title. These projects (divided by the company into 'two distinct bodies of performance work': multi-site performance and studio performance[25]) are concerned with the kinds of site that might be opened up within or alongside a city's spaces by a combination of low-grade technology, the choreographed spatial presence and absence of the performers and audience (who, by means of recording and replaying techniques, may not share the same spaces at the same times), and language that slips playfully between textual, performative and geographical spaces. Avoiding the urge of the City of Culture events for a polished and final spectacle, the work of Pearson/Brookes appears to be continually in process (within and between each project); the performance and its documentation are presented simultaneously, and both are inflected and renegotiated through the encounter with the audience.[26]

Similarly working alongside officially sanctioned events, and deliberately operating in the cultural margins, were the 14 commissions for the 'Small Acts at the Millennium' project (curated by Tim Etchells, Adrian Heathfield and Lois Keidan), which adopted a site-specific approach in order to tease out alternative meanings in this arbitrary yet oddly significant moment. Through deliberately low-key projects such as Daniel Gosling's three-week 'destinationless' hitch-hike, punctuated by performative interventions at motorway service stations (*10.1.00>>30.1.00>>> <*), and Mike Pearson's intimate guided tour of his home village of Hibaldstow, north Lincolnshire (*Bubbling Tom*), 'intended for an audience who need know nothing of the niceties and conventions of contemporary theatre and art practice' (Pearson in Heathfield 2000: 176), the performance series enters into a discourse of commemoration, simultaneously seeking to mark the millennium while implicitly critiquing other, 'bigger' acts of commemoration. The millennium is invoked here as an impetus for creating, challenging and asserting a range of 'official' and 'counter-' memories. Further, in the light of the formal shift for which I want to argue in site-specific practice, it is worth noting that many of the 'small acts' (and, indeed, the multi-site works of Pearson/Brookes) chose a particular frame for encountering place: that of the journey.

The Journey Motif

The journey, and more specifically the walk, has emerged as perhaps the most prominent motif of site-specific practice at the beginning of the twenty-first century.[27] For a growing number of theatre and performance art practitioners – including Graeme Miller, Janet Cardiff, Wrights & Sites, and Lone Twin – the journey offers a version of the site-specific that is shifting, unfixed; a literal exploration that seems to invite direct connections with a metaphorical exploration. Some of these practices engage explicitly with Situationist agendas.[28] Wrights & Sites, for example, has developed a mode of the 'mis-guided' walk that draws much of its inspiration from Guy Debord's concept of the *dérive* (or 'drift').[29] In *An Exeter Mis-Guide* (2003; produced mainly as a book, to accompany a number of small-scale walking performances), the company proposes a series of instructions and provocations for reorienting oneself in a series of familiar and less-visited spaces around the city. 'Allow yourself to be stopped and diverted', the project suggests; 'look for ruins on which the future can be built' or 'walk until your anger runs out. Then mark the spot' (2003: 10, 14, 88).

Other journeying practices, however, are decisively not drifts. Rather, they assign personal and social narratives to the precise routes taken. A recent example is the theatre artist and composer Graeme Miller's *LINKED* (2003), which makes an 'invisible' but marked intervention into the socially and politically constructed site of the M11 link road. Billed as 'a landmark in sound – an invisible artwork – a walk',[30] *LINKED* constitutes a sound map of the 400 east London houses, including the artist's own, that were demolished to make way for the new road. Spectators (or, more precisely, walkers or participants; there is no live performance presence) tune in, via headphones and a receiver, to a set of narratives recorded with ex-residents, edited by Miller and transmitted from various points along the three-mile route.

99

Inventories of the objects of domestic spaces (layers of wallpaper, the 'table that Joe's got in the middle of his room') combine with histories of residency and movement ('83, every house was inhabited'[31]) and names of pets now buried under the busy road to produce an odd sense that the activity of the walker is somehow triggering these recollections (despite the knowledge that the transmitters are operating anyway, regardless of the presence of anyone to overhear).

The site of *LINKED* is the result of the awkward intersection of its spoken texts of remembered spaces with the physical space of the link road, a space described by Miller in a talk given shortly before the work opened[32] as one 'resistant to narrative', in which 'stories don't seem to hang'. This suggests one claim that might be made for the prominence of the journey motif in current site-specific performance: that it serves as a productive format through which to examine contemporary experiences of apparently non-compliant or recalcitrant spaces, which seem closed to the kinds of culturally located inquiry that have previously been associated with site-specific theatre. The journey holds a seductive promise for practitioners and critics: that the site of performance has the capacity to operate between places.[33]

Rethinking Site

From the sculptor Richard Serra's famous assertion that 'to move the work is to destroy the work' (cited in Kaye 2000: 2) to Wrights & Sites member Cathy Turner's suggestion that it might actually be 'no more than a set of footprints in the sand',[34] site-specificity has been differently conceptualized depending on the aesthetic imperatives, political convictions and spatial sensibilities of its practitioners. What does seem apparent across the range of work, however, is that *site* does not operate simply as a synonym for place or space. Rather, it is an idea that is often produced as a result of the performative framing of more than one place, as in Miller's *LINKED* or McLucas and Shanks' *Three Landscapes Project*. 'Site' seems to incorporate a set of productive spatial metaphors, whereby practitioners use their focus on geographical space to explore a range of theatrical, conceptual, political and virtual spaces. Thus the potentially restrictive *specificity* of the work is expanded to allow for ambiguity and multiplicity.

At the beginning of this chapter, at the risk of generalization, I pointed to what I see as two broad shifts in site-specific theatre: a shift in form (from *inhabiting* to *journeying*) and a shift in the nature of inquiry (from *this place* to broader questions of *site*). In addition to the prominence of the journey motif, then, what characterizes much recent work is not an attention to the cultural resonances of one particular place but an active rethinking of how *site* is constituted. A glance at a few examples illustrates some productive routes of inquiry that site-specific theatre is taking. The 'mis-guiding' practice of Wrights & Sites, for instance, is developing in a new project that attempts to move from Exeter to 'anywhere'. In *A Mis-Guide to Anywhere* (2006), the company has set itself the provocatively impossible task of usefully adapting its site-specific strategies to a generic model, exploring the 'dynamic between the specific and the general, in connections and differences, in scale' (61). Whether the task itself is achievable or not is perhaps beside the point; more interesting will be the problems and slippages that such a project encounters and what these might reveal about our assumptions of the nature of site. A rather different example is provided by the 'strange spaces' of recent work by Station House Opera. The production *Roadmetal, Sweetbread* uses pre-recorded film to construct a site that sits within, or alongside, the physical performance space occupied by the performers and audience. The filmed material, showing the same performers in the same costumes moving through the same performance space (including backstage and foyer areas; re-filmed for each version of the show), is brought into a playful and increasingly uneasy relationship with the live material as each acquires, challenges and loses the status of 'reality'. More recently, Station House Opera has been interested in investigating further possibilities of this kind of in-between space; *Live From Paradise* is performed simultaneously to three audiences in different cities, with each space visible to the others via live video broadcast. This ongoing experiment poses the questions of where the performance might be located and how the nature of the theatrical site is conceived.

While, for Una Chaudhuri, 'a complex engagement with the significance, determinations, and potentialities of place courses through the body of modern drama' (1995: 3), *site* seems to incorporate a concern with particular geographical places with an interrogation of how art, and in our case performance, creates a space of encounter. Questions of *what* and *how* site 'means' are teased apart by all of the practices addressed here in different ways, and it is in this sense that the dynamics of site-specific theatre are important. Whether *site* signals the same meanings now as it did in the 1960s when minimalist sculptors alerted viewers to their own situation, or in the 1980s when theatre-makers began to experiment with the alternative possibilities it seemed to offer, site-specificity remains a useful concept (and set of practices). In large part this is because it enables us to think through what would seem to be pressing questions: of the local and the global, of what Britain might mean in relation to (and as part of) changing understandings of Europe, of cyberspaces and their implications for our relationships to physical spaces, and of contemporary versions of dislocation. It also permits entry into a debate around *theatreness*, raising questions of what theatre has been and might be in the future. Site-specific theatre, like the sites that it conceives, enacts and disrupts, might best be conceived of as in process, always under negotiation.

Notes

1   To date these have been *Tropicana* (2004–5) and *Amato Saltone* (2005–6). Prior to its work with the National Theatre, Shunt had created performances at its previous temporary home under the railway arches at Bethnal Green as well as in a range of other venues.
2   Bryden followed up this experience with another large-scale site-specific performance, *The Big Picnic* (Harland and Wolff Engine Shed, Govan, Glasgow, 28 September–13 November 1994). Both this and *The Ship* were also screened on BBC television (*The Ship* first broadcast BBC2, 26 December 1990; *The Big Picnic* first broadcast BBC2, 22 June 1996).
3   The comment appeared in a review of Shunt's *Tropicana* (*Guardian*, 23 October 2004). Billington continues: 'when the show matches the space, as in Bill Bryden's remarkable 1990s play set in a defunct Glasgow shipyard, the result can be astonishing. But Tropicana, although skilfully performed, offers little more than mild titillation for jaded theatrical appetites.'
4   Different versions of the label have been preferred in different contexts. A recent symposium at the University of Exeter, for example, opted for 'site-based', though most of the questions it posed circulated around just the term 'site' ('Site/Sight – Source/Resource', 11–12 September 2004). See the introduction to Miwon Kwon's *One Place After Another* (2002) for an argument for the value of the range of terms other than site-specific (in addition to those already mentioned, Kwon refers to 'site-determined', 'site-referenced', 'site-conscious', 'site-responsive' and, later, 'context-specific').
5   See Cathy Turner (2004) for an exploration of the critical possibilities of two discourses that she suggests are complementary: archaeology and psychoanalytic theory.

6 Kwon usefully traces this genealogy (2002: 11–31). In a performance context, Nick Kaye (2000) draws on the legacies of minimalist sculpture to inform his discussions of architects, visual artists and theatre companies.

7 One example often cited in this context is Robert Morris's *Untitled* (1965), consisting of a set of mirrored cubes in which the viewer is reflected.

8 Both companies are still engaging with site-based work (and, indeed, IOU recently mounted *PLOT*, an exhibition of images from its 30 years of making performance in unusual locations). See the company websites at www.ioutheatre.org and www.stationhouseopera.com.

9 David Wheeler, interview with author, 15 February 2002.

10 These are documented in Kaye's *Site-Specific Art* (2000: 170–81).

11 Brith Gof was founded by Mike Pearson and Lis Hughes Jones in Aberystwyth, Wales, in 1981. Clifford McLucas joined the company in 1989 and remained a prominent figure there until his untimely death in 2002. The company was formally closed in 2004. It is most often remembered for its large-scale site-specific performances and its ethical commitment to the geographical and social landscape of Wales.

12 In particular, the mass privatization and 'modernization' of the UK's industries, and the cutting of public arts funding.

13 McLucas sets out the terms of this model in his documentation 'Ten Feet and Three Quarters of an Inch of Theatre' (Kaye 2000: 125–37). See also Cathy Turner (2004), who discusses the model at more length.

14 Pearson later developed his work on the potential for active connections between performance and archaeology in collaboration with the archaeologist Michael Shanks. Their proposal for a new 'blurred genre' is published as *Theatre/Archaeology* (2001).

15 As Pearson notes (Pearson and Shanks 2001: 106), following the Cardiff performances the production was 'restaged in a sand quarry in Italy, in a disused crane factory in Germany, in an empty ice-rink in Friesland and in Tramway in Glasgow'.

16 This and subsequent quotations are taken from the performance text of *Haearn*, as recorded in the televised document of the show (see note 17, below).

17 Of course, the television format in which a version of *Haearn* was also made produces its own scale and priorities that seem, at times, to be at odds with those of the live event (*Haearn (Iron)*, BBC and S4C, 1993). As a site, according to McLucas, 'television deals best and is happiest with small, intimate, light, fluid things' (interview, 6 October 2001).

18 A concern with rural and to some extent marginal 'timespaces' developed in later work in which McLucas was engaged. For example, following a series of projects in rural Wales, towards the end of his life McLucas collaborated with the archaeologist Michael Shanks on *The Three Landscapes Project*, which attempted to use time-based media other than live performance to represent a series of places: Hafod, a picturesque landscape

in west Wales; the site of an archaeological dig in Sicily; and the San Andreas fault in California. Mike Pearson, meanwhile, established the company Pearson/Brookes with Mike Brookes and created a number of works, discussed later in this chapter, that use various modes of documentation and live performance to fold together different spaces and times. These later works of both Pearson and McLucas are significantly more low-key than the large-scale industrial work associated with Brith Gof: provisional, fleeting and frequently focused on the private sphere.

19   In a talk given at Lancaster University on 27 January 2006, artistic director Tim Etchells pointed to 'landscape' as a significant idea in much of Forced Entertainment's work ('Text/Action/Landscape: Connections and Processes in the Work of Forced Entertainment').

20   See Sarah Gorman's chapter in this volume for further discussion.

21   Welfare State is currently in the process of reviewing its artistic agenda and reorganizing itself and its work in the light of John Fox's retirement from the company in March 2006.

22   We might read this as another version of some of the imperatives of public art; for more on these, and their potential contradictions, see Malcolm Miles, *Art, Space and the City* (1997).

23   There are comparisons to be made with the 1951 Festival of Britain. See David Matless (1998: 267–72) for a reading of the festival through questions of place and identity.

24   Built on the Meridian Line at Greenwich, London, to celebrate the millennium, the Dome opened to the public on 1 January 2000, housing exhibits in a series of themed 'zones'. The much-publicized expense of the project, together with the low visitor numbers, made it controversial. The Dome closed on 31 December 2000 and plans are under way to turn it into a sports and entertainment stadium to be used as part of the 2012 Olympics.

25   This distinction was made in a talk ('Who Are You Looking At?') given by Mike Pearson and Mike Brookes at the PARIP conference, Bretton Hall, University of Leeds, 3 July 2005.

26   See Heike Roms's chapter in this volume for further discussion.

27   This trend might be connected to discourses of walking in other contexts: some diverse examples are Michel de Certeau's model of 'Walking in the City' in *The Practice of Everyday Life* (1984), Rebecca Solnit's *Wanderlust* (2001) and Francesco Careri's *Walkscapes* (2002). There is, of course, an important body of work in visual art that uses walking as process, structure and object of inquiry; the practice of Richard Long is at the forefront of such work (see Long 2002). And, in a dramatic context, Una Chaudhuri suggests that 'the master trope of modern drama is that image of transformation which nevertheless inscribes the power of the old: the journey' (1995: 53); walking is not the only version of the journey employed in her examples, but it remains a significant one.

28 Situationist International was a political and artistic group prominent in the late 1950s and 1960s. It asserted that capitalism has led to a stifling 'society of the spectacle' (the title of a key work by SI's unofficial leader, Guy Debord) and sought ways of connecting art and everyday life.
29 The *dérive*, or drift, was one of the techniques outlined by Debord as a means of working against the power of the spectacle; it involves mapping the city in terms of its 'psycho-geography' by ignoring one's habitual motivations for moving and instead walking according to the influences one finds in the urban space at the time. See Guy Debord (1958). 'Theory of the Dérive', *Internationale Situationniste* 2. This article is also available widely on the internet, for instance at http://library.nothingness.org.
30 See the project website: www.linkedM11.info.
31 Quotations from *LINKED* are drawn from my notes taken while doing the walk.
32 On 13 April 2003, as part of the Civic Centre symposium hosted by the research project 'Performance Architecture Location' (based at Roehampton University), 9–16 April 2003 (see www.civiccentre.org).
33 Miwon Kwon traces a comparable genealogy of site-specificity in visual art, suggesting that, whereas the 'site' of art contexts was once a discrete and bordered place, it is now more likely to be an itinerary than a map. She points to the potential of nomadic artistic practices to produce a concept of site as 'an intertextually coordinated, multiply located, discursive field of operation' (2002: 159), though she does warn against the romanticism that is often associated with 'the image of the cultural worker on the go' (160).
34 Response to questionnaire, discussed in Wilkie (2002).

Primary reading

Fox, John (2002). *Eyes on Stalks*. London: Methuen.
Heathfield, Adrian, ed. (2000). *Small Acts: Performance, the Millennium and the Marking of Time*. London: Black Dog.
Hill, Leslie, and Paris, Helen (2006). *Performance and Place*. Basingstoke: Palgrave Macmillan.
Kaye, Nick (2000). *Site-Specific Art: Performance, Place and Documentation*. London: Routledge.
Kwon, Miwon (2002). *One Place After Another: Site-Specific Art and Locational Identity*. Cambridge, MA: MIT.
Pearson, Mike, and Shanks, Michael (2001). *Theatre/Archaeology*. London: Routledge.
Wrights & Sites (2003). *An Exeter Mis-Guide*. Exeter: Wrights & Sites.
Wrights & Sites (2006). *A Mis-Guide to Anywhere*. Exeter: Wrights & Sites.

Fiona Wilkie

Further reading

Careri, Francesco (2002). *Walkscapes*. Barcelona: Editorial Gustavo Gili.

Casey, Edward (1993). *Getting Back into Place: Toward a Renewed Understanding of the Place-World*. Bloomington, IN: Indiana University Press.

Chaudhuri, Una (1995). *Staging Place: The Geography of Modern Drama*. Ann Arbor, MI: University of Michigan Press.

Coult, Tony, and Kershaw, Baz, eds. (1983). *Engineers of the Imagination: The Welfare State Handbook*. London: Methuen

de Certeau, Michel (1984). *The Practice of Everyday Life*. Berkeley: University of California Press.

Harvie, Jen (2005). *Staging the UK*. Manchester: Manchester University Press.

Hetherington, Kevin (1998). *Expressions of Identity: Space, Performance, Politics*. London: Sage.

Hodder, Ian, and Shanks, Michael, eds. (1995). *Interpreting Archaeology*. London: Routledge.

Long, R. (2002). *Walking the Line*. London: Thames and Hudson.

Mason, Bim (1992). *Street Theatre and Other Outdoor Performance*. London: Routledge.

Matless, David (1998). *Landscape and Englishness*. London: Reaktion Books.

Miles, Malcolm (1997). *Art, Space and the City: Public Art and Urban Futures*. London: Routledge.

Pearson, Mike (1998). 'My Balls/Your Chin', *Performance Research* 3:2, 35–41.

Relph, E. (1976). *Place and Placelessness*. London: Pion.

Solnit, Rebecca (2001). *Wanderlust: A History of Walking*. London: Verso.

Turner, Cathy (2004). 'Palimpsest or Potential Space? Finding a Vocabulary for Site-Specific Performance', *New Theatre Quarterly* 20:4, 373–90.

Wiles, David (2003). *A Short History of Western Performance Space*. Cambridge: Cambridge University Press.

Wilkie, Fiona (2002). 'Mapping the Terrain: A Survey of Site-Specific Performance in Britain', *New Theatre Quarterly* 70:2, 140–60.

Chapter 6

Staging an Urban Nation: Place and Identity in Contemporary Welsh Theatre

Heike Roms

Summer in the city. A heatwave.
Traffic snarls.
A dog sleeps in the shade of a park.
He wakes in the cool of a thunderstorm but when the rain clears he's
    lost.
The rain has washed away the scent, the trail, the path that will lead
    him home.
He now roams the city
a stray dog
one of many
a lost dog
dreaming of home
a raindog. (Pearson et al. 2003: 40)

Raindogs (Chapter, Cardiff, 2002) was conceived as the result of a collaboration between Welsh playwright Ed Thomas and Wales-based performance group Pearson/Brookes.[1] A meditation on the *unhomely* nature of the contemporary city, it featured a collection of short poetic texts by Thomas and Pearson, which the two recited in front of a large projection screen showing CCTV footage of a succession of black-suited male performers standing still among the bustling multitude that engulfed them on the streets and squares of Cardiff's city centre. The loss of a sense of place and belonging of which the writing spoke and the lonely dissociation of the men from their surroundings portrayed in the films were reinforced by the performance's formal design. Specific in its reference to a particular site (the city of Cardiff) and yet decidedly not site-specific (i.e. performed at site), the work presented its urban locations as a series of panoptic visions, offering us a recognizable view of the world (our world) that lay just outside of the theatre walls, and yet locating us firmly outside of its frame, thus making us share the performers' sense of displacement from it.

In its representation of urban space as a problematic, *Raindogs* marked a significant shift in contemporary Welsh theatre that passed almost unnoticed at the time. The work could simply be regarded as another example of the renewed interest in the theme of the contemporary city that has lately emerged across the British theatre and performance scene, were it not for the fact that it was created by artists whose past work had been committed wholly to developing a theatrical representation for a different spatial problematic, that of Wales as a nation. One of Pearson/Brookes's directors, Mike Pearson (b. 1949), had in the past been the artistic co-director of Brith Gof (a Welsh idiom translating as 'faint recollection'), 'probably Wales's internationally best-known performance company' (Harvie 2005: 44), whose pioneering site-specific productions – including *Gododdin* (Cardiff, 1988), *Pax* (Cardiff, 1991), *Haearn* (Iron) (Tredegar, 1992) and *Tri Bywyd* (Three Lives) (Lampeter, 1995) – as Charmian Savill notes, were 'inspired by their need to reinscribe Welsh social, mythic, literary, political and historical representation' (Savill 1997: 105).

Playwright and director Ed Thomas (b. 1961) is another well-known Welsh theatre artist of whom it was said that his former company, Y Cwmni (Welsh for The Company, later renamed Fiction Factory), like Brith Gof, 'could only exist in present-day Wales because the nature and status of Welshness is what it is all about' (Adams 1996: 52). Thomas's major plays – including the so-called *New Wales Trilogy* of *House of America* (St Stephen's, Cardiff, 1988), *Flowers of the Dead Red Sea* (Tramway, Glasgow, 1991) and *East from the Gantry* (Tramway, Glasgow, 1992), as well as *Song from a Forgotten City* (Chapter, Cardiff, 1995) and *Gas Station Angel* (Newcastle Playhouse, 1998), all premiered by his company under his own direction – set out to invent a new cultural mythology from a dismantling of traditional views of Welsh identity. It could be argued therefore, with some justification, that Pearson and Thomas's apparent break with their commitment to an investigation of Welsh nationhood and their turn towards the city as location and subject matter is indicative of a wider change in theatre in Wales, a change that critic David Adams, long-time observer of the scene, summed up as: 'we've had ten years being obsessed with [Welsh] identity, it's time to move on' (see Thomas 2002: 128).

The decade to which Adams alludes here refers to the years between 1988 and 1998, a time he calls 'a mini Golden Age of Welsh theatre' (1996: 126). The period was bracketed at the start by 'an exceptionally good year' (ibid.) for theatre in Wales, which included in particular two works that have become defining landmarks for the era's addressing of the problem of identity: Brith Gof's seminal *Gododdin*, the first of its large-scale site-specific shows, and Ed Thomas's first and still best-known play, *House of America*. But the period ended with two major developments in the political and cultural sphere in Wales which have had a decisive impact on the country's theatre scene, not least on the work of Brith Gof and Ed Thomas. The year 1998 saw the creation of the National Assembly for Wales, and only months later the Arts Council of Wales published its infamous *Drama Strategy for Wales* (1999), which meant the removal of revenue funding from half of the Arts Council's theatre clients (including Brith Gof[2]) in order to support the planned creation of two mainstream Welsh national theatre companies (see Owen 2004: 386–9). These developments presented a radical shift in arts policy concerning the link between theatre and nationhood, from a time in the early 1990s when the eclectic diversity of theatre companies in Wales was widely regarded, in the words of the then drama officer at the Welsh Arts Council, Mike Baker, as the 'real incarnation of a national theatre of Wales' (1990: 119) to a time at the closing of the decade when this diversity was replaced by a greater focus on a small number of flagship companies, whose role was conceived of as that of a more simplified and streamlined 'national theatre' of self-representation.

Just as the process of devolution reinvigorated a debate on national identity and its theatrical representation in Wales within the institutional realm of cultural policy making, theatre-makers – including Pearson and Thomas – increasingly turned away from the kind of national narratives that had dominated Welsh theatre in the 1980s and 1990s (some may indeed argue that even before devolution the importance of these narratives was exaggerated). Thomas has openly expressed his disappointment with the process of devolution: 'The optimism many of us felt in the late 1990s about the cultural possibilities for Wales has by now evaporated' (Davies 2005: 43). But the reasons probably run much deeper than this: Thomas and Pearson's complex and questioning theatre practice, which had increasingly emphasized the eclecticism and hybridity of Welsh identity, is profoundly at odds with what Roger Owen has identified as the '*faux*-populist institutionalization of Welsh theatre, the impoverishment of its local diversity and the marginalization of intellectually challenging and stimulating work' (Owen 2004: 396) that have developed in response to the challenges of greater self-government in Wales.

At the same time, however, I wish to argue that there is in fact a continuity in the thematic and formal concerns of Pearson and Thomas's theatrical practice between the 1990s and their more recent work that the talk of the end of 'an obsession with Welsh identity' is in danger of overlooking. I will aim to show that at the heart of the theatre-making of both artists has been an ongoing inquiry into the problems of place and its relation to identity. This inquiry is not an expression of the often-quoted essentialist notion of a particular Welsh 'sense of place' or *brogarwch*, 'a care and love for the locality and its people' that finds its various manifestations in the place-sensitive genres of site-specific or community-based theatre (Baker 1990: 119). Rather, it has been a response to what Una Chaudhuri has called 'a new *platiality*, a recognition of the signifying power and political potential of *specific places*' (1997: 5), that is the product of particular historical, cultural and political configurations. Such 'platiality' has acquired special significance for a country such as Wales whose geography has long been culturally dominated and economically exploited by forces outside of itself.[3] The result is the conception of place as problem, or, to be precise, the conception of the problem of place as home (and homeland) that runs through Pearson and Thomas's earlier oeuvre, symbolized through the signifying power and political potential of specific places. This concern has not been abandoned in their recent work, but rather reconfigured and rethought in relation to a new 'platial' context – that of the city. As Alyce von Rothkirch proposes in her review of *Raindogs*: 'It is a Welsh urban culture in which place does not automatically confer a sense of belonging and community, which, in the context of Welsh discourses of place and community, is doubtless an interesting departure' (2003).

I do not wish to ignore the fact, however, that the aesthetic approaches Pearson and Thomas chose for their representation of a problematic of place had for most of their careers been very different. With Brith Gof, Pearson had pioneered site-specific performance work in Wales, which became a prominent genre precisely because of its perceived potential to bring into correspondence the place of representation and the represented place in an attempt to create theatre work that expresses particular localized concerns. Thomas, on the other hand, never attempted to move out of the representation framework of the conventional theatre space, instead subjecting this space to increasing scrutiny. Both exemplified two different aesthetics – site-specific performance and new writing – around which the lines of the debate about contemporary theatre in Wales seemed irrevocably drawn throughout most of the 1980s and 1990s. For the advocates of the former, the word on stage was associated with an authoritarian (often equated with a predominantly English) cultural and aesthetic tradition; for the advocates of the latter, site-specific theatre was culturally marginalized as an experimental form with limited audience reach.[4] With hindsight, however, their mutual concern with the relationship between questions of place and questions of theatrical representation (which they share with other Welsh theatre artists, including playwrights such as Ian Rowlands, Dic Edwards and Gary Owen and performance practitioners such as Eddie Ladd, Marc Rees and Volcano Theatre) moves the two approaches much closer together and makes Pearson and Thomas's collaboration on *Raindogs* the obvious development of both their paths.

Virtual Reality Wales

In 1995, in a scathing attack on what he regarded as the stifling cultural nationalist agenda dictated to writers in Wales, Welsh playwright Mark Jenkins (1995) coined the phrase 'Virtual Reality Wales' to describe an invented place that only existed in stage representations and that to him presented a crass simplification of the highly fragmented reality of the country's contemporary cultural landscape. The phrase could indeed serve as an apt description for the places evoked in the works of Brith Gof and Ed Thomas during the 1990s – yet in their cases not in spite of, but precisely because of, their recognition of the deeply incongruous and continually changing nature of contemporary Welsh identities. Both had set themselves a difficult task: to represent something which did not yet exist, a future Wales that would be a home for a different idea of identity. In Ed Thomas's dramas, this place is dreamt up by a group of displaced characters, not just excluded from but often disempowered by traditional notions of Welshness. In Brith Gof's site-specific performances, this place is an increasingly hybrid site which aims to contain the ever more complex relations between the Welsh-speaking and English-speaking cultures of Wales and their different claims on a Welsh national identity.

How strong this sense of Wales as a place yet to come was in the work of both theatre-makers in the 1990s emerges clearly from their programmatic writing of the time. In an early essay on 'Wales and a Theatre of Invention', Thomas (1991) drafts his vision of how a new form of theatre could contribute to the creation of a new Wales, echoing the influential thesis of Welsh historian Gwyn Alf Williams on the need for a constant reinvention of Wales in the face of a series of historic ruptures:[5] 'In a Wales that only exists in the hearts and minds of those who desire it and who see that existence based on constant re-invention, any new Welsh theatre must be a theatre of invention, with its own new language, form and style' (Thomas 1991: 17).

As Katie Gramich has pointed out, for a playwright who is thus devoted to cultural reinvention, 'the canvas of [Thomas's] works is not lavish but restricted, the atmosphere of his plays fetid with a sense of claustrophobia' (Gramich 1998: 159). The dramas[6] are played out in a series of closed-in (often eponymous) places – not referring to specific locations, but none the less recognizable as 'platial' metaphors for the Welsh condition: hotel rooms (*Song from a Forgotten City*, *Stone City Blue*), a slaughterhouse engulfed by water (*Flowers of the Dead Red Sea*), and, most frequently, houses, encroached upon by an open-cast mine (*House of America*), derelict and surrounded by snow (*East from the Gantry*), or half fallen into the sea (*Gas Station Angel*). The plays derive their impact from the interplay between these beleaguered locations and the expansiveness of the (mostly doomed) spatial visions of their heroes, through which Thomas tests various models for a 'virtual reality Wales'. This interplay is already at work in Thomas's first piece for the theatre, *House of America*, where the tension between limitation and expanse, home and escape, is encapsulated in the double figure of the title. In this story of a dysfunctional, fatherless[7] (i.e. rootless) family in the South Wales valleys, the 'house' in its double sense of shelter and kin becomes a place of inevitable destruction for the characters, who find themselves both overwhelmed by the external cultural and economic forces of the present (the open-cast mine appears to offer employment but in the end only contributes to the devastation of the place) and haunted by the returning ghosts of their own past (in the shape of the murdered father, literally revealed by the advancing mine). Thomas here reconfigures what Chaudhuri has identified as the central 'geopathological' problem for all modern drama (1997: 8): home appears as both the *condition for* and the *obstacle to* identity. That this problematic of home serves as a metaphor for the problematic of homeland in Thomas's work is recognized by Anna-Marie Taylor, for whom in 'Thomas's crazed Lewis family cooped up in their *House of America* [we see] south Wales gone mad in its post-industrial decline' (Taylor 1997: 112). A vision of America serves temporarily as a figure of escape and recovery to two of the characters, the young Sid and his sister Gwenny: it stands for everything that Wales is not – rebellion, freedom from the shackles of an oppressive past, a shelter for outsiders. But their American Dream taken to its final conclusion turns out to be an impotent, even destructive one, leading to the foreshadowing of a monstrous future signified through an incestuous pregnancy (Williams 2002: 434).

America appears as such an ambivalent symbol in many of Thomas's early plays: the home of a potentially liberating (although always only borrowed) imaginary, but also the origin of an all-pervading cultural and economic force that threatens to level cultural difference. In a later play, *Gas Station Angel*, in many ways the hopeful mirror image of the bleakness of *House of America*, the dream of America is replaced by myths drawn from closer to home, including traditional Welsh stories and European folklore (see Williams 2002), replacing a failed vision of exile with a new and reinvigorated image of home. The drama again features a besieged locale in the form of a house, 'whose other half has fallen into the sea' (*Gas Station Angel*: 2) – only this time, fuelled by pre-referendum optimism, Thomas allows his characters to leave this embattled place (and, as von Rothkirch has pointed out [2006: 137], to leave behind a certain kind of Welsh nationalism that had become entrenched in a purely oppositional stance) and dream of building a new, confident house of Wales in a changing, decentred Europe: 'De-lotteried. De-governed. Ungoverned. Free' (Thomas 1998: 72).

Central to Ed Thomas's conception of a 'theatre of invention' is the manner in which the different places that are thus represented in his work are mapped onto the dimensions of the theatre space itself. Thomas, as much a director as he is a writer, creates works for the theatre that unravel the problematic of place by responding to and challenging the specifics of their own particular home, the stage. Whilst

House of America still pays tribute to the self-contained world of theatrical naturalism, later plays, beginning with *Flowers of the Dead Red Sea*, repeatedly call attention to the fit (or misfit) between dramatic space(s) and stage space in an increasingly self-referential manner.[8] *Gas Station Angel*, for example, demands an environment that is continually changing and changeable: the stage directions talk of 'an ever fluid landscape [. . .] dislocated, unreal, fantastic, functional, witty and full of possibility. Beds turn into cars, mountain becomes beach [*sic*] airport becomes supermarket [. . .]. Transformation is everything . . .' (Thomas 1998: 2).[9] Thomas's plays thus aim to make transparent and productive their contingency on the audience's imaginative complicity in the creation of their make-believe – vital for the working of a theatre that hopes to transform theatrical imagination into political reinvention.

In 1997, Mike Pearson outlined a new aesthetics for Welsh theatre that, in the link it draws between theatrical and political place, figured as real and virtual respectively, and its dependency on the structures of representation and spectatorship, contains a number of interesting parallels to Thomas's vision. He describes the role of such a new theatre as creating:

> an idealized world where wrongs can be righted, injustices repealed, new agendas set [. . .]. Performance may begin to resemble a 'special world' [. . .], all the elements of which [. . .] are conceived, organized and ultimately experienced by its ordering of the participant [. . .]. We may all – performers and spectators – eventually have to ask, 'Who is who?', 'Whom do I watch?', 'What's going on here?' – in a virtual Wales. [. . .] To challenge and to create identities may be its ultimate objective. (Pearson 1997: 97–8)

Unlike Ed Thomas, however, Brith Gof moored this aesthetic and political programme in the use of 'other places [. . .] for performance. In such constructed situations, free from the laws and by-laws of normative theatre practice, other things, real things, can happen' (ibid.). The company had begun right from its establishment in 1981 to reject purpose-built theatre spaces because, as its artistic co-director Cliff McLucas claimed, 'the Welsh-speaking community may see them as "colonial outposts"' (McLucas and Pearson 1999: 83), as there had been no indigenous tradition of playhouses in Wales. Instead, throughout its history the company adapted locations in which, as Pearson proposed, 'a Welsh, particularly a Welsh rural audience, would feel more at ease in' (Kaye 1996: 210) – here too we find a discourse of home deeply woven into the work. The locations included barns, chapels and farmhouse kitchens and, in its later site-specific practice, post-industrial sites such as railway stations (*Pax*), disused car factories (*Gododdin*) and abandoned iron foundries (*Haearn*), all regarded as metonymies for Wales at large. Jen Harvie argues that it is through the choice of such locations of deep familiarity that Brith Gof has come to epitomize what she regards as site-specific performance's particular power to act as a vehicle for identity:

> Fundamental to Brith Gof's work, therefore, was a commitment to exploring Welsh identities, first, in the 'real', lived environments where memories which produced those identities were located [...] and, second, in environments of social, industrial, and economic activity (or forced inactivity) which so significantly constituted many people's – especially men's – experience of Welsh identity at that time of accelerated decline in Wales's mining, steel production and heavy manufacturing industries. (Harvie 2005: 45)

But the link between location, identity and performance was not as straightforward as this may suggest. The more differentiated and hybrid Brith Gof's understanding of Welsh identity became – extending its conception of Welshness increasingly beyond traditional notions of a rural, Welsh-speaking culture towards the post-industrial, English-speaking and urban aspects of contemporary Wales – the less obvious became the cultural association between identity and location and the more complex the relationship between performance and its site.[10] Indeed, this relationship became ever more interrogated, reworked and elaborated in both Brith Gof's practical and theoretical explorations of 'site-specificity' in the 1990s (e.g. Kaye 1996). It was frequently not the locations that invested the performances with a sense of identity, as Harvie proposes, but the performances that made these locations and the histories associated with them representative of such an identity. *Gododdin*, for instance, took as its starting point the earliest poem in the Welsh language, Aneirin's *Y Gododdin*, which commemorates the defeat of a band of Celtic warriors by a dominant invading army in 600 BC, and placed it in the disused Rover car factory in Cardiff. The performance thereby established a link between the mythical narratives of cultural birth, defeat and rebirth which the Welsh-language culture had cultivated and the contemporary decline of a predominantly English-speaking industrial culture in Wales, referring to both as symbols for a Welsh identity that was conceived as a hybrid of past and present, rural and industrial, Welsh and English.[11]

Within Pearson's notion of a 'virtual Wales', a liminal space of potency, identity appears not as a given object to be represented, but as the joint product of the work of the spectators and the performers, created, experienced and challenged in performance. This aspect presents an important element of Brith Gof's later performances, made just prior to the Welsh referendum in 1997, yet one which is often overlooked – it emphasizes that the company became increasingly concerned with Welsh identity as a potentiality rather than as an already existing reality. This potentiality had no home (as yet) in any of the culturally significant locations of the company's earlier work, but was itself a provisional home that would be actualized in the event of performance itself.

Without wanting to underestimate the unquestionably significant role that site-specific considerations played in Brith Gof's work, just as important as the history of the locations it chose for its performances[12] was what they allowed the company to do, namely to encourage a different kind of audience–performer interaction.[13] Brith Gof hoped to be able to investigate the workings of theatrical representation 'free from the laws and by-laws of normative theatre practice' (Pearson 1997: 98) so that it could reorder the way in which theatrical representation joins notions of identity to the process of the audience's identification – vital for the working of a theatre that aimed to challenge and recreate long-established cultural attachments. It is this desire which unites Ed Thomas's and Brith Gof's otherwise very different theatre practice in the 1990s: inventing a virtual Wales for them was less about representing an identity that is already given than about imagining and creating a sense of identification with an identity that was yet to come.

Cardiff Noir

In 2005 Cardiff celebrated its centenary as a city and 50 years as the Welsh capital. Its relation to the nation has always been a fraught one: Cardiff is geographically and culturally located in close proximity to England, and as a port has always maintained stronger links with the rest of the world than with its Welsh hinterland, which for many has called into question its suitability as a capital.[14] The dispute that first arose when this role was decided upon was revived in the wake of devolution: when searching for a location for the Welsh Assembly, Swansea and every other major town in Wales were again thought to have historically more justifiable claims than Cardiff's to becoming the seat of government.[15] But the city is undergoing major changes: once a thoroughly anglicized and overwhelmingly working-class town, Cardiff has attracted a new middle class, many of whom are Welsh speakers employed in the media and government. Symbolic of the transformation is the bay area, where, adjacent to the neighbourhood that still houses one of the oldest multicultural communities in Britain, one of Europe's largest waterfront developments now includes the Senedd, the new home for the Assembly, designed by Richard Rogers.

James Donald has written about the importance of the literary imaginary for the construction of the modern city: 'In order to imagine the unrepresentable space, life, and languages of the city, to make them liveable, we translate them into narratives' (1997: 181). Whilst for a long time a blank and uncharted space, Cardiff has recently experienced a range of narrative translations, notably in the works of its new urban noir novelists,[16] but increasingly also in the works of dramatists. *Cardiff East* (Royal National Theatre, London, 1997) by Peter Gill (b. 1939) and *Ghost City* (Chapter, Cardiff, 2004) by Gary Owen (b. 1972) are two plays that speak of Cardiff's metamorphosis. Whilst Gill's play upholds the possibility of a working-class community threatened by the new urban order, Owen, a representative of the younger generation of Welsh playwrights, depicts fragmentation, failed communications and latent violence as the defining experience of contemporary urban life.

Ed Thomas had turned to Cardiff as a location once before *Raindogs*. *Song from a Forgotten City* (1995) is, more than any of his previous plays, firmly located in a real, existing topography: the text mentions famous landmarks in Cardiff, from the Hayes Island public toilets to the Angel Hotel (Thomas 2002: 13, 11), the latter of which serves as the setting for the play. Yet it is not really Cardiff's urban landscape that appears to interest the writer, but its status as a capital and as a metonym for the nation at large. Thomas's familiar search for a new Wales is figured here as the search for a new city, 'emblematic of the quest for a new, modern, urban, Welsh culture, not one based on an outmoded rural idyll' (Gramich 1998: 170). The play features one of Thomas's male dreamers, a poet called Carlyle, whose imaginings of a great metropolis continue the playwright's earlier preoccupations: 'A place where something good might happen. [. . .] A place where you aint treated like a piece of shit. A place where you're not a fuck-all squared. A place that counts on the scale of things. Is noted for something good. Is not invisible' (58). Later on in the play, the invention of this city is even more openly equated to the birth of a new Wales in the shape of a nativity scene:

Carlyle: She wants to give birth in the city. She wants it to happen in the city because she wants to give birth to a country. Without a city she can't have a country. She can only imagine the pain of birth. But she wants to give birth. She wants a country. She imagines the city. A metropolis. (116)

But the optimism that is expressed in the symbol of the birth is muted by the realities of Cardiff's (and therefore Wales's) cultural invisibility: 'This city aint grown up yet. It's a junior city, still on free school milk, not on the map, the cool map, the map of cool, any fucking map!' (58). Thomas himself writes against this invisibility by conjuring up his imagined Cardiff from the narrative repertoire of noir elements: against a seedy setting of suppressed violence, *Song* celebrates excess, gender confusion and erotic desire, all conventionally associated with a transgressive urbanism, as potentially emancipating from the shackles of a static and outlived cultural tradition ('singing, dancing, winning at rugby').

For Pearson/Brookes too, *Raindogs* was not the first time the artists turned their attentions to the city of Cardiff. The work was the third in a series of performances by the company that derived its material from contemporary life on Cardiff's city streets and shifted its focus of attention to questions of urbanity, civic space, public behaviour and visibility.[17] The earlier works, *Carrying Lyn* (Chapter, Cardiff, 2001) and *Polis* (Chapter, Cardiff, 2001), were both staged as multi-site performances, utilizing a complex intersection between urban environment and the theatre space. In *Carrying Lyn*, a group of men carried disabled transgender performer Lyn Levett across Cardiff on a crowded day, whilst the audience in the theatre watched documentation of this journey brought to them at regular intervals by cycle couriers directly from the streets. The theatrical reconstruction thus took place within a 15-minute time delay of the live event, a delay that was both revealed and confounded by the eventual arrival of the performers in the theatre space (Pearson and Jeff 2001). In *Polis*, the audience itself was put in charge of the documentation: several groups of spectators watched and documented different events occurring simultaneously in different locations in the city. Taken back to the theatre, their recordings were then assembled to create a multi-perspective impression of the city on one particular night.

As I have argued elsewhere in reference to *Polis* (Roms 2004), issues of Welsh nationness continued to inform this work, but *Polis* marked a transition from a cultural understanding of such nation-hood (for which the tensions between Wales's different constituent cultures has always been difficult to reconcile, even in models of cultural hybridity) to one based on a conception of citizenship, a transition effected by the process of devolution. The political intent of the work is manifest in its title: *Polis* set out to explore the idea of the 'political' in its double association with urbanity and citizenship, as implied in the traditional notion of the 'polis'. Extending Brith Gof's earlier explorations of the theatrical mechanisms of identification, this was a work conceptualized by Pearson *as* a kind of 'polis', in which an ad hoc and provisional community would be built from the experiences and contributions made in the encounters between performers, spectators and the urban everyday.

The most remarkable aspect of Pearson/Brookes's city projects, however, was their utilization of the theatre space. When the spectators of *Carrying Lyn*, who were waiting in Chapter's theatre for the slowly approaching performers, rushed outside to welcome them and then accompanied the group into the black box studio where we jointly watched the video documentation of this arrival, we in effect witnessed the return to the space of the theatre of a group of artists whose past work had become practically synonymous with a radical exit from that very space. But this was a return that brought with it the experiences made elsewhere, a reconfiguration of the intentions of the site-specific work rather than its abandonment. Borrowing from Chaudhuri, we can describe this approach as a 'transgression *qua* transgression, a sign that the enclosure of the theatre is not airtight, that theatrical boundaries are permeable' (1997: 45). This work no longer attempts to escape the mechanics of theatrical representation by moving outside of conventional theatre spaces – only to find that these mechanisms were often being reinforced by this very move.[18] Instead, Pearson/Brookes now called attention to their working by involving the spectators in their construction.

But where *Polis* still suggested the possibility of an identification through participation that had been so important to Brith Gof's political programme – even if, by relocating the audience's encounters from the streets into the theatre space and thereby from a live moment to its mediated reproduction, the performance revealed it in its ambivalence as both a desire for a genuine exchange and as a desire to control it – *Raindogs* withdrew that possibility altogether. In *Raindogs*,

the audience was confined to being witnesses rather than participants, encountering the urban landscape entirely through its mediatized
representation. We may assume that this was a deliberate break
with current site-specific practice. Much of this practice that engages
with the city (including Pearson/Brookes's earlier works) utilizes theoretical principles first articulated by Michel de Certeau in *The Practice
of Everyday Life*, which privilege the ground-level performance of the
urban pedestrian as a potential enactment of a resistant practice.
Raindogs, however, offered us the city only through the panoptic
perspective of the omnipresent surveillance camera, the symbol of a
detached power – a perspective that promises control, but removes
us from the opportunity to inscribe meaning into the city by moving
through it in the way de Certeau had theorized. A sense of dissociation and dislocation is performed in the very medium itself:
this is a territory of exile, where the performance is divided between
screen and stage and the spectator finds no 'home' to rest her or
his gaze.

If *Raindogs*[19] articulated a shift in Pearson's preoccupation with
spectatorial identification away from methods of participation and
physical engagement, it did the same to Ed Thomas's concern for
imagination. These raindogs no longer dream of a new metropolis –
they stand still, physically and imaginatively. The city that surrounds
them is a location that is confining, not unlike the locations of Thomas's
earlier work, but this place is ultimately also unknowable and un-
changeable.[20] There is also a loss of faith in historical development:
narrative progression is replaced by a cyclical structure that circles
through a series of repetitions back to its beginning. Familiar literary
tropes of the modern city as the ultimate unhomely place are reworked in Thomas's and Pearsons's poetic texts: a city awash with
rain and litter, lost loves and disappeared locations. Some of this
material makes a reappearance in Ed Thomas's latest play, *Stone City
Blue* (Clwyd Theatr Cymru, 2004), his first text written for the stage
after an absence from the theatre of six years: 'I'm just a stray dog
cruising the city' (Thomas 2004: 19). What in *Raindogs* had been a
series of third-person narratives is now an obviously autobiograph-
ically coloured reflection on personal identity and its fragility and
fragmentation: four performers represent four aspects of the same
character, who, trapped in an anonymous hotel room in Cardiff in
one long night, relives parts of his life that have brought him to the
point of suicide. But even this text, intimate, confessional, deeply
personal and intentionally obscure, seems to unfold in a hidden dia-

logue with the political landscape in Wales by articulating a sense of dislocation and paralysis that strikes a chord more widely.

Framing the work as urban noir,[21] Thomas and Pearson stage what literary critic Toni Bianchi has called the emergence of 'the pathology of national decay' in the wake of Welsh devolution: 'Dispossession, the usurpation of place by empty space, and the sense of impotence to reclaim the spaces we inhabit', which are represented in these works, mark not the end of an obsession with national identity, but a bleak view of its current malady.

Notes

1   Mike Pearson and Mike Brookes.
2   After McLucas's death in 2002, Brith Gof formally closed in 2004. Pearson had left the company in 1998, and McLucas continued as sole artistic director until his death in 2002, attempting with performances such as *Y Dyddiau Olaf/Y Dyddiau Cyntaf* (Lampeter, 1998) and *Draw, draw yn . . ./ On Leaving* (Lampeter, 1999) to create a series of site-specific works in non-urban locations in order to re-engage the company with its Welsh-language constituency. Ed Thomas moved away from theatre to work in film and television in 1998, a move he attributes partly to the effect of the *Drama Strategy*; see Davies (2005: 45).
3   Under English rule since 1284 and tied to England by the Acts of Union of 1536, Wales has often been called 'England's first colony'. The historical accuracy of this label has divided the cultural debate in Wales since at least the 1970s, when Michael Hechter's controversial study *Internal Colonialism* (1975) attempted to describe the political and economic inequalities between the English centre and the Celtic peripheries in Britain as the product of a form of colonial rule. The debate has of late been revived in a passionately fought discussion about whether or not one may see the contemporary experience of Wales therefore as post-colonial. See Jane Aaron and Chris Williams, eds. (2005) *Postcolonial Wales*. Cardiff: University of Wales Press.
4   See, for examples, the discussion in Ruth Shade (2004). *Communication Breakdowns*. Cardiff: University of Wales Press.
5   'A country called Wales exists only because the Welsh invented it. The Welsh exist only because they invented themselves. They had no choice. [. . .] From birth, they lived with the threat of extinction. Until our own days, they have survived. They survived by making and re-making themselves and their Wales over and over again.' Gwyn A. Williams (1988 [1985]). *When Was Wales? The History, People and Culture of an Ancient Country*. Harmondsworth: Penguin, 2, 5.

6   Ed Thomas is a first-language Welsh speaker but has written only one play in Welsh, *Adar Heb Adenydd* (Cardiff, Dalier Sylw, 1989).
7   For a discussion of the gendered aspects of Ed Thomas's work see Gramich (1998) and Williams (2002).
8   See my discussion of this aspect in Heike Roms (1998). 'Caught in the Act: On the Theatricality of Identity and Politics in the Dramatic Works of Edward Thomas' in Hazel Walford Davies (ed.) (1998). *State of Play: 4 Playwrights of Wales.* Llandysul: Gomer Press, 131–44.
9   In a later version these stage directions are summarized in the following: 'It moves through the real and the imagined in a fluid way. I suppose that's all there is to say' (Thomas 2002: 296).
10 For a full discussion of this see Roms (2004).
11 It was therefore not as much of a radical change at it may appear at first when Brith Gof in the later part of the 1990s started creating performances in empty multi-purpose sheds on new industrial estates (*Prydain: The Impossibility of Britishness*, Cardiff, 1996).
12 It might be expected that in comparison with the history-rich 'real' sites the theatre for Brith Gof would be presented as a place without history, but, on the contrary, it is rather the excess of history that has left the stage 'ploughed to exhaustion' (Pearson 1997: 95), which motivates the company's departure from it.
13 Already in Brith Gof's early work during the 1980s, performances in chapels used the spatial configuration of the preacher facing the congregation, and a show in a cattle mart (*Rhydcymerau*, Lampeter, 1984) placed the audience like buyers surrounding the spectacle of a livestock auction to use the familiarity of its concomitant social configuration to help stimulate the spectators' identification with the theatrical event. Similarly, in the later work, the use of non-theatrical sites allowed Brith Gof to experiment with different audience configurations, using standing and shifting crowd formations.
14 See Rhodri Morgan (1994). *Cardiff: Half-and-half a Capital.* Llandysul: Gomer; Peter Finch (2002). *Real Cardiff.* Bridgend: Seren; Siôn T. Jobbins (2005). 'Caerdydd Cardiff: How the City Became a National Capital', *Cambria* 7:2, 16–17.
15 BBC News (1999). 'Building a New Assembly', *BBC News* Website, 6 April 1999, http://news.bbc.co.uk/1/hi/events/wales_99/the_welsh_assembly/310031.stm (accessed 19 September 2006).
16 John Williams, Duncan Bush, Sean Burke and others; see Bianchi (2003).
17 Other performances in the series were *Polis* (2001) (see Roms 2004); *Raindogs* (2002) and *Who Are You Looking At?* (2004), the latter two in collaboration with Ed Thomas.
18 That site-specific work does not necessarily break with the conventional theatrical representation apparatus merely by moving out of a conventional theatre building is by now a well-rehearsed critique, astutely articulated first by Chaudhuri (1997).

19 *Raindogs* was inspired by Cardiff's (failed) bid to become Cultural Capital
of Europe in 2008. Ironically, the campaign for *Cardiff 2008* used as its
slogan a rather ambiguous quotation from *Song from a Forgotten City*:
'Take me somewhere good' (Thomas 2002: 20).
20 For a perceptive discussion of the gendered aspects of *Raindogs*, particularly the imagining of the city as 'woman', see von Rothkirch (2003).
21 This sense of paralysis is not the prerogative of the urban. In works such
as *Scarface* (Chapter, Cardiff, 2000), Eddie Ladd enacts a similar sense of
dislocation from a place of familiarity in reference to her family's farm in
West Wales. See Rothkirch (2006) for a full discussion.

Primary reading

Ladd, Eddie (2000). *Scarface Programme Notes*. Cardiff: Chapter Arts Centre.
Pearson, Mike (2004). 'Raindogs', DVD supplement, *Performance Research* 9:4.
Pearson, Mike, and Jeff, Paul (2001). 'Pearson/Brookes: Carrying Lyn', *Per-
formance Research* 6:3, 23.
Pearson, Mike, Brookes, Mike, and Thomas, Ed (2003). *Raindogs*, *Platform* 1,
40–2.
Thomas, Edward (1994). *Three Plays: House of America, Flowers of the Dead Red
Sea, East from the Gantry*, ed. Brian Mitchell. Bridgend: Seren.
Thomas, Ed (1998). *Gas Station Angel*. London: Methuen.
Thomas, Ed (2002). *[Selected] Work '95–'98*. Cardigan: Parthian. (Includes *Song
from a Forgotten City, House of America, Gas Station Angel*.)
Thomas, Ed (2004). *Stone City Blue*. London: Methuen.

Further reading

Adams, David (1996). *Stage Welsh. Nation, Nationalism and Theatre: The Search
for Cultural Identity*. Llandysul: Gomer.
Baker, Mike (1990). 'Transporting a Sense of Place' in David Cole (ed.), *The
New Wales*. Cardiff: University of Cardiff Press.
Chaudhuri, Una (1997). *Staging Place: The Geography of Modern Drama*, Ann
Arbor, MI: University of Michigan Press.
Bianchi, Toni (2003). 'The Welsh Novel Noir', *Welsh Literature Abroad* website,
www.welshlitabroad.org/features (accessed 7 September 2006).
Davies, Hazel Walford, ed. (2005). *Now You're Talking: Drama in Conversation*.
Cardigan: Parthian.
de Certeau, Michel (1984). *The Practice of Everyday Life*. Berkeley: University of
California Press.
Donald, James (1997). 'This, Here, Now: Imagining the Modern City' in Sallie
Westwood and John Williams (eds.), *Imagining Cities: Scripts, Signs, Memory*.
London: Routledge.

Gramich, Katie (1998). 'Edward Thomas: Geography, Intertextuality, and the Lost Mother' in Hazel Walford Davies (ed.), *Now You're Talking: Drama in Conversation*. Cardigan: Parthian, 159–73.

Harvie, Jen (2005). *Staging the UK*. Manchester: Manchester University Press.

Jenkins, Mark (1995). 'Virtual Reality Wales', *New Welsh Review* 30, 74–7.

Kaye, Nick (1996). 'Interview with Cliff McLucas and Mike Pearson (Brith Gof)' in Nick Kaye, *Art into Theatre: Performance Interviews and Documents*. Amsterdam: Harwood Academic, 209–34.

McLucas, Clifford, and Pearson, Mike (Brith Gof) (1999). 'Interview' in Gabriella Giannachi and Mary Luckhurst (eds.), *On Directing: Interviews with Directors*. London: Faber and Faber.

Owen, Roger (2004). 'Theatre in Wales in the 1990s and Beyond' in Baz Kershaw (ed.), *The Cambridge History of British Theatre*. Cambridge: Cambridge University Press, vol. 3, 485–97.

Pearson, Mike (1997). 'Special Worlds, Secret Maps' in Anna-Marie Taylor (ed.), *Staging Wales*. Cardiff: University of Wales Press, 85–99.

Roms, Heike (2004). 'Performing *Polis*: Theatre, Nationness and Civic Identity in Post-Devolution Wales', *Studies in Theatre and Performance* 24:3, 177–92.

Rothkirch, Alyce von (2003). 'Cardiff's Anti-Flâneurs', *New Welsh Review* 59, 74.

Rothkirch, Alyce von (2006). '"Art Can Save Culture:" Welsh Stagings of Place in Selected Works by Eddie Ladd and Ed Thomas' in Thomas Rommel and Mark Schreiber (eds.), *Mapping Uncertain Territories: Space and Place in Contemporary Theatre and Drama*. Trier: Wissenschaftlicher Verlag Trier, 127–41.

Savill, Charmian C. (1997). 'Brith Gof' in Anna-Marie Taylor (ed.), *Staging Wales*. Cardiff: University of Wales Press, 100–10.

Taylor, Anna-Marie, ed. (1997). *Staging Wales*. Cardiff: University of Wales Press.

Thomas, Edward (1991). 'Wales and a Theatre of Invention' in Neil Wallace (ed.), *Thoughts and Fragments about Theatres and Nations*. Glasgow: Guardian Newspaper Publication, 15–17.

Williams, Jeni (2002). 'Fantastic Fictions: Wales and Welsh Men in the Plays of Ed Thomas' in Ed Thomas, *[Selected] Work '95–'98*. Cardigan: Parthian, 409–54.

Chapter 7

The Landscape of Contemporary Scottish Drama: Place, Politics and Identity

Nadine Holdsworth

As Scotland began to reassess and reimagine itself in the light of political and constitutional change following the end of 18 years of Conservative rule in 1997 and the subsequent vote for devolution that ushered in a new Scottish Assembly in 1999, Scottish theatre flourished. A new generation of Scottish dramatists, including David Greig (b. 1969), David Harrower (b. 1967) and Zinnie Harris (b. 1973), joined established playwrights such as Liz Lochhead (b. 1947), Sue Glover (b. 1943), Rona Munro (b. 1959) and Chris Hannan (b. 1958), making an impact not just on Scottish stages, but on stages through- out the world. Responding to the challenges posed by political, cul- tural, environmental and economic change, as well as providing intricate and intimate portrayals of personal, family and community relations, these playwrights invigorated conceptions of Scottish theatre as the country sought to redefine itself as a small, but important, nation within Europe in the context of rapid globalization. Writing in the immediate aftermath of the devolution vote, Harrower and Greig highlighted the role playwrights could play as cultural commentators: 'Scotland has voted to redefine itself as a nation. To redefine our- selves we need to understand ourselves, exchange ideas and aspira- tions, confront enduring myths, expose injustices, and explore our past. The quality, accessibility, and immediacy of Scottish theatre make it one of the best arenas in which these dialogues can take place' (1997: 15).

One of the ways that Scottish playwrights have explored the nation's history and present has involved evoking particular places and land-scapes. This preoccupation is perhaps unsurprising given the prob-lematic history and legacy of land ownership and the exploitation of natural resources in Scotland, but these depictions also often resonate with an imaginative terrain, as Greig admits: 'All writers develop relationships with a place. This relationship is at once about solid things – a house on a street, a town, a landscape – and at the same time is about a less immediately real geography; a geography of the imagination' (1994: 8). From the urban cityscapes of Hannan's *The Evil Doers* (1990) and *Shining Souls* (1996), to the isolated rural set-tings of Harrower's *Knives in Hens* (1995) and *Dark Earth* (2003), to the coastal peripheries of Sharman MacDonald's (b. 1951) *Winter Guest* (1995), these Scottish landscapes speak to and of characters as they navigate their personal, social, gendered and national identities. It is tempting to say that, of course, all plays/performances do this to an extent, but I'm arguing that there is a marked trend amongst many contemporary Scottish playwrights and theatre-makers to theatricalize multifarious sites, geological formations and landscapes as a way of articulating the diversity of Scotland. This preoccupation is nowhere more evident than in the refusal to locate the newly formed National Theatre of Scotland in a building situated in an urban centre; instead, it is free to roam throughout Scotland's urban, rural, coastal and island communities. This decision was epitomized by its opening event, *HOME* (2006), 10 productions of the same name that inhabited sites including a disused shop in Stornoway, a former Nissen hut near Inverness, a ferry from Lerwick, a derelict council housing block in Aberdeen and the Queen's Hall in Edinburgh. As Mark Fisher noted: 'It recognized that Scotland is a nation of ferry boats and tower blocks, ballrooms and council houses, fishermen and politicians – a landscape too diverse to be summed up in any centralised world view' (2006: 24).

Whilst I acknowledge the crucial multiplicity of landscapes that appear in contemporary Scottish theatre, there are reoccurring motifs, and in this chapter I am particularly concerned with recent Scottish plays that draw on the metaphorical resonance and cultural signific-ance of the Highlands and islands: places that exist on the edge, on the border of the nation, locations often remote and isolated, that throw questions of personal and national identity into sharp relief.

Cultural theorists have long acknowledged that the Highland landscape is central to the cultural imagining of what Scotland is in terms of topography, climate and natural resources. As David McCrone writes, 'The "Scotland" of our imaginations remains not only rural but largely Highland' (2001: 60), highlighting the irony that 'the part of Scotland which had been reviled as barbarian, backward and savage found itself extolled as the "real" Scotland' (2001: 39) following the Enlightenment period. Promoted as a key icon in the marketing of Scotland by the heritage and tourist industries, the seemingly timeless romantic myth of a sparsely populated wilderness, rugged landscape, lochs and mountains has lodged itself in the popular imagination, regardless of the fact that this landscape-dominated conception of Scotland is a social and cultural construct.[1]

When thinking about cultural representations of the Highlands it is important to consider what they might signify for Scotland. Crucially, the Highlands have been politically contested sites, as evidenced by key historical events such as Culloden, the Clearances, and the impact and consequences of the discovery of North Sea oil off Scotland's shores there in the early 1970s.[2] It is a place associated with many of the battles and narratives of resistance embedded in the Scottish psyche in the face of the greater political and economic might of England following the 1707 Act of Union. For a nation intent on defining itself as other to its English counterpart, the Highlands serve as a useful marker of difference – geographically, culturally and linguistically. Hence, the historian T. M. Devine argues that the Highlands are integral to the national self-image, but also that their galvanizing potential offered an astute political move, as 'Any vigorous assertion of national identity would, however, threaten the English relationship on which material progress was seen to depend and so Highlandism answered the emotional need for the maintenance of a distinctive Scottish identity without in any way compromising the union' (1999: 244). According to Peter Womack (1989), the Highlands have additionally acquired a heightened significance in terms of values and ethics because of their location on the periphery of core social, political and economic power situated in the Lowlands and across the border in England. As such, whilst the core is associated with commerce, politics, and materialistic and individualistic attitudes, Womack suggests that the periphery aligns itself with human concerns such as emotional intelligence, idealism and ethical accountability.

There is a long tradition of novelists and playwrights drawing on the fertile setting of an island as a heightened microcosm of society, a utopian or dystopian space detached from the normal rules of engagement, where aberrant behaviour can flourish or liberation be sought.[3] An island offers an opportunity 'to leave behind one's constricting official identity and assume a playful and temporary innocence' (Womack 1989: 154). In this sense, the island becomes a refuge, a retreat, an interval from the demands of modern life. An island setting can offer a contained space to explore the challenges of globalization, environmental issues and the breakdown of civil society or provide a potent metaphor of an untouched place where simpler times might survive or be nurtured. Concerns with how these literal and imagined Highland and island landscapes engage with contemporary conceptions of personal, gender and national identity form the broad backdrop to this chapter, as I discuss plays that consider ideas around individual and social responsibility, imprisonment and freedom, self-examination and self-discovery, the local and the global, political idealism and political compromise.

Commissioned to write her first play, *The Seal Wife* (1980), by the Edinburgh Lyceum, Sue Glover has subsequently produced *An Island in Largo* (1980), *The Bubble Boy* (1981) and *Sacred Hearts* (1994), alongside work for radio and television. Her most critically and commercially successful piece, *Bondagers* (1991), is widely recognized as a contemporary Scottish classic. She has primarily produced historically situated plays that draw on mythology and folklore in their focus on female protagonists and communities. As Ksenija Horvat writes, 'Mixing history and mythology, Glover offers a powerful criticism against the double standards of patriarchal society where the feminine is always seen as the other, the inferior, the chaotic and the godless, something that needs to be subdued and tightly controlled' (2005: 147). *The Straw Chair* (1988) epitomizes these concerns in the play's central narrative about how Rachel, the real-life wife of James Erskine, lord advocate during the mid-eighteenth century, is abducted and taken to the tiny island of St Kilda (known as Hirta to the locals) after she discovers her husband's Jacobite sympathies and refuses to keep quiet.

Glover admits, 'I like my characters cut off, marooned spatially or psychologically, or both' (cited in Rose and Rossini 2000: 244). In *The Straw Chair*, the island serves as a literal prison, but also as a microcosm of wider forces of socio-economic, patriarchal and geographical status. It is a space where relationships flourish and the characters go on journeys of political and self-discovery. The island of 'rough and mountainous terrain' (Glover 1997: 74) is a character in the piece, a remote, isolated, barren environment with an unforgiving climate. Its dwellings are similarly harsh, with little furniture and beds carved out of the rock-face. Glover conveys the sense that the natural environment defines and infuses every aspect of life on the island. For instance, the lack of distinction between inside and outside space is emphasized by fluid staging that shifts between the island landscape and the domestic arena inhabited by Aneas, the recently appointed minister to Hirta, and Isabel, his young wife.

The play focuses on the relationship forged between Rachel, Isabel and a local woman, Oona, whom Lord MacLeod, the island's landlord, appoints to guard Rachel. Rachel treats Oona with contempt for her class and islander status, and Oona refers to Rachel as her 'skua' (119), an aggressive, predatory bird traditionally caught by men who take out its eyes, sow up the sockets and condemn it to a slow death – a theatrical metaphor for the fact that 'the future of all three is controlled by the power of the absent male hierarchy' (McDonald 1997: 500).[4] For Rachel, the island is her purgatory, a place of damnation, 'a hellish, stinking isle' (87) from which she is desperate to escape, either literally or through her opportunistic retreats into alcohol abuse. An angry victim of mutually reinforcing class and patriarchal systems, her six-year abduction has left her mentally fragile, a state of mind Glover captures with language that flails between polite society hostess, tormented prisoner and raging harpy. Rachel realizes that her family and former confidantes must think her dead, but throughout the play, her feisty disruptive presence asserts her liveness.

At 17, Isabel has never travelled beyond Edinburgh before arriving on the island, and Glover depicts her as a naïve woman determined to embrace all the responsibilities that her new role as a minister's wife entails. Her relationship with Aneas is tentative, awkward and, when they arrive on the island, unconsummated. 'On the island, however, she finds a freedom, an authority, and even an awakened sexuality that escaped her in her uncle's house in Edinburgh' (Scullion 2000: 105). Rachel tells Isabel of life beyond the island and her closeted upbringing in Edinburgh. She tells her about oyster cellars and parties and encourages her to find liberation, to dance, sing, and experiment sexually with her husband. Whereas Aneas dismisses Rachel as 'a Godless, mischievous, evil creature' (106) who fails to fulfil her wifely duties of subservience and obedience, Isabel believes her story of political intrigue and defies Aneas by continuing to see her.

On the island, Aneas and Isabel discover things about themselves, each other, the wider political system and their powerlessness. There is an interesting reversal here, as both Isabel and Aneas grow more worldly-wise through their interactions with the remote island than they have living in cosmopolitan Edinburgh. Isabel's experience ignites and fosters her growing curiosity, independence and ability to articulate her past experiences and present desires. As Isabel makes a journey from viewing the island as an abomination to appreciating its idiosyncrasies, Glover confirms Isabel's attachment to the island and her bodily familiarity and confidence with the island's terrain by having her remove her stockings and shoes like the other islander women. Isabel also asserts her growing independence by joining the local women on their voyage to the inhospitable island of Boreray to collect puffins and goose eggs, where they will be free from the constraints of domesticity.

Aneas not only grows to appreciate his wife's subjectivity, but also realizes MacLeod has brought him to the island to quell any potential seeds of rebellion and that his unquestioning subservience to patriarchal, religious and class-based power relations has blinded him to Rachel's pitiful plight and wider political forces. Banished from the island in disgrace, after revelations about Isabel's attempt to smuggle a letter on Rachel's behalf, both Isabel and Aneas leave profoundly touched by their experiences and far less naïve about the machinations of power, their desires and their individual agency.

Adrienne Scullion has argued that 'Scottish drama is habitually concerned with the nature and politics of community, with the moment of inclusion in, or exclusion from, that community as recurrent narrative spine' (2000: 102). This is undoubtedly true, but in many recent examples, such as Stephen Greenhorn's (b. 1964) *Passing Places* (1997), playwrights problematize the very notion of what and who constitutes a *Scottish* community through the presence of travellers, economic migrants, refugees, tourists and overseas workers.[5] These characters undermine the myth of community as something that is static, known, and untouched by migration and globalization. Whereas Scullion identifies the way Scottish culture has previously been 'preoccupied with issues of colonialism, marginalism, and parochialism' (2000: 114), there is increasing evidence of Scottish playwrights exploring Scotland's place within a global culture, a global community and global advanced capitalism.

Glover's *Shetland Saga* was first performed at the Traverse Theatre as part of the official Edinburgh Festival programme in August 2000. Set in the microcosmic space of the Shetland Isles, the play explores the response of a small island community when a Bulgarian fishing trawler, the *Ludmilla*, is stranded in its harbour after its skeleton crew decide to occupy the vessel and hold their fish cargo to ransom in the hope of securing essential supplies and wages.[6] Hoover, a hotel owner and global trader who supplies goods and services to the *Ludmilla*, his niece Mena, a warm-hearted 18-year-old, and her friend Brit represent the Shetlanders. Industrious Angel, Svetan, a moody engineer, and Natka, a feisty fish-guttter, represent the Bulgarians. Glover stresses the impact of political and economic migration and internationalism on the Shetland Isles as Hoover's hotel on the quay has a New Zealand chef and welcomes international holiday-makers, and there are reports of 'Poles, Russkies, Latvians, Africans' in neighbouring Ullapool (Glover 2000: 16).

Through *Shetland Saga*, Glover examines the widespread upheavals caused by the new world order ushered in by events across Europe in 1989, especially the myth of free trade within a global economy, and ruminates on notions such as belonging, community, displacement and national identity. She creates a picture of Bulgaria trying to find its place as an emergent capitalist country in the post-1989 environment, but also underlines the tensions between its communist past and its plans to resituate itself as a democratic global player in the free market. As the Bulgarian trio refer to the black economy, rocketing inflation, strictures on freedom of speech, and high levels of unemployment, homelessness and poverty, and as the menacing presence of the Bulgarian secret police confirms their fears of reprisal for taking industrial action, Glover indicates that there has been only partial implementation of democratic processes following perestroika. The reality for the crew, caught up in the new rules of global trade, is that the boat is a commodity and they are expendable as other workers wait to take their place. Equally, the unfettered access to goods and riches promised by global capitalism has failed to materialize, so the Bulgarians recycle the waste of contemporary consumer capitalism that appears in the charity shops and rubbish dumps in Shetland.

In *Shetland Saga*, national identity is a complex and evolving phenomenon. Glover sets out clear national markers through language, diet and codes of hospitality, but at the same time acknowledges commonality through shared jokes, alcohol and secrets. The Bulgarians assert their difference from the Russians (fearing the Shetland community see them as interchangeable), just as the Shetlanders assert their distinctiveness from the rest of Scotland. There is also an ambiguity in that the Bulgarians define themselves in terms of a nation they are absent from, with the island setting underscoring their estrangement, and where they are charged with treason. The

Shetlanders also have mixed responses to their place of origin. Despite plans to go travelling with Brit, Mena feels a connection to Shetland, whereas Brit 'would leave for good' (32) to join her brother and other peers who have migrated.

Glover theatrically embodies the cultural divide and initially fraught relationship between the Bulgarians and the Shetlanders in the physical agility required to negotiate the precarious gangplank that connects the *Ludmilla* to the quay. Exhibiting the qualities of humanitarianism and decency Womack (1989) identifies as characteristic of the Highland sense of ethical responsibility, the Shetlanders become increasingly willing to cross the gangplank, and adept at doing so, as they share food, coffee and alcohol with the crew. Language is also an important indicator of both cultural difference and growing cultural understanding. Angel uses the term 'monoglot' as a term of abuse to Svetan and urges him to learn English, which he does as his relationship with Mena develops. In the beginning of the play, there are scenes reminiscent of the famous one in Brian Friel's *Translations* (1981) between Maire and Yolland when they have a conversation at cross-purposes due to a misunderstanding over the meaning of 'always' (see chapter 2). Mena and Svetan communicate beyond the bounds of language and national borders, but still misunderstand their respective connections to the sea. Svetan presumes that Mena must have salt in her blood because she is a Shetlander, whereas she admits 'I live on an island, but I'm no sailor' (29).

Despite cultural differences and misunderstandings, dislocation of families, through death, migration or economic necessity, unites the characters, and through the play Glover considers the possibility of nurturing close-knit relations beyond familial and cultural borders. The potential for an increasingly hybrid, composite and fractured national identity is specifically illustrated when Hoover jokingly recalls having 'a great time in Ullapool. Bloody wonderful! Some Polish celebration or other. Or it might have been a Scottish one. Can't remember' (19):

> It is commonly argued that it is in religious or secular ceremonies, in moments of collective celebration through community events, that the markers of identity are most strongly evident. But here Glover recognizes that in post-war, post-industrial, regional Europe the markers of nationhood are at the very least blurred or 'fuzzy' – even in the most heightened and externalized demonstration of community. (Scullion 2001: 382)

The longer the Bulgarians stay the more integrated and part of the community they become as the locals embrace the outsiders, provide for them and offer them refuge. Critics frowned on this rather rosy picture, a sentiment summarized by Benedict Nightingale: 'I ended up feeling that any half-way needy refugee would only have to stop in Shetland for a violinist to emerge from the woodwork, ceilidhs to be thrown, and marriage proposals to flow as freely as single malt' (2000: 18). As a result, many critics overlooked the brutal undercurrent of global capital Glover explores. For instance, the Bulgarians face trial for treason and the threat of physical harm for daring to expose the inconsistencies in Bulgaria's marketing of itself as a newly democratic, free-market economy, and Mena commits murder and perjury to protect them. The final image of the play sees Angel on the phone to Bulgaria, an image highlighting his enforced dislocation from his homeland and the distressing realization that unsatisfactory phone calls will constitute contact with his family after standing up for his workers' rights – rights ignored by the British government, as Glover presents it, pursuing a protectionist agenda to secure trading relations with Bulgaria. Glover thus refuses to ignore the prevalence of problematic aspects of rigid national borders, epitomized by the application of dubious trade and immigration laws, as she simultaneously evokes the possibility of cross-border sympathies and relationships.

The playwright David Greig has secured an enviable reputation for both the quality of his writing and his prolific output. Coming to critical attention with *Europe* (Traverse 1994), he continues to develop a relationship with the Traverse with plays including *The Architect* (1996) and *The Speculator* (1999). He has produced *Caledonia Dreaming* (1997) for 7:84, *The American Pilot* (2005) for the Royal Shakespeare Company (RSC) and *The Cosmonaut's Last Message to the Woman He Once Loved in the Former Soviet Union* (1999) and *Pyrenees* (2005) for Paines Plough. Greig has generated this output alongside co-founding Suspect Culture, one of Scotland's leading touring companies, with Graham Eatough in 1990. For Suspect Culture, he has produced *One Way Street* (1995), *Airport* (1996), *Timeless* (1997), *Mainstream* (1999), *Candide 2000* (2000), *Casanova* (2001), *Lament* (2002) and *8000m* (2004).[7] He is also dramaturg for the National Theatre of Scotland.

Through his work Greig questions what Scotland and Scottish identity might mean in the current climate by evoking particular Scottish histories, cultural memories, archetypes and global signifiers, combined with considerations of belonging and the complexities of nationalism. He couples this commitment to location, however elusive, with an examination of factors such as the forces of international capital, technological change, commodity fetishism, globalization, ethical accountability and American imperialism. At the same time, his work has a profoundly human dimension as he returns to themes such as the struggle to communicate, the possibility of love and the force of desire. Theatrically, Greig traverses territory between the intimate and the epic and combines a sensual appetite for the intricacies of language and a sharp aesthetic sensibility. Dan Rebellato has observed that many of Greig's plays are set in the 'non-places' of supermodernity theorized by French anthropologist Marc Augé: train stations, airports, bars and corporate hotels.[8] This is undoubtedly true, but for the purposes of this chapter I'm interested in two plays that break this mould with their quintessentially Scottish Highland settings: *Victoria* (2000) and *Outlying Islands* (2002).

The poetic epic *Victoria* (RSC, Pit Theatre, London, 2000), comprises a triptych set in 1936, 1974 and 1996 interconnected by reoccurring characters, themes, key phrases and the theatrical motif of fire as a variously destructive, regenerative and cleansing force. Billington, one of many critics who admired the play's ambition and scope, writes that 'In an age of mini-dramas, it is heartening to find a play that tackles nothing less than the state of Scotland' (2000: 5). Whereas Paul Taylor recognizes the play's concern with 'the almost gravitational pull of the landscape on the people and the contrasting desire to take flight from it' (2000: 18), *Victoria* is about much more than a relationship to place. Through the microcosm of a small, coastal Highland community, Greig traces the various political agents that defined the landscape throughout the twentieth century, from the landed gentry to multinational corporations. He threads the play through with ideas around the tyranny of capital, the exploitation of natural resources, the reverberations of history, political idealism, community and environmental responsibility, and the search for a stable identity in relation to overarching themes of genetic inheritance, gender and class. Greig distinguishes and divides the characters through their socio-economic status, political affiliations and struggles between puritan repression and reckless libertarianism, but the theatrical use of doubling highlights connections between characters and across historical periods.

In *Victoria* there is a repeated metaphor of a failure to connect with the wider world, when a wireless produces white noise and television reception fails, but it becomes increasingly clear that the Highland community is not immune from the forces of history. The first play, set in 1936, catches individuals, the Highlands and the world on the eve of massive personal, social and political upheaval. Greig represents the old order through Lord Allan, whose father participated in the Clearances. Lord Allen's heir, David, returning to the Highlands with Margaret, his fiancée, rebels against his outmoded class privilege and espouses Nazism, naturism and a good degree of self-loathing. He attempts to fraternize with the local estate- and farm-workers, but is not beyond using his position of power to rape and silence his servant, Shona, or to wipe out his genetic heritage by paying Euan, an idealistic communist farm-worker, to provide sperm to inseminate Margaret. The final image of the first play sees David hanging from a butcher's hook in the grounds of his family estate. Euan and Oscar, his opportunist friend, have executed him the night before they join the International Brigade in the Spanish Civil War. He is shown surrounded by rich industrialist holiday-makers, his wife and father; the image signals a seismic social shift, as well as prefiguring the fight against fascism in Spain and, shortly afterwards, the Second World War.

As the play unfolds, Greig resists easy polarizations between right and wrong, largely through Oscar, who remains the one consistent character. Oscar returns from Spain as the moral touchstone, but the audience knows that as a young man he abandoned his pregnant girlfriend, murdered David, went to fight for his own selfish rather than idealist reasons, and contributed to Euan's death through his fear-induced paralysis in Spain. Personal motivations, histories and politics are murky and ambiguous, a concern that pervades the rest of the triptych.

The second play is set in 1974 at the height of resurgent Scottish nationalism following the discovery of oil, 'black gold', off the coast of Scotland in the late 1960s, which gave credibility to the view that Scotland could be self-supporting as an independent nation. The play revolves around the aftermath of a plane crash on the side of a mountain. As the local police officer and community amass evidence from the wreckage, the people reassess their lives in the presence of unexplained destruction and death. Margaret, now an elderly aristocrat, still occupies the estate with her hapless son Jimmy, but they have run out of money and need to sell up. As their privilege erodes, Margaret considers a proposal by Oscar, now a local councillor, to turn the house into an adult educational establishment, a community resource for people from the islands to stem the tide of out-migration.

Oscar thinks Margaret should give something back to the community, but fails to anticipate the disruption caused by his entrepreneurial son, Euan.

As an unashamed capitalist relentlessly pursuing profit regardless of the personal, social or environmental cost, Euan marks a shift from the collectivism of his father's generation to an encroaching Thatcherite stress on individual gain. A Ferrari-driving show-business manager, he has bought into the American Dream of meritocracy and materialism. He returns to the Highlands and his parent's council house with his folk-singer protégé, Connolly. Seduced by the beautiful landscape and clutching at new-age philosophy, Connolly offers to buy the estate to turn it into a hippie commune. For him it represents a chance to feel connected to something of permanence amidst an existence based on transient success, touring and hotel rooms. However, he too does not bank on the malevolent presence of Euan.

Frustrated with what he regards as Scottish parochialism and lack of ambition, Euan exclaims 'Scotland is nowhere. Nowhere in any league' (Greig 2000: 74). The plane crash and his discovery of the mysterious American Victoria excite him as he sniffs an opportunity to make money from oil. Greig highlights the shift from collective consciousness to a desire for personal gain by situating a hopeful, idealistic speech by Oscar immediately after a desperate Norrie shoots Connolly in the hand to raise insurance money for Euan to buy the estate, which sits on an oil well. Oscar recalls a story of barbers prepared to fight in the Spanish Civil War: 'I said to myself. In this city everyone's a worker now. Even barbers are prepared to die for socialism. To kill for it. Surely we have to win' (121). Oscar and millions of his contemporaries killed for a purpose, as part of a fight for a better world in Spain or the Second World War, whereas his son is prepared to have someone shot for monetary gain.

In the final part, set in 1996, Greig highlights the complex, ambiguous and contradictory nature of the political landscape and national identity in the mid-1990s. There is a sense of expectancy, a whiff of change in the air that prefigures the devolution vote of 1997. A constant reference to the movement of goods and people suggests the shrinking world in a new global economy, and Greig signals its precariousness by referencing the volatility of markets, interest rates and the devaluation of currency, all influencing Euan's decision to expand his quarry business. Profiting from devastating the land, Euan becomes a target for the environmental movement that rose to prominence in the 1990s. Whilst he rages about the irony of protestors from outside the community fighting to protect a *natural* landscape *manufactured* for profit, he uses money to insulate himself from opposition, hiring the directionless Norrie and uncommitted Patrick as security guards, and an intelligent, sharp-talking marketing consultant, Kirsty. By the end of the play, the local council agree to the quarry's expansion after Kirsty softens Euan's public image and persuades him to fund a business training centre for young people. Greig ensures these promises, however laudable, have a hollow ring as, in an echo of the Clearances, Euan orders Norrie to burn the protestors' camp, unaware that Norrie has switched allegiances and has plans to let the fire spread to the control room operating the quarry's machinery.

Victoria is the restless heroine who, played by the same actress, connects all the pieces, even though she does not remain the same character. Each feels an inexplicable connection to the place as if she is 'like a stone half in the ground' (180), but also a restless desire to be elsewhere. According to Billington 'she becomes a shifting symbol of Scottish spirituality, freedom, and oneness with nature and the past, an instinct that, through the generations, runs counter to Puritanism, the profit-motive and the desire to plunder Scotland of its natural resources' (2000: 5). This is a rather romantic reading of Victoria's function in the piece, as she could also be accused of abandoning, exploiting and disregarding her geographical and familial heritage. In the first play, she is the flirtatious daughter of the local minister, an object of desire seduced by Oscar and romanticized by Euan, who gives her money to escape to Argentina with her unborn child. In the second play, geologist Victoria (Vicky) emerges unscathed as the sole survivor from a group of American oil prospectors killed in the plane crash. She joins forces with Euan to exploit the land's natural resources, but her increasing isolation and retreat into Eastern mysticism suggest unease with her actions. In 1996, the new Victoria, Vicky's directionless daughter, shows a reckless disregard for her life, wealth and history. Arriving with her boyfriend, David, after four years away, she tries to locate herself in the landscape:

Victoria: I wanted you to see this place.
Mountains. Sea. Forest.
This is where I grew up.
I wanted you to see me in this place.
What do I look like?
David: Part of the scenery. (132)

She also searches for a sense of self in relation to her father's materialism and Oscar's political conviction. In a moving speech to Oscar's ghost, Victoria admits that her apathetic generation means defeat for Oscar's ideals and, unable to cope with the weight of responsibility, the 'Weight of your life. Weight of this place' (172), she burns the weight of history, along with Oscar's body, as she throws the documents recording his life and thousands of pounds onto the fire. In a symbol of destruction and rebirth, she attempts to destroy 'All I am. On the fire', before returning to Spain (179).

Greig's intense, atmospheric and erotic play *Outlying Islands* premiered in July 2002 at the Traverse and transferred to the Royal Court in London later in the same year. Greig was inspired to write the play by Robert Atkinson's *Island Going* (1949), an account of two students visiting the Outer Hebrides over a 10-year period to capture sightings of rare birds. Greig admitted being 'intrigued by the idea of these young posh boys in the 1930s encountering the culture of the Hebrides which was, and still is a very strong, discreet culture' and being fascinated by 'the unique hybrid of Christianity and paganism that characterizes some Scottish islands' (cited in Rimmer 2002: 16). The result is a play set in the summer of 1939, on the eve of the Second World War, when two young Cambridge ornithologists arrive on a remote, uninhabited Scottish island 40 miles from the mainland.

With them during their month-long stay are Kirk, the owner of the island's leasehold, and Ellen, Kirk's niece. The government instructs John and Robert to survey the island's bird population, but it becomes clear that their visit has far more sinister undertones when Kirk reveals that Porton Down, the Ministry of Defence's chemical weapons research centre in Wiltshire, has plans to requisition the island.[9] The island, like the rest of the world, is about to change forever as humanity embarks on a path of unimaginable destruction. In *Outlying Islands* Greig evokes something of the loss of innocence this will entail. Whilst setting his play in 1939, he offers a complex mediation on the 'tensions between social obligation and individualism, humanism and environmentalism, morality and desire, religion and paganism, tradition and modernity' (McMillan 2002: 12) that chime with contemporary debates on such wide-ranging issues as genetic engineering, global warming, nuclear power, the profit motive, the ethics of war and sexual liberation. He also presents a disturbing account of the powerful and transformative potential of the island experience and the Highland landscape.

Sam Heughan as John in *Outlying Islands*
Photo: Douglas Robertson

As Glover does in *The Straw Chair*, Greig constructs the island as a character – compelling yet remote and inhospitable in its exposed terrain and harsh climate. For Robert, a gifted ornithologist, the appeal of the island is the chance to observe rare birds, whilst John wants to learn from the more senior and accomplished Robert. Yet they both, in different ways, are seduced by the island, not least because its isolation creates a space of possibility free from the demands and morality of the mainland. As the play unfolds, they embark on a journey of self-discovery, pushing at the limits of their existence to explore what it is to be human: to experience desire, love and the presence of death.

John and Robert are radically different characters, 'the gambler and the saver' (Greig 2002b: 27), and during their exchanges Greig sets up a battle between John's aims to respect and preserve the status quo and Robert's aggressive adherence to a Darwinist philosophy of the survival of the fittest. John is inhibited, unconfident and desperate to behave in an appropriate, respectful way towards the island and its inhabitants. In contrast, Robert is bullish, irresponsible and provocative. He is restless and erratic and refuses to be constrained by social niceties or conventional morality. Greig constructs Robert as a force of nature, at one with the birds he documents, through repeated theatrical imagery of him stalking the island, diving into the sea and sitting perched observing his surroundings and companions. The opening sequence of the play establishes their differences as John treads carefully, unpacking belongings wrapped in newspaper, and mends the door to shore up their dwelling in a former pagan church. In contrast, Robert swims in the freezing water, causes an explosion by setting light to peat he previously doused in paraffin, and takes a petrel nesting in an old candle box and sets her free.

For Robert, the remote island is a sanctuary where he feels alive to the core of his being. He is free to swim naked, masturbate in the open air, and live the nocturnal existence required to observe and photograph birds as they fly, nest, feed their young and prepare to migrate south. He describes the island as a 'whole, pristine, unobserved, unsullied, pure environment' (68), and it offers an opportunity for him to embark on a study not only of birds, but of human behaviour. Learning of the government's plan to exploit the remoteness of the island by turning it into one large laboratory, Robert is shocked and appalled, not least by Kirk's mercenary attitude. The island represents Kirk's livelihood and he is only interested in establishing the compensation due for its contamination and loss.

Whereas John appeals rationally to Kirk, explaining that 'the island is a haven, it's unique, it's a wilderness' (52), Robert becomes increasingly aggressive, and Kirk dies after Robert semi-suffocates him and induces a heart attack. Even then, Robert remains dispassionate, loyal to the island and its wildlife rather than the dead leaseholder, whilst John lamely tries to brush over Robert's actions and his own complicity in them. Unlike Robert, John finds himself overwhelmed by the remoteness of the island and the feelings ignited in him both by watching a man die and by his romantic love for Ellen. Whilst he longs for the safety of the mainland, he also relishes the opportunity

Laurence Mitchell, Robert Carr and Sam Heughan in *Outlying Islands*
Photo: Douglas Robertson

to relinquish his inhibitions as he becomes embroiled in an erotically charged three-way relationship.

Prior to coming to the island, Ellen has led a sheltered life under her uncle's authoritarian control, with attempts at escape restricted to regular cinema-going and a quirky fascination with Stan Laurel. On the island, she experiences a sexual awakening, a process accelerated by the death of her uncle, which releases her from the conventional life he planned for her. In the presence of death, she becomes more aware of what it means to be alive. Robert interprets her mourning in Darwinist terms:

> if we were in a church or amongst society you would pretend, maybe even truly feel, something completely different. But here – in a natural environment – death means exactly what it should. More room for the young. (75)

Observing Robert bathing naked and masturbating, aware of his gaze, Ellen becomes conscious of her body as an object of desire. In the face of Robert's Darwinist thesis that she will seek out the best sexual mate, she undermines this competitive ethos by confessing her desire for both men; a pursuit of unrestrained sexual freedom John associates with the island, claiming 'When we're on the mainland. You'll see things more clearly then' (63). Refusing to frame her desires as anything other than natural, Ellen gently seduces John on the island's only table, regardless of the fact that Robert returns and watches them make love in the firelight. The realization that this unfettered life is unsustainable prompts Robert to hurl himself off a cliff into a stormy sky, his final speech capturing his motivation to be at one with the forces of nature:

> Imagine.
> Living without time.
> Because time, Johnny, time belongs to the land.
> Not to the sea and the air.
> Imagine entering their world.
> Imagine that.
> No beginnings and no endings.
> Limitless.
> Imagine departing from the land. (109)

As the mainland beckons, there is an attempt to restore a conventional and safe moral compass: John tells the captain that Robert fell and Ellen requests time to pay her respects to her dead uncle. As history rapidly ushers in the horrors of the Second World War, Ellen and John leave their temporary 'home', a space that has taught them about the joys of being human, just as history is about to discover the chilling potential of taking Robert's Darwinist philosophy to its extreme.

Thinking about Scottish theatre now, it is interesting to look back at Glover's *Straw Chair*, produced a decade prior to devolution, in comparison with the other post-devolution plays explored in this chapter. Whereas *The Straw Chair* generates a profound sense of stasis through characters literally bound by the wider forces of economic status, social roles and patriarchy despite evidence of individual change and growth, all the other plays are concerned with crucial moments of historical change and flux. In *The Straw Chair*, the Highland and island setting evokes a literal and metaphorical prison, a dislocation from the discourses of power and influence. In *Victoria*, *Outlying Islands* and *Shetland Saga*, the occupation of the periphery is suggestive of other possibilities, other priorities, other modes of being and living that are indicative of a wider national agenda of self-reflection and change. Throughout history, the Highlands have been a site of national self-consciousness, political battle and contestation, so perhaps it is unsurprising that Scottish playwrights returned there to explore the human potential to evolve and adapt as new futures beckoned.

Notes

1. For further discussion see Womack (1989) and the chapter on 'Highlandism and Scottish Identity' in Devine (1999).
2. Events that form the core focus of John McGrath's seminal Scottish play *The Cheviot, the Stag and the Black, Black Oil* (1973).
3. Some famous examples include Shakespeare's *The Tempest*, Charlotte Perkins Gilman's *Herland* (1915), William Golding's *Lord of the Flies* (1954) and, more recently, the television show *Lost* (2004–).
4. For a further consideration of the feminist aspect of Glover's play see Ksenija Horvat and Barbara Bell (2000). 'Sue Glover, Rona Munro, Lara Jane Bunting: Echoes and Open Spaces' in Aileen Christianson and Alison Lumsden (eds.), *Contemporary Scottish Women Writers*. Edinburgh: Edinburgh University Press, 65–78.
5. For a discussion of *Passing Places* see Nadine Holdsworth (2003). 'Travelling Across Borders: Re-Imagining the Nation and Nationalism in Contemporary Scottish Theatre', *Contemporary Theatre Review* 13:2, 25–39.
6. The play was rooted in a long tradition of 'klondykers' from Eastern Europe visiting the coast of the Scottish West Highlands, primarily to receive surplus fish caught by local fishermen. They themselves did not fish in European Union waters. However, during the 1990s there were concerns with poor insurance, substandard vessels and boats/crews abandoned without supplies, such as Glover presents.
7. For a discussion of Suspect Culture's work see Dan Rebellato (2003). '"And I Will Reach Out My Hand with a Kind of Infinite Slowness and Say the Perfect Thing": The Utopian Theatre of Suspect Culture', *Contemporary Theatre Review* 13:1, 61–80.
8. See Dan Rebellato's introduction to Greig (2002a: 13); Marc Augé (1995). *Non-Places: Introduction to the Anthropology of Supermodernity*. London: Verso.
9. This is based on historical events, as the Highlands were used by the British government to test chemical weapons. For example, in 1942 the government used the island of Gruinnard to test anthrax. No one was permitted to visit the island, other than to check on the level of contamination, until 1990.

Primary reading

Glover, Sue (1997). *Bondagers and The Straw Chair*. London: Methuen.
Glover, Sue (2000). *Shetland Saga*. London: Nick Hern.
Greenhorn, Stephen (1998). *Passing Places* in Philip Howard (ed.), *Scotland Plays: New Scottish Drama*. London: Nick Hern, 137–226.
Greig, David (2000). *Victoria*. London: Methuen.
Greig, David (2002a). *Plays: 1*. London: Methuen.
Greig, David (2002b). *Outlying Islands*. London: Faber and Faber.
Hannan, Chris (1991). *The Evil Doers*. London: Nick Hern.
Hannan, Chris (1996). *Shining Souls*. London: Nick Hern.
Harrower, David (1995). *Knives in Hens*. London: Methuen.
Harrower, David (2003). *Dark Earth*. London: Faber and Faber.
McDonald, Sharman (1995). *Plays: One*. London: Faber and Faber.

Further reading

Atkinson, Robert (1949). *Island Going*. London: Collins.
Billington, Michael (2000). 'Plundered Land of Freedom', *Guardian*, 29 April, 5.
Devine, T. M. (1999). *The Scottish Nation: 1700–2000*. London: Penguin.
Fisher, Mark (2006). 'National Antics', *Guardian*, 27 February, 24.
Greig, David (1994). 'Internal Exile', *Theatre Scotland*, autumn, 8–10.
Harrower, David, and Greig, David (1997). 'Why a New Scotland Must Have a Properly-Funded Theatre', *Scotsman*, 25 November, 15.
Horvat, Ksenija (2005). 'Scottish Women Playwrights Against Zero Visibility', *Études Écossaises* 10, 143–58.
McCrone, David (2001). *Understanding Scotland: The Sociology of a Nation*. London: Routledge.
McDonald, Jan (1997). 'Scottish Women Dramatists since 1945' in Gifford Douglas and Dorothy McMillan (eds.), *A History of Scottish Women's Writing*. Edinburgh: Edinburgh University Press, 494–513.
McMillan, Joyce (2002). 'Outlying Islands', *Scotsman*, 5 August, 12.
Nightingale, Benedict (2000). 'An Intricate Pattern of Island Life', *The Times*, 8 August, 18.
Rimmer, Louise (2002). 'I'm Shocked By What My Plays End Up Saying', *Scotland on Sunday*, 11 August, 16.
Rose, Margaret, and Rossini, Emanuela (2000). 'Interview with Sue Glover' in Valentina Poggi and Margaret Rose (eds.), *A Theatre That Matters: Twentieth-Century Scottish Drama and Theatre*. Milan: Edizioni Unicopli, 242–4.
Scullion, Adrienne (2000). 'Contemporary Scottish Women Playwrights' in Elaine Aston and Janelle Reinelt (eds.), *The Cambridge Companion to Modern*

British Women Playwrights. Cambridge: Cambridge University Press, 94–118.

Scullion, Adrienne (2001). 'Self and Nation: Issues of Identity in Modern Scottish Drama by Women', *New Theatre Quarterly* 17:4, 373–90.

Stevenson, Randall, and Wallace, Gavin (1996). *Scottish Theatre Since the Seventies*. Edinburgh: Edinburgh University Press.

Taylor, Paul (2000). 'The Main Event: Possible Worlds', *Independent*, 28 April, 18.

Womack, Peter (1989). *Improvement and Romance: Constructing the Myth of the Highlands*. Basingstoke: Macmillan.

Part III

The Body, Text and the Real

Chapter 8

The Body's Cruel Joke: The Comic Theatre of Sarah Kane

Ken Urban

Take as representative these three moments from the plays of Sarah Kane:

In *Blasted* (1995), a journalist named Ian undergoes atrocities to rival those found in Shakespeare's *Titus Andronicus*. In a bombed-out hotel room in Leeds, an unnamed soldier rapes Ian, then sucks out the journalist's eyes and eats them. Ian, blind and driven by hunger, unearths a baby's corpse from the floorboards and feasts on the remains. Having sated himself, he decides to take the baby's place in the ground. He lowers himself into the hole until only his head protrudes from the grave. Just when Ian hopes to die 'with relief', 'it starts to rain on him'. To this final indignation, Ian exclaims, 'Shit' (60).[1]

In the chaotic crowd scene that ends *Phaedra's Love* (1996), Kane's adaptation of Seneca, Theseus unknowingly rapes and murders his stepdaughter Strophe, while an angry mob cuts off the penis of his son Hippolytus, who stands accused of raping his stepmother Phaedra. Oblivious to his own hypocrisy, Theseus joins the crowd in disembowelling his son Hippolytus, but then realizes the identity of the woman he murdered. Theseus asks God's forgiveness before slitting his throat. Hippolytus observes the carnage around him and just before a vulture descends to make a meal of him, he delivers the play's final line, 'If there could have been more moments like this' (103).

Tinker, the central character of *Cleansed* (1998), tortures Rod and Carl, a gay couple interned in a university-turned-prison. In an attempt to test their love, Tinker forces Rod to watch his lover lose first his tongue, then his hands, and then finally his feet. But this is not enough for Tinker. His final act is to remove Carl's penis and then graft it onto a woman's body in a perverse sex-change operation. The beneficiary of this surgery wakes up only to be told by Tinker, 'I'm sorry. I'm not really a doctor' (146).

Acts such as these are barely imaginable, and picturing such incidents on the stage is perversely even more difficult, for they come close to exceeding what theatre is capable of representing. Such graphic moments are not merely a hallmark of Kane's work. Explicit violence is one of the common features of the new writing scene that emerged in London during the 1990s with playwrights such as Mark Ravenhill, Martin McDonagh and Anthony Neilson. Rather than an anomaly, the 1995 production of Kane's first play *Blasted* at the Royal Court retrospectively became *the* defining moment of a new aesthetic in British theatre. Though initially dubbed the 'New Brutalists' or 'Nihilists', Kane's generation would be best known as the purveyors of 'in-yer-face' theatre, thanks to Aleks Sierz, who championed their work.[2]

Kane's career was brief, her canon small: five plays and one screenplay; but since her suicide in 1999, many critics and artists claim that her work altered the landscape of British drama.[3] Her work is never usually described as funny, and given the above descriptions, it is not hard to see why.[4] While her final two plays (1998's *Crave* and *4.48 Psychosis*, posthumously produced in 2000) are driven by language, not narrative or spectacle, the bleakness of their worldview is equally punishing, the violence residing in images created by the text. However, this chapter argues that the comic plays a central role in Kane's aesthetic project. One of her earliest pieces, *Comic Monologue* (first staged in Bristol and Edinburgh in 1991), was about a woman who is orally raped by her date, Kevin. Though Kane would dismiss these early monologues as 'juvenilia', *Comic Monologue*'s juxtaposition of suffering and humour sets the tone for her plays.[5]

A moment of gallows humour follows a startling incident of rape or mutilation in Kane's work. In phenomenological terms, humour *brackets* the violence for the viewer, forcing a reassessment of that violence, not as a release from the intensity of the spectacle, but as a reinforcement of its spectacular power. In Kane's theatre, the laugh is as important as the gasp. Yet the laughter that a Kane play fosters, to quote one reviewer of *Cleansed*, leaves 'silent cracks in a battered disfigured face' (Peter 1998). In other words, it is an experience that reminds us that laughing can hurt. Kane's brand of comedy demonstrates the relationship between comedy and the body, reaffirming the cruelty at the heart of the humour. But rather than dramatizing hopelessness or cynicism, as her detractors have claimed, Kane's plays stage the body's cruel joke, and in doing so, demonstrate the possibilities of an ethics grounded in materiality.

The 'Incongruity Theory of Humour'

Originating in the eighteenth century and elaborated in the writings of Immanuel Kant, Arthur Schopenhauer and Søren Kierkegaard, the 'incongruity theory of humour' remains a pervasive account of what makes us laugh.[6] This theory finds humour emerging from the disparity between our own expectations, our understanding of the world, and what the joke or gag forces us to imagine or consider. Comedy, therefore, is the art of defamiliarization. Defined by Russian Formalist critic Viktor Shklovsky as art's ability 'to create a special perception of [an] object', defamiliarization challenges our perception of the world (1965: 18). The technique of defamiliarization makes the known 'unfamiliar' and 'difficult', and this process allows us to see things in an unexpected way (1965: 12). Comedy thrives on unmooring assumptions. When we expect an air of solemnity, and instead get the stink of the fart; when we expect a light-hearted chat, and instead get a vivid description of a mass murder; when we expect serious investigative reporting, and instead hear a question about political hairstyles: frustrated expectations breed comedy.

You don't have to look far in Kane's work to find the humour of incongruity. The opening line of her first play features Ian walking into a 'very expensive hotel room in Leeds' and remarking to his companion Cate, 'I've shat in better places than this' (3). In *Phaedra's Love*, Strophe tells the portly Hippolytus that his stepmother Phaedra has accused him of rape. His response: 'A rapist. Better than a fat boy who fucks' (88). In *Cleansed*, when the tortured lover Carl has his hands cut off by the faux-doctor Tinker, the stage directions read: 'Carl tries to pick up his hands – he can't, he has no hands' (129). Even in her (arguably) bleakest play, *4.48 Psychosis*, the depressive narrator relays a comic dream: 'I went to the doctor's and she gave me eight minutes to live. I'd been sitting in the fucking waiting room half an hour' (221). These defamiliarizing moves create laughs even in the darkest of scenarios.

The Humour of the Illogical

Kane's plays demonstrate a fondness for the logic of the illogical. What appears to be a choice is not a choice at all; what appears to be common sense is completely nonsensical. Yet because of the characters' extreme circumstances, the statements appear completely rational to the speaker, but to the audience, the lines produce a smile, a chuckle, even a laugh. For instance, after the soldier violates him, the blind Ian tells Cate, '[If I] Don't shoot myself I'll starve to death' (54). Speaker A in *Crave*, a probable paedophile, tells the underage object of his affection, 'Only love can save me and love has destroyed me' (174). In *4.48 Psychosis*, the patient who seeks treatment for her depression concedes the absurdity of her mental state: 'I have become so depressed by the fact of my own mortality that I have decided to commit suicide' (207). These paradoxes of false choices and illogical logic are distilled in Grace's memorable line to her dead brother in *Cleansed*, 'Love me or kill me, Graham' (120).

The extreme situations of these characters – Ian's ravaged body, A's desire for a young girl, the patient's psychosis, Grace's need for her dead brother – force logic to an illogical end. For Ian, nothing can save him, so his choices are death by gunshot or starvation. For A, the means of his salvation bring destruction. For the patient, a fear of death culminates in a wish for death. And for Grace, her brother reciprocates with either love or death.

Kane's detractors may concede a humorous pithiness to her writing, but their principal criticism does not focus on her perceived lack of humour, but rather her lack of hope. In the face of catastrophe, Kane renders her characters devoid of options; they are doomed, critics contend, and this is especially true for her female characters. In the case of Grace, for instance, the object of her desire is an impossible one, and therefore, her sole option is destruction. If political theatre, following playwright David Greig's formulation, must present an audience with the possibility of change, Kane's critics find that by exploring such extreme states, her work denies any possibilities for change.[7] That argument, however, fails to see Kane's use of humour as part of a larger authorial strategy that produces laughter in painful moments to do more than confound expectations. In these plays, humour crucially emerges from physical cruelty; it is the body that it is at centre of Kane's comic tendencies.

The Body in Comedy

The body as a subject of humour has a long and illustrious history. From Chaucer's *The Miller's Tale* to Jonathan Swift's *A Modest Proposal*, from François Rabelais and his *Gargantua* to the creators of *South Park* and their cartoon creations, the abject body remains a source of amusement. Even Samuel Beckett, the writer most often named as Kane's significant literary precursor, enjoyed humour of the bodily variety. The title character of Beckett's 1951 novel *Molloy*, for example, consistently confuses a woman's vagina and anus. Of his mother, Molloy says, it is she 'who brought me into this world, through the hole in her arse if my memory is correct. First taste of the shit' (1955: 6). Here, birth becomes excretion and life a flavour most foul. Age, however, does not improve Molloy's understanding of the female anatomy. During intercourse with a woman who is named either Ruth or Edith, Molloy realizes she has 'a hole between her legs, oh not the bunghole [he] had always imagined, but a slit', and after a series of awkward fumblings, Molloy exclaims, 'Perhaps after all she put me in her rectum. [. . .] Perhaps she too is a man' (1955: 56–7). To Beckett's protagonist, a hole is a hole, and understanding the biological differences between male and female is, at best, unlikely, at worst, impossible.

What humour does in a moment like that of Beckett's novel is deflate the high with the low. It undermines the idealized domain of the intangible by juxtaposing it with the grotesque truths of the body. In *Molloy*, Beckett subverts his protagonist's elevated discourse with materiality, one's grand introduction conflated with 'shit', one's lover reduced to a confusing choice of orifices. Philosopher Simon Critchley calls this comic strategy 'the return of the physical into the metaphysical' and for him, 'humour functions by exploring the gap between *being* a body and *having* a body' (2002: 43). If material reality is the state of 'being a body', then 'having a body' is the projection of metaphysical or extra-physical qualities onto that body. Laughter, in Critchley's formulation, comes when 'the pretended tragical sublimity of the human collapses into a comic ridiculousness which is perhaps even more tragic' (2002: 43). In short, when the body's 'baseness' topples the 'deep' abstractions of metaphysics, tragic laughter erupts.

While some theorists see our love of laughing at the body as liberatory, most famously Mikhail Bakhtin in his concept of the carnivalesque, Critchley's formulation is more telling in that it reveals the comic's anti-metaphysical tendencies and its ethical implications. While metaphysics imagines an escape from the material world, comedy refutes that possibility; it returns us to the realm of the physical, reminding us that this is all there is. This is not to say humour quashes that desire to transcend, but that the comic bursts the bubble of that delusion, if only momentarily. That is the wisdom that humour brings: the 'body' that dreams of Spirit is really the body that shits.

Cruelty and the Comic

Lest we confuse the faecal with the radical, humour unseats metaphysics from its lofty perch through cruelty. Humour always has an object; a joke always has a butt. The humour of Beckett, Rabelais and Chaucer, and the humour of racists, xenophobes and homophobes, both share an obsession with the body. While the intentions might be vastly different, the means are the same: the cruel undermining of the target. Philosopher Henri Bergson, in his classic 1900 essay *Laughter*, defines humour as rigidity and repetition. A person transformed into a thing produces laughter. When the athlete becomes a human football, or when an office worker acts like a calculator with legs, we laugh. But comedy for Bergson, and this is an overlooked aspect of his argument, has as its methodological impulse cruelty. 'Comedy can only begin', Bergson writes, 'at the point where our neighbor's personality ceases to affect us. It begins, in fact, with what might be called a growing callousness to social life' (1999: 121). He argues that laughter intends 'to humiliate', to make 'a painful impression' on its target: 'It would fail in its object if it bore the stamp of sympathy or kindness' (1999: 176). While laughter can be affirmative, serving as a 'corrective' for a social ill, his theory also illuminates that other kind of laughter, that of the powerful taking aim at the powerless: when white laughs at black, native mocks foreigner, straight demeans gay. In both types of laughter, comedy is born of cruelty.

Bergson's theory complements Critchley's notion of humour as 'the return of the physical' by illuminating laughter's unmasking of the metaphysical as cruel in its intention. Cruelty is typically understood as the wilful causing of pain. But Antonin Artaud's body of writings demonstrates cruelty's potential as both an aesthetic and an ethic. Cruelty, for Artaud, is the force that violently awakens consciousness to a truth that has remained unseen or unspoken, or wilfully repressed. It is with Artaud and Bergson in mind that philosopher Clément Rosset argues that 'cruelty is in every case a mark of distinction', but only when 'we understand cruelty not as pleasure taken in cultivating suffering but as a refusal of complacency toward any object' (1993: 18).[8] Cruelty, in this Artaudian sense, is rigour: the refusal to look away, no matter the pain that it causes to others or the self.

When humour returns the stink of the physical to the realm of the metaphysical, it produces a laugh and a sting. The object feels the wind being knocked from its sails, and this is true even when the tellers of the joke themselves are the intended targets. When the joke is on us, we are reminded, sometimes violently, that who we think we are and who we are is not the same thing. The joke's cruelty not only punctures our carefully maintained veneer; it makes us aware of the insurmountable gap between perception and reality. Regardless of humour's object, in returning the physical to the metaphysical, laughter diminishes us all, for materiality is finite, weak and ultimately failing. If the 'body' that dreams of Spirit is really the body that shits, then it is ultimately the body that ceases to be. The body's cruel joke, it appears, is on all of us.

Ethical Possibilities

The telling of the body's cruel joke – that reminder of life's finitude created when materiality levels metaphysics – is at the heart of Kane's comic theatre. Humour brackets moments of extreme violence, the onstage body in pain commingling with the laughing bodies of the audience, but it is a humour that allows no release. It does not relieve us of the pain, but rather intensifies it. This is the ethical turn in her work, which makes a space for change.

Ultimately, Kane's critics are correct: her work is not political (and by extension, not feminist) in any traditional sense. No programme is espoused; no solutions are proposed. Characters do not represent any clear divide between good and evil, victim and victimizer; there is no clear message, no commitment to a specific goal. A 'pure' political theatre – assuming there is such a thing – would be aligned with morality, while Kane's plays represent an ethical theatre. Ethics must be understood as opposed to morality's interpretation of the world. Gilles Deleuze makes the distinction between the two concepts this way: 'The difference is that morality presents us with a series of constraining rules of a special sort, ones that judge actions and intentions by considering them in relation to transcendent values (this is good, that's bad . . .); ethics is a set of optional rules that assess what we do, what we say, in relation to the ways of existing involved' (Deleuze 1995: 100; see also Deleuze 1988). While morality is aligned with law, and actions are evaluated by a set of metaphysical ideals, ethics is contextual; its 'optional rules' assess actions in relation to the here and now, to the material set of circumstances in which we find ourselves.

The political activist and philosopher Alain Badiou refines Deleuze's distinction by arguing forcefully that ethics can never be understood in universal terms. Instead, 'there is', he writes, 'only the ethic-of (of politics, of love, of science, of art)' (2001: 28). For Badiou, the maxim that best encapsulates ethics is, 'Do all that you can to persevere in that which exceeds your perseverance', which he shortens to, 'Keep going!' (2001: 47, 52). It is a call that echoes Beckett's famous dictum, 'You must go on, I can't go on, I'll go on' (1955: 414).

When understood in this light, the possibility of reading Kane's humour as ethical becomes clearer. In *Blasted* and *Cleansed*, the two plays that make up her abandoned trilogy,[9] Kane's comedy forcefully asserts its ethical possibilities. Witnessing the body's cruel undermining of metaphysics in these two plays dramatizes an ethics in the face of catastrophe.

Blasted

The genesis and development of *Blasted* had three significant phases. First, it began as a play about a rape in Leeds. Ian takes a mentally troubled young girl, Cate, to a hotel. Ian and Cate's ongoing relationship is founded in abuse. During the first two scenes, Ian attempts, first by words and then by deeds, to force Cate into having sex with him. Ultimately, Ian rapes Cate, and the morning after, she flees the hotel.

During the early stages of writing the play, Kane watched the genocide in Bosnia unfold on the evening news and wanted the play to confront that horror.[10] The play's domestic conflict, Kane decided, must take on an international hue. A Serbian soldier named Vladek breaks into the hotel room, taking Ian prisoner at gunpoint. In the 1993 drafts of the play, when the soldier enters, the hotel exists in

Neil Dudgeon as Ian in the 2001 revival of *Blasted* at the Royal Court
Theatre
Photo: Courtesy of the Royal Court

two spaces concurrently: home (Leeds) and abroad (Serbia). Vladek
derides Ian, 'This is a Serbian town now. Where is your passport?
[. . .] You are an Englishman, a journalist, staying in a foreign hotel
and you do not have a passport?'[11] To demonstrate his disgust for the
English journalist, Vladek urinates on the bed, at which point a 'huge
explosion' rocks the room.

However, when *Blasted* opened at the Royal Court Theatre Upstairs in January 1995, the play had undergone a crucial change. The soldier is no longer called Vladek; in fact, he is never given a proper name. When he breaks into the hotel, instead of designating the nationality of the invading troops, he simply tells Ian, 'Our town now', and that 'our' is never defined except in so far that is definitively not 'English'. While descriptions of the violent conflict conjure images of the Bosnian genocide, Kane stripped all identifiable ethnic designations from the play. When the 'huge explosion' bombs the room out of existence, a force not defined by any nation or state has invaded Leeds. The play's setting is now a metaphorical third space, both Leeds and Serbia, while crucially neither. No longer domestic or international, *Blasted* becomes an allegory about masculinity and violence.

The play's transformation – from a defined location into an indefinite transitional space – affects how the audience views the events of the play both before and after the explosion. The play's first rape, when Ian forces Cate to acquiesce to sex, initially appears individuated: one man's cruel act against a woman. The soldier's rape of Ian, where he sodomizes Ian and then repeats the act using Ian's own revolver, is rendered symbolic, a representation of the violence occurring outside the hotel room. The soldier tells Ian what soldiers did to his girlfriend Col, and then re-enacts that violation on Ian's body. The repetition of rape – the description of Col's rape by soldiers, the staging of Ian's rape by the soldier, which is then repeated using the gun – transforms individual acts into allegorical symbols, Ian's rape standing in for all the genocidal events described by the soldier. Ian's violated body becomes the means by which the atrocities occurring outside become visible. The soldier teases Ian after his violation: 'Can't get tragic about your [own] arse' (50). What is tragic, however, is how the singular represents the multiple. The consequence of the metaphorization of Ian's rape is that Cate's rape earlier in the play retrospectively becomes symbolic: part and parcel of the same violent causal chain.

What *Blasted* does is articulate the coherence between individualized acts of rape and strategic programmes of war. Kane stated in an interview: 'What does a common rape in Leeds have to do with mass rape in Bosnia?' And the answer appears to be 'Quite a lot' (Stephenson and Langridge 1997: 131). And this is a statement that she extended elsewhere: 'The logical conclusion of the attitude that produces an isolated rape in England is the rape camps in Bosnia, and the logical conclusion to the way society expects men to behave is war' (quoted in Sellar 1996: 34). In this view, violence is omnipresent and the play suggests that a culture that sanctions mass murder abroad inevitably allows crimes of rape to occur at home.

Humour punctuates the wounding of bodies in *Blasted*, for even in this nightmare, Cate and Ian still tell jokes. The soldier eats Ian's eyes and then kills himself. But Ian is not left alone. Cate returns to the remnants of the hotel room, carrying a crying baby that a woman gave her. The now-blind Ian begs Cate to give him the soldier's gun so he can finish the job that the soldier began. Cate, however, informs Ian, 'It's wrong to kill yourself' because 'God wouldn't like it.' Ian's reply: 'No God. No Father Christmas. No fairies. No Narnia. No fucking nothing' (55). To Ian, God is no more real than the fundamentalist fantasies of a C. S. Lewis novel. Cate and Ian's theological back-and-forth continues with Cate claiming God is necessary for life to have meaning, while Ian takes the Enlightenment high road, arguing that 'everything's got a scientific explanation' (56). It is the classic dispute between religion and science, but the body undercuts the solemnity of this 'Is There A God' debate.

In the 2001 revival of the play at the Royal Court, actor Neil Dudgeon's Ian made his case for science as his eye sockets bled, while Cate's plea for metaphysics was undercut by a hungry baby's loud cries, Kelly Reilly delivered her lines as she paced around the damaged hotel room, desperately looking for sustenance for the infant. Given the dire circumstances, how could God's existence even matter?

The audience's laughter came at the debate's conclusion. Cate gives in to Ian's request. Ian puts the gun in his mouth, but in a rare instance of good manners, he removes the gun and tells Cate, 'Don't stand behind me' (56). A beat. Then laughter. The tragedy of a man committing suicide is underscored by the bloody realities of blowing your head off. If Cate stood behind Ian, she would find herself getting very messy; the physical undermines the metaphysical. But there will be no blood, no gore. Ian pulls the trigger and it only clicks, empty of bullets. A satisfied Cate tells Ian, 'Fate, see. You're not meant to do it. God – ' (57). But if metaphysics appears to have scored a victory, the audience is in on a joke that Ian literally can't see. Cate herself took the bullets out of the gun, her faith in God's plan not so steadfast. Upon hearing Cate invoke God, Ian hurls the gun and yells, 'The cunt' (57). Again, laughter. But just as the empty gun hits the floor, Cate realizes the baby has died in her arms. And in that moment, laughter ceases, giving way to tragedy. If the truth of the body reasserts itself first to produce humour, it then serves as a reminder of the body's ultimate truth: its eventual demise.

Blasted does not end with the baby's death. There is still one final joke to tell. Cate buries the baby and leaves Ian in a quest for food. Now alone, Ian pursues a final solution to his pain. He devours the baby's corpse and then climbs into the grave. Ian's suffering is not yet complete:

> *He dies with relief.*
> *It starts to rain on him, coming through the roof.*
> *Eventually.*
> Ian: Shit. (60)

Poor Ian can never find peace. The laughter here comes from the combination of the visual (rain disturbing Ian's repose) and the verbal (Ian's expletive). But it is an uncertain moment: is Ian dead? The stage direction reads: 'he dies with relief . . . eventually'. On the page, the rain appears to have interrupted that eventuality. In performance, Ian's status is even less clear. In the 2001 revival, Ian let out a final groan, as if he was finally passing on, but nothing in the physical reality of the space – the lighting, sound or set – connoted a transition from one world to another.

This lack of clarity in text and production suggests that it does not, in fact, matter whether Ian is alive or dead: 'Punish me or rescue me makes no difference', Ian earlier told Cate (54). If Cate is vindicated, and there is an afterlife, then Ian's discovery is that it is no better than this world. In death, people are still hungry; people still get wet. If he remains alive, his chance of finally dying 'with relief' has been thwarted by a simple act of nature. In either case, Ian's rain-soaked head uttering 'shit' produces laughs. Metaphysical comfort is again squashed by the reality of bodily discomfort.

Cleansed

Kane's next play for the Royal Court, 1998's *Cleansed*, exceeds the spectacular horrors of her first play. Set in a university which functions as a concentration camp, the play charts Tinker's violent subjugation of those interned within its perimeter fence. The hints of naturalism found in *Blasted* are abandoned completely. The characters of *Cleansed* use a language that is flint-like in its starkness, making

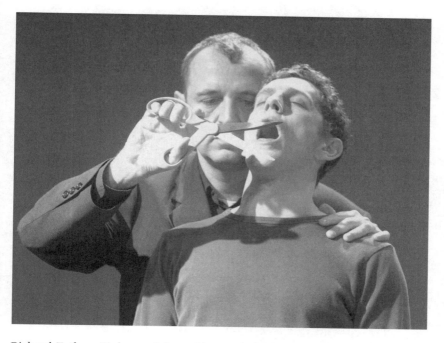

Richard Toth as Tinker and Scott Blumenthal as Carl in *Cleansed* directed by Ken Urban
Photo: Tom Nick Cocotos

individual lines open to endless interpretation and allowing for little verifiable back-story. Stage directions almost outnumber the lines of dialogue. One of the reviewers of James Macdonald's original production said, 'Half the time the play could be an installation in an art gallery' (Benedict 1998).

In the play's 20 scenes, Tinker takes over the role of university guardian following fellow inmate Graham's fatal overdose. He uses that newfound power on the inmates: Rod and Carl, two men who express their love for each other on the college greens; Grace, who has come to retrieve the belongings of her dead brother Graham; and a young boy, Robin, who can neither write nor read. In between administering bodily punishments to these four people, Tinker masturbates before a nameless stripper who performs for him in the university sports hall now converted into peep-show booths. Only in these moments can Tinker express any affection or compassion, and

161

Ken Urban

Carrie Keranen as the Woman and Richard Toth as Tinker in *Cleansed*
directed by Ken Urban
Photo: Tom Nick Cocotos

given the circumstances, these scenes take on humorous tones. To the woman peddling her wares behind a partition, Tinker implores, 'I'll be anything you need. [. . .] Please. I won't let you down' (122), but when the audience last saw Tinker, he cut off the tongue of one of the inmates. The juxtaposition of brutality and cliché defamiliarizes Tinker, transforming him into the executioner who wants to be loved. Yet his sentimental longings reveal Tinker to be as trapped as the inmates that he tortures. Tinker's shifting roles in the institution suggest a degree of mobility. Throughout the play, he appears as a drug dealer, as the doctor in charge of the university sanatorium, and as the head torturer controlling an unseen death squad. But despite these positions of authority, the joke is on Tinker. He can take on any role at the university except the one he wants most: the lover whose love is reciprocated.

What Tinker *is* capable of doing is testing the limits of the inmates. In the case of Rod and Carl, Tinker witnesses the lovers exchanging rings as a sign of love. Carl tells Rod, 'I'll always love you', and

162

though Rod takes a more cynical view of relationships – 'Anyone you can think of, someone somewhere got bored with fucking them' – the pair seal the exchange with a kiss (110–12). Tinker tests the veracity of the lovers' bond through fanatical acts of torture. Carl, after being beaten and sodomized by a pole, betrays Rod, crying out for Tinker to kill Rod, not him. Tinker spares Rod, but cuts off Carl's tongue. Carl tries to apologize to Rod for his betrayal, but with every attempt, Tinker further mutilates Carl: when Carl writes a message to Rod in the mud, Tinker cuts off his hands; when Carl performs a dance of love for Rod, Tinker cuts off his feet. The piling up of Carl's body parts becomes almost comical, and in fact, the culmination of this bodily defilement is laughter, for when Carl's feet are cut off, Rod's response is to laugh. If Bergson locates laughter's origin in the humorist's 'growing callousness to social life', Kane suggests that laughter is born out of life's growing callousness. In the case of Rod, the sheer excess of bodily defilement pushes Rod out of his body and he is transformed into a 'cold' observer, looking down at the sheer ridiculousness of it all. He experiences what Bergson calls 'a momentary aesthesia of the heart' (1999: 11). Unable to stop the escalating violence, Rod can only laugh at it.

With Grace, Kane shows a different side of Tinker's violent megalomania. Tinker wants to honour Grace's desire for Graham, but in literalizing her wishes, he ravages her body as he does Carl's. Grace arrives at the university, demanding to see her dead brother's clothes, but after putting them on, she breaks down and tells Tinker that she is staying and that he should treat her as a patient. Grace desires her brother to such a degree that Graham appears to her as a spectral presence. She consummates her incestuous desire, but the metaphysical comfort that Grace finds in her male half is rendered abject when Tinker literalizes her wishes. Tinker perceives Grace's desire for her brother as a wish to be him physically. Tinker castrates Carl and grafts his penis onto Grace's body. As she 'touches her stitched-on genitals', Tinker tells Grace, 'Nice looking lad. Like your brother. I hope you – What you wanted. [. . .] I'm sorry I'm not really a doctor' (145–6). The brutal joke is not only the obviousness of Tinker's statement, for no sane doctor would behave as Tinker has, but also the sincerity of Tinker's apology. Kane pushes Tinker's twisted logic to its conclusion: Tinker gives Grace what she wanted, for she has become her brother. Only looking at Grace's mutilated body, listening to her struggle to spit out that she 'felt it', does Tinker realize he might have been wrong. Again there is laughter, which is then silenced when Carl awakes, emitting 'a silent scream' of pain.

Despite the physical tortures depicted in the storylines of Rod, Carl and Grace, the play's cruellest scene, in fact, perhaps, the cruellest scene of Kane's canon, is saved for the young boy Robin. Grace has been teaching Robin to write and count, and Robin has fallen in love with her. Tinker's jealousy and sexual frustration cause him to lash out at the boy. In scene 15, Tinker holds a knife to Robin's throat, demanding to know if Robin has succeeded where he has failed. 'You fuck her', he asks, 'Fuck her till her nose bleed?' But what gets the audience to laugh is Tinker's next line: 'I may be a cunt but I'm not a twat' (139). In colloquial British use, 'cunt' is a rough expression for 'asshole' or 'jerk', while 'twat' is a stronger form of 'idiot' or 'moron'. What Tinker is saying is, I might be a horrible bastard, but don't, Robin, think me a fool. However, the terms Tinker uses are both shocking slang terms for the female genitalia. That Tinker in a moment of extreme anger attempts such linguistic precision in his invective is funny, but humour also arises from the context. Robin cannot re-spond to Tinker's claim; there is a knife pressed to his throat.

The humour of this moment also serves as a mirror for Tinker's misogyny. The desire for Grace that pains Tinker to such violent extremes reveals itself as both an identification with, and a repulsion from, women: I am a cunt, Tinker proclaims, but then he undermines that identification by contrasting it with something altogether lower, a twat, seemingly indifferent that both terms represent an unflattering synecdoche for the female sex. Tinker's conundrum is that the thing he desires and the thing he wants to destroy are one and the same, and that internal conflict expresses itself as inhumane cruelty to others. But in this moment, that cruelty is rendered comical.

Yet, if Tinker's line invites laughter, it does so only to accentuate the cruelty that follows. Tinker discovers the box of chocolates that Robin has bought for Grace, and Tinker forces Robin to eat every single chocolate in the box. Tinker tosses the chocolates to Robin like a dog, and Robin obediently eats every piece, gulping down the sweets as he cries, distraught as his gift to Grace is turned into the means of his humiliation. In the original 1998 script, Kane specifies that Robin needs to eat 12 chocolates, but in the revision that she made to her play before her death, she included another laugh and a gasp: there is another layer of chocolates hidden underneath the first.

What makes the scene so difficult is that it is real and it is lengthy. Unlike the cutting off of the tongue, hands and feet, unlike the sex and masturbation, this act is actually occurring on stage. There is no way to 'fake it'.[12] As a director and occasional actor herself, Kane was undoubtedly aware of this fact. Reading it on the page does not prepare you for the scene's duration. Methodically, Tinker dispenses the 24 chocolates until nothing remains of Robin's gift. He must eat them all so that there is no possibility of a generous act, so that literally nothing remains for Robin to give. Crucially this scene concludes with a joke. Forced to gorge himself on chocolate, Robin pisses himself. Tinker forces Robin's face in the mess and then instructs him to burn all the books that Grace was using to instruct him. When Grace enters and sees the fire, Robin smiles and explains the scene this way, 'Sorry. I was cold' (141). Robin reduces his torture to a simple bodily need for warmth. But humour again gives way to tragedy. Grace is oblivious to the irony of Robin's statement; she has just undergone electroshock therapy and bits of her brain have been burnt out.

The 'Dianoetic Laugh', or 'the Laugh of Laughs'

As I have argued, the comic is an integral component to Kane's work, humour and violence working in tandem to increase the play's impact on an audience. The laughter produced in an audience becomes a place where the larger ethical possibilities of her plays emerge. But Kane purposefully puts perhaps the cruellest, perhaps most liberating laughter in the mouths of her characters.

In *Blasted*, Cate is prone to fits. Early in the play, when Ian is aggressive with her, Cate stutters and, much to Ian's horror, blacks out. During these episodes, Cate 'bursts out laughing, unnaturally, hysterically, uncontrollably', eventually 'com[ing] around as if waking up in the morning' (9). This happens twice, but Cate has no memory of these moments, comparing the sensation to both an orgasm and what she imagines death feels like. When the baby dies in her arms near the play's end, her response is again to burst into laughter. Kane again describes the sound: 'unnatural', 'hysterical' and 'uncontrollable'. This outburst, like the eating of the chocolates, is lengthy, the stage direction reading, 'She laughs and laughs and laughs and laughs and laughs' (57). Again, in performance, it is about duration, the sheer volume and length of the laughter. Cate is fully awake, not as she was in the earlier spells; she has not fainted or had an episode. Here, she laughs knowing she is laughing. It is her response to the loss of the baby, indeed, to her situation in the world.

In *Cleansed*, when Rod watches Tinker remove Carl's feet, Rod responds with laughter. In performance, it is startling to see Rod's response since it first appears so cruel. But in context, given the extremity of the situation, it is impossible to imagine what other response Rod could have at this point.

The sound of Rod laughing as Carl lies helpless, another means of communication stripped from him; the sound of Cate laughing as she holds the dead baby, unable to stop herself: this is a specific kind of laughter. The laughs that Kane's work induces in an audience stick in the throat, no sooner uttered than silenced by shock. We laugh at Tinker's jokes to Grace and Robin, or Ian's frustration at being rained on, but we grow quiet in the violence that follows. Cate and Rod's laughter, by contrast, is uncontained. This is laughter laughing at the world's futility, laughter laughing at the revelation of life's finitude, laughter laughing at the cruellest of jokes; this is, in short, laughter laughing at laughter itself. Beckett calls this the 'dianoetic laugh'. 'It is the laugh of laughs', Beckett writes in his 1953 novel *Watt*, 'the laugh that laughs – silence please – at that which is unhappy' (1953: 48).[13] In this 'laugh of laughs', laughter becomes the affirmation of nothingness. The audience, however, does not laugh at these moments; the incongruity of a man laughing at his lover's pain or a woman laughing at the dead baby in her arms does not make us smile. For the audience, these are the plays' most tragic moments, for these moments teach us that laughing is, in fact, a cruel matter. In those moments when we witness the laugh that laughs at unhappiness, comedy's cruel ethics is revealed to us in all its anti-metaphysical glory. The world is meaningless. The only response is to laugh. And, of course, to keep going.

Conclusion: Fuck Saint Sarah

Kane's suicide at the young age of 28 casts a long shadow on our understanding of her work. This painful fact coupled with her rapid introduction into the canon of 'important writers' has led to a somewhat monochromatic portrait of her plays, where her pain authenticates or validates her work. Her early death leaves just a canon of five plays and one screenplay. That work can easily ossify under the burden of an 'accepted' reading, particularly when that locates profundity in relationship to biography (Iball 2005; Luckhurst 2005).

I fear transforming Sarah into a saint. Saints are precious, their words, holy; they are venerated to the point of being untouchable, imprisoned in halos that cut them off from the rest of the living and the dead. But what is most odious about saints is their lack of humour. If there is anything funny about saints, it is that they are too earnest to find anything funny. Sarah was not, is not, and should never be a saint. Works for the stage must be grappled with, fought with and reimagined; they cannot be directed or interpreted with the reverence once reserved for scripture. Perhaps by considering the comic elements of her plays, we can return a sense of humour to our image of a writer who is sadly no longer alive to remind us of it herself. 'Perhaps I know best', Nietzsche wrote in a note from 1855, 'why man alone laughs; he alone suffers so deeply that he *had* to invent laughter. The unhappiest and most melancholy of animals is, as fitting, the most cheerful' (1968: 91). Nietzsche's statement, I think, is one with which Kane would cheerfully agree.

Notes

1   All quotations from Sarah Kane's plays are taken from *Complete Plays* (2001).
2   See Sierz (2000). For an alternative reading of 1990s British theatre and culture, see Urban (2004).
3   For examples of positive appraisals of Kane's work, see Ravenhill (2005), Rebellato (1999), Saunders (2002, 2003) and Urban (2001).
4   In production sometimes, there can be humour, but it is often of the unintentional variety, coming from a more literal-minded execution of Kane's nearly impossible stage directions, the most infamous perhaps being the rats in *Cleansed* which are supposed to eat a severed hand and carry away feet. Rats, as German director Peter Zadek learned, cannot be trained to carry out such feats.
5   Mel Kenyon, Kane's agent, told Graham Saunders that Kane saw the 'very early monologues' as 'juvenilia', and following Kane's wishes, the estate has been steadfast that these monologues (*Comic Monologue, Starved, What She Said*) not be performed or published. See 'Conversation with Mel Kenyon' in Saunders (2002: 143–53).
6   See Morreall (1987) and Critchley (2002: esp. 2–6).
7   For David Greig's assertion about political theatre, see Edgar (1999: 66). For examples of this criticism of Kane's work, see 'Conversation with Phyllis Nagy' in Saunders (2002: 154–62) and Wandor (2001: 232–7).
8   While Rosset never mentions Artaud by name – a reading of Nietzsche is his prime concern – his understanding of cruelty owes a sizeable debt to Artaud's writings. See Artaud (1958).

9   The third play of the trilogy focused on nuclear war and had the working
     title of *Viva Death*. Kane finished a first draft of the play, but then aban-
     doned it.
10   In Kane's words: 'I'd been doing it [working on *Blasted*] for a few days
     and I switched on the news one night while I was having a break from
     writing, and there was a very old woman's face in Srebrenica just weep-
     ing and looking into the camera and saying – "please, please, somebody
     help us, because we need the UN to come here and help us". I thought
     this is absolutely terrible and I'm writing this ridiculous play about two
     people in a room. What's the point of carrying on?' Quoted in Saunders
     (2002: 38–9).
11   Kane began *Blasted* during her year on the MA in playwriting at Birming-
     ham University and the play's first two scenes were given a workshop
     presentation at the end of the course. There are two 1993 drafts of the
     play: one draft was used for the rehearsals and the workshop perform-
     ance, while the other one contains a number of corrections in Kane's
     handwriting. While there are differences between the two, in both ver-
     sions, the soldier is named Vladek and he refers to Leeds as a 'Serbian
     town'. My thanks to Graham Saunders for making these materials avail-
     able to me.
12   It could be argued that an actor could hide the chocolates in some way,
     and that the scene could occur without the actor actually eating them,
     but that, I would argue, defeats the power of the scene. This moment is
     about the physical ingesting of the chocolates – the audience's witness-
     ing of both Robin *and* the actor playing Robin eating the sweets – and
     the duration of that event. When I directed the play, we attempted to
     stage the moment in a way that Victor Villar-Hauser, the actor playing
     Robin, didn't need to eat all the chocolates. But we quickly learned the
     scene did not work if we 'cheated'. Just as 'body art' or radical perform-
     ance art requires the performer to undergo the experience on stage, so
     it is for the actor playing Robin in *Cleansed*. The power of this scene on
     stage was brought home to us when an audience member fainted during
     the eating of the chocolates.
13   Critchley (2002) makes much of Beckett's notion of laughter.

Primary reading

Kane, Sarah (1991a). *Comic Monologue*. Unpublished manuscript.
Kane, Sarah (1991b). *Sick: Three Monologues (Comic Monologue, Starved, What
     She Said)*. Unpublished manuscript.
Kane, Sarah (1993). *Blasted*. Unpublished manuscript.
Kane, Sarah (1994). *Blasted* in Pamela Edwardes (ed.), *Frontline Intelligence 2:
     New Plays for the Nineties*. London: Heinemann, 1–51.

Kane, Sarah (2001). *Complete Plays: Blasted, Phaedra's Love, Cleansed, Crave, 4.48 Psychosis and Skin*. London: Methuen.

Further reading

Artaud, Antonin (1958). *The Theatre and Its Double*. New York: Grove Press.
Badiou, Alain (2001). *Ethics: An Essay on the Understanding of Evil*. London and New York: Verso.
Bakhtin, Mikhail (1984). *Rabelais and His World*. Bloomington, IN: Indiana University Press.
Beckett, Samuel (1953). *Watt*. New York: Grove Press.
Beckett, Samuel (1955). *Three Novels: Molloy, Malone Dies, The Unnamable*. New York: Grove Press.
Benedict, David (1998). Review of *Cleansed*, *Independent on Sunday*, 10 May.
Bergson, Henri (1999). *Laughter: An Essay on the Meaning of the Comic*. Copenhagen and Los Angeles: Green Integer Books.
Critchley, Simon (2002). *On Humour*. London: Routledge.
Deleuze, Gilles (1988). 'On the Difference between the *Ethics* and a Morality' in *Spinoza: Practical Philosophy*. San Francisco, CA: City Lights, 17–29.
Deleuze, Gilles (1995). *Negotiations*. New York: Columbia University Press.
Edgar, David (1999). 'Provocative Acts: British Playwriting in the Post-War Era and Beyond' in David Edgar (ed.), *State of Play, Issue One: Playwrights on Playwriting*. London: Faber and Faber, 1–36.
Iball, Helen (2005). 'Room Service: En Suite on the *Blasted* Frontline', *Contemporary Theatre Review* 15:3, 320–9.
Luckhurst, Mary (2005). 'Infamy and Dying Young: Sarah Kane, 1971–1999' in Mary Luckhurst and Jane Moody (eds.), *Theatre and Celebrity 1660–2000*. London: Palgrave, 107–24.
Morreall, John, ed. (1987). *The Philosophy of Laughter and Humour*. Albany, NY: State University of New York Press.
Nietzsche, Friedrich (1968). *The Will to Power*, ed. Walter Kaufmann. New York: Vintage.
Peter, John (1998). 'Short Stark Shock', *Sunday Times*, 10 May.
Ravenhill, Mark (2005). 'Suicide Art? She's Better than That', *Guardian*, 12 October.
Rebellato, Dan (1999). 'Sarah Kane: An Appreciation', *New Theatre Quarterly* 59, 280–1.
Rosset, Clément (1993). *Joyful Cruelty: Toward a Philosophy of the Real*. New York and Oxford: Oxford University Press.
Saunders, Graham (2002). *'Love Me or Kill Me': Sarah Kane and the Theatre of Extremes*. Manchester: Manchester University Press.
Saunders, Graham (2003). ' "Just a Word on the Page and there is the Drama": Sarah Kane's Theatrical Legacy', *Contemporary Theatre Review* 13:1, 97–110.

Sellar, Tom (1996). 'Truth or Dare: Sarah Kane's Blasted', *Theater* 27:1, 29–34.

Shklovsky, Viktor (1965). 'Art as Technique' in Lee T. Lemon and Marion J. Reis (eds.), *Russian Formalist Criticism: Four Essays*. Lincoln, NE, and London: University of Nebraska Press, 5–24.

Sierz, Aleks (2000). *In-Yer-Face Theatre: British Drama Today*. London: Faber and Faber.

Stephenson, Heidi, and Langridge, Natasha (1997). 'Interview with Sarah Kane' in *Rage and Reason: Women Playwrights on Playwriting*. London: Methuen, 129–35.

Urban, Ken (2001). 'An Ethics of Catastrophe: The Theatre of Sarah Kane', *Performing Arts Journal* 69, 36–46.

Urban, Ken (2004). 'Towards a Theory of Cruel Britannia: Coolness, Cruelty and the 'Nineties', *New Theatre Quarterly* 80, 354–72.

Urban, Ken (forthcoming). 'Cruel Britannia' in Graham Saunders and Rebecca D'Monte (eds.), *Cool Britannia: British Political Drama in the 1990s*. London: Palgrave.

Wandor, Michelene (2001). *Post-War British Drama: Looking Back in Gender*. New York and London: Routledge.

Chapter 9

Physical Theatre: Complicite and the Question of Authority

Helen Freshwater

'Physical theatre' is a notoriously problematic term, and resistance to its application has grown despite – or perhaps because of – its frequent use by critics, commentators and practitioners, and its regular appearances in programmes, listings, reviews and critical commentary in the media since the mid-1980s. Even companies such as DV8 (whose director, Lloyd Newson, claimed that they were 'one of the first groups in Britain to call their work physical theatre') have distanced themselves from the phrase, declaring that overuse has rendered it meaningless (Giannachi and Luckhurst 1999: 109). Others argue that it has been reduced to a marketing tool (Murray 2003: 34). This ubiquity is not matched by similarly extensive coverage in published academic analysis, though there is a slowly growing field of scholarly engagement with the form. As a result there are many questions left to answer about its development in Britain and its relationship to continental European, American and eastern traditions; the influence of contemporary international practices and training; and the links between the numerous companies whose work has been labelled physical theatre.[1] This chapter aims to explore some of the issues which are raised by the critical response to these practices through a reading of the work of Théâtre de Complicité, or Complicite, as they are now known. First, however, it is necessary to examine what we do know about this kind of work, and to assess some of the challenges which attend its analysis.

Foremost amongst these challenges is the difficulty of defining physical theatre. The significant differences between even the most well-known and long-lived British theatre companies who have had their work described as physical theatre – such as Shared Experience, Kneehigh Theatre, Complicite and DV8 – make the problems inherent in any attempt at taxonomy apparent. As a result, scholars tend to shy away from presenting a one-size-fits-all formula, preferring to talk of 'physical theatres', a 'loose movement of practitioners, teachers and theorists', 'family resemblances' between different companies, or several interrelated but distinct strands of practice (Murray 2003: 35, 3; Lark 1999: 236; Heddon and Milling 2006: 162). Nevertheless, assertions that physical theatre cannot be codified, or that its sheer diversity renders it all but indefinable, often preface attempts to describe this quality and the creative processes that produce it. For example, Dymphna Callery identifies several shared practices, focusing upon the principles that inform the construction of a piece and its relationship to an audience. She notes that physical theatre gives the actor a central creative role, and that it is often devised by an ensemble. Callery also observes that this kind of work seeks to exploit theatre's liveness and its theatricality, as it eschews both naturalism's techniques of literal reproduction, and the passive spectatorship naturalism is perceived to encourage (2001: 5, 15).[2]

Physical theatre has also been associated with a rejection of conventional disciplinary categories and techniques, as well as an anti-establishment politics. Ana Sanchez-Colberg's 1996 reading of 'the road towards a physical theatre' interprets contemporary work through the frame of the historical avant-garde's commitment to transgression (1996: 40–56), whilst Jen Harvie connects DV8's embodiment of the form with a commitment to addressing the experience of social exclusion (Harvie 2002: 69). Others claim to have identified links between an 'anti-textual' stance in contemporary performance and a politics of liberation (Hornby 2002: 355–6). All of these claims invite critique, of course, but physical theatre's relationship to text has remained central to existing discussions of its definition.[3] For Callery, physical theatre is dependent upon development processes that begin with a somatic impulse, rather than intellectual engagement with a script (2001: 205–7). Sanchez-Colberg also associates a focus upon the corporeal with a 'devaluation of language and a move towards a non-verbal idiom', extending this point to suggest that this is part of a broader cultural perception that language can be a tool in social subjugation; an alienating 'coercive institution' that serves to distort our understanding of reality (1996: 41–2). Within this ideological framework, moving 'beyond words' often seems to imply challenging the imposition of authoritarian control; giving expression to the unsaid and the unsayable; releasing the imagination; and rooting out unconscious physical habits that distort the body's movement (Murray 2003: 72–8; Callery 2001: 3).

To date, there has been no attempt at a systematic investigation of these claims, but it is clear that – as far as the physical theatre practitioner is concerned – these objectives can only be realized through an ongoing commitment to physical training. This investment in training is what provides contemporary British physical theatre with a recognizable generic signature.[4] It also distinguishes physical theatre from the tradition of body-focused performance art that emerged during the same period.[5] But this identification of the central importance of training for any definition of physical theatre presents the researcher with another set of questions and challenges. For example, the transmission of performance techniques through workshops complicates investigations into issues of ownership, and may confound efforts to establish origins or genealogies of influence. As a result, critics prefer not to attribute the development of physical theatre to a single practitioner or theorist, and invoke a wide range of traditions, techniques and training when discussing possible sources of influence. None the less, recent studies of Jacques Lecoq's imaginative, non-prescriptive pedagogy bear convincing witness to the significant role his emphasis upon play, improvisation, ensemble work and mask has had in shaping physical theatre. Many well-known practitioners whose work has been labelled physical theatre have attended his school in Paris since it opened in 1956, and members of successive generations of performers – including Steven Berkoff, Simon McBurney and Carolina Valdez (one of the founder members of Theatre O) – testified to the importance of his work on his death in 1999 (Berkoff 1999: 5; Esslin 1999; Valdez 1999: 8).[6]

Training at Lecoq's school has not been the only route into physical theatre, however. Other European traditions and theories have also inspired practitioners and fed into the development of the form, including Jerzy Grotowski's 'poor theatre'; Antonin Artaud's vision of a theatrical language 'intended for the senses and independent of speech', articulated in *The Theatre and Its Double* (Artaud 1958: 38); Vsevolod Meyerhold's Biomechanics; the collaborative practice of Bertolt Brecht and his exploration of 'gestus'; Tadeusz Kantor's 'Theatre of Death'; Eugenio Barba's exploration of ritual forms; and Dario Fo's politicized reworking of *commedia dell'arte*.[7] Moreover, if we shift our focus from theatrical imports, it is possible to locate early British experiments in physical theatre in the visions of Edward Gordon Craig, whose work anticipated a shift from verbal to corporeal expression, and in the stylized, expressionist experiments of director Terence Gray and the Little Theatre movement of the 1920s, as Christine Lark demonstrates.[8]

Clearly, emphasis upon any one of the above practices leaves others neglected. Lark argues that theatre scholars and critics have failed to acknowledge the wealth of cross-disciplinary connections between avant-garde dance and physical theatre.[9] Conversely, Murray suggests that a focus upon experimental dance and theatre overlooks the influence of popular performance traditions of *commedia dell'arte*, circus and vaudeville (Murray 2003: 35).[10] Asian and American practices have also had a substantial impact upon the development of physical theatre in Britain, but a full analysis of the connections between these diverse traditions and contemporary physical theatre has yet to appear, as does a comprehensive assessment of the form's reflection of broader cultural conceptions of the body, or its position in relation to other contemporary theatres.[11]

There are several possible explanations for the relatively limited analysis of the history and growth of physical theatre – or physical theatres – in Britain. It certainly seems that the broad range of practice that has been given this label, the diversity of sources of influence and inspiration, and the complexity of tracing the origins of particular techniques and approaches have all contributed to the tentative and provisional statements made about its history and growth in existing publications. Moreover, although the alleged 'anti-textual' bias of contemporary performance (identified by Richard Hornby 2002: 355–8) requires further analysis, it does appear that many practitioners consider writing about their work to be inimical to its achievements, as the types of training and dissemination which are associated with physical theatre privilege knowledge that may be primarily – or indeed exclusively – understood *Through the Body*, as Callery's book puts it (2001: 3).[12]

There may be other ways, however, of explaining why physical theatre has not yet been given much attention in the scholarly sphere. Harvie has argued recently that the disproportionate – and dominant – historiographical emphasis upon British theatre's literary credentials has reduced our understanding of the material aspects of theatre production, leading to the neglect and suppression of alternative histories. In *Staging the UK*, Harvie proposes that this dominant narrative serves to perpetuate the perception of British theatre as uniquely literary, and that it is 'symptomatic of an anti-theatrical – if not an anti-dramatic – prejudice', which leads us to overlook 'aspects of theatre that are material, embodied, physically expressive, and produced through the work of a group' (Harvie 2005: 114).[13] This is a serious omission: physical theatre now has an established position in the theatre industry in Britain, and a significant history of its own. The last twenty years have seen phenomenal growth in the number of opportunities for performers to train in physical theatre techniques within the UK; a steady proliferation of companies who describe what they do as physical theatre; and the form's gradual, but inexorable, move from the fringe towards the mainstream. Students now have access to well-established training methods and a large pool of shared knowledge, as well as numerous examples of current practice. Complicite celebrated their twenty-first birthday in 2005, and several physical theatre productions have reached the West End, such as Frantic Assembly's *Sell Out* (1998) at the New Ambassadors Theatre and Shared Experience's *After Mrs Rochester* (2003) at the Duke of York's. Failure to recognize the contribution physical theatre continues to make to the development of contemporary theatre would diminish any account of current British theatre. None the less, the prejudice that Harvie describes is still alive and well. As we will see, many in the critical establishment continue to have difficulty in responding to physical theatre, and in recognizing the contribution the form has made to the contemporary theatre scene.

This chapter addresses this phenomenon through an examination of the assumptions and attitudes that have distorted the reception and appreciation of contemporary physical theatre. It concentrates upon journalistic coverage of Complicite's work in order to assess the response to their practice in the media. It also addresses the company's own contribution to the construction of their public image, analysing the statements made about Complicite's work by its artistic director, Simon McBurney (b. 1957). Together, the media coverage and McBurney's accounts of his experiences with the company raise important questions about the role of the director and the contribution of the performer in physical theatre, as well as illustrating some of the beliefs which continue to limit understanding of the relationship between scripts and performance, authority and interpretation. The chapter attempts to unsettle some of these beliefs through analysis of the company's practice in performance and assessment of accounts of their work in rehearsal. It suggests alternative methods of evaluating this relationship, and finally points us in the direction of a more mature assessment of the achievements of physical theatre.

I have chosen to focus upon Complicite because they are central to the development of contemporary physical theatre in Britain. Indeed, many commentators are happy to declare that they are the most significant, and the most influential of all British physical theatre companies (Callery 2001: 6; Heddon and Milling 2006: 178–82; Murray 2003: 97–109). Formed in 1983 by Simon McBurney, Annabel Arden, Fiona Gordon and Marcello Magni, the company received critical acclaim quickly: *More Bigger Snacks Now* (1985) won the Perrier comedy award at Edinburgh and was broadcast on the television chat show *Wogan*. This was followed by a series of short pieces including *Food-stuff* (1986) and *Anything for a Quiet Life* (1987). McBurney observes that the company was a loose, anarchic and frequently volatile collective during this period, and presents the more focused collaboration produced during their 15-week season at the Almeida in 1989 – which resulted in a well-received production of Dürrenmatt's *The Visit* – as a defining moment in their history (O'Mahony 2005).

The revival of *The Visit* at the National Theatre in 1991 was also highly significant for the company, as it marked the start of a relationship that has been central to their mainstream success. Complicite's connection to the National was secured with the *Street of Crocodiles*, which went into development at the National Theatre Studio in 1991, and cemented by several further productions, including *Out of a House Walked a Man* (1994), *The Caucasian Chalk Circle* (1997), *Measure for Measure* (2004) and a revival of *A Minute Too Late* (2005).[14] The company now enjoys international acclaim, having presented their work across Europe, and in Israel, the USA, Canada, the West Indies, Argentina, Chile, Peru, Columbia, Ecuador, Hong Kong, Australia and India. *Mnemonic* (1999) – which began life as a co-production with the Salzburg Festival – was the first of the company's shows to receive support from a major international arts festival, and since then productions have been funded by a veritable flotilla of international arts institutions.[15] Over the years their productions have won numerous awards, and several have proved popular enough to transfer to the West End and Broadway.[16] The company's website also highlights the range of work they have produced, noting their forays into other media.[17] What has remained constant, however, is the company's stated commitment to collaboration and ensemble work. The website contains an exhaustive and detailed catalogue of the numerous performers, writers, designers, technicians and administrators who have worked with Complicite, and the brief introductory page states: 'What is essential is collaboration. A collaboration between individuals to establish an ensemble with a common physical and imaginative language' (Complicite 2006).[18]

Despite the company's huge popular success, the acclaim they enjoy and the range of work they have produced, considered analysis of their practice in the media has been in short supply. Reviewers either appear to lack the critical vocabulary to respond to their work appropriately, or seem to be so in awe of their achievements that they produce hagiography rather than analysis, leading to unconsidered repetition of the claims made by the company. For example, Complicite have always stressed that they do not apply, or have, a single set 'technique', or 'method'. This is an account that reviewers are happy to endorse and perpetuate, as an article by Lyn Gardner – which has been selected for reproduction on the website – indicates. Gardner asserts that the essence of Complicite is 'impossible to pin down', and notes, 'Not only are Complicite productions different from everybody else's they are also vastly different from each other. There may be revivals of successful productions, but the next show will never offer more of the same. Complicite have always taken delight in multiplying the uncertainties, keeping us and them on their toes' (Gardner 2002). This commitment to constant change is reflected in the way in which productions grow and develop during a run, and in the ever-changing constellation of collaborators. But it is possible to identify reoccurring themes and a distinctive style in Complicite's work, and failing to interrogate the company's insistence upon the importance of change leaves several interesting questions unaddressed.[19]

More problematic than this tendency to unreflective reiteration, though, is the anti-theatrical prejudice that continues to exist in some quarters of the critical establishment. Traces of this prejudice are not hard to find. For example, in an interview on a special edition of *The Late Show* (which followed the development of *Street of Crocodiles* during the eight-week devising and rehearsal period) critic Michael Billington conceded that Complicite had convincingly demonstrated their 'often brilliant and dazzlingly acrobatic, athletic, physical, mimetic skill' during their first eight years as a company, but registered his uncertainty about the value of these achievements: 'They've also bred I think in me and one or two other people too a counter-reaction, a feeling, yes, but where is this taking us? [. . .] Is the moral concept of theatre being subordinated to a display of technique?' Reflecting upon audience response to the company's production of *The Visit* at

Cesar Sarachu as Joseph in Complicite's *Street of Crocodiles*
Photo: Joan Marcus

the National Theatre in 1991, he recalled: 'people came out of the production [. . .] saying, "Aren't they wonderful? Aren't they brilliant?" Not as far as I remember saying, "Isn't the play fantastic?"' He concluded that he sometimes suspected that the company's technique was 'overlaying the content' (*Late Show* 1992).

Billington's commentary acknowledges that his response is out of kilter with the broad enthusiasm for Complicite's work amongst audiences, but his suspicion that physical technique might be displacing engagement with 'the play' has proved enduring. The value system that informs these kinds of judgements and narratives was explicitly articulated by Billington in another television interview some twelve years later, as he discussed the work of another young British theatre company, Shunt:

> I am a bit worried at the moment about the fact there is a strong anti-text movement in the British theatre. Text is inherently rich, stimulating, ambiguous, full of ideas, full of moral conflict. That to me is what theatre finally comes down to and that's when theatre begins to work on your mind and your imagination. You go and see people prancing around in a gymnasium doing amazing physical theatre and you come away but you – well I anyway – don't feel changed by the experience. What I want is a theatre that is going to upset me, disturb me, change my view of the world. And in the end I think that happens with language. (*Culture Show* 2004)

Billington is careful to acknowledge the subjective nature of his judgement, but it is possible to view his response in the context of a much older, and wider, tradition.

As Marvin Carlson points out, many of the historical models that address the relationship between literature and theatre, or the script and performance, give text the dominant position in this pairing. This results in performance being considered as a successful illustration or translation of a script at best, and a corruption or a betrayal of it at worst (1985: 5–11). This approach is particularly apparent in the critical discussion that surrounds modern productions of Shakespeare, as W. B. Worthen demonstrates in *Shakespeare and the Authority of Performance*. This exploration of the descriptions of performance circulating in contemporary Shakespearean scholarship, in actor training and amongst directors shows that the 'intentional fallacy' – the notion that all interpretation should defer to authorial intention – is still in regular use:

> The sense that performance transmits Shakespearean authority remains very much in play, most strongly perhaps when the ostensibly free and disruptive activity of the stage is at hand. [. . .] 'Shakespeare' – sometimes coded as the 'text', its 'genre', or the 'theatre' itself – remains an apparently indispensable category for preparing, interpreting and evaluating theatrical performance, at least as much for practitioners as for scholars and critics. (Worthen 1997: 3)

Worthen establishes that the success of a production is frequently measured against the text of the play: a text that stands in for its 'literary identity, an identity that lies outside and beyond performance' (26).

Given the effective deconstruction of the intentional fallacy in academia, it is rather depressing, if not entirely surprising, to find many theatre reviewers still measuring productions against a play-wright's wishes: or rather what they perceive these to have been. Certainly, casting an eye over the critical response to Complicite's two high-profile Shakespearean productions *The Winter's Tale* (1992) and *Measure for Measure* (2004), it cannot be said that the radical reassessment of the concept of the author delivered by critical theory in the 1970s and 1980s has had any discernible impact upon the majority of British theatre reviewers (see Foucault 1977; Barthes 1977). Although reviewers of *The Winter's Tale* all paid some form of tribute to the company's energy, their cohesion as an ensemble and their creativity, none was unequivocal in their praise. The reviews' language reveals that many critics thought of the company as being in competition, or in a battle, with the script: some argued that the text had been 'sacri-ficed' to Complicite's theatricality (Wardle 1992; Hewison 1992; Nathan 1992). Others criticized the company's failure to ensure that 'bravura display remains subservient to plot and character', addressing what they perceived as an imbalance, or inversion, of the proper relation-ship between performance and script (Nightingale 1992). Accordingly, some complained that the company was merely deploying the script as 'an upmarket pretext for an exhibition of inventiveness', rather than 'using its skills to explore and illuminate Shakespeare's play' (Taylor 1992). Delivery of the verse came in for criticism, and some reviewers judged the demonstrative physicality of McBurney's Leontes to be particularly excessive (Spencer 1992; Taylor 1992; Billington 1992). These reviews display the critical attachment to the notion of a production that would be appropriately faithful to the text, conjuring up the figure of Shakespeare himself in order to measure the distance between Complicite's command of theatrical artifice and this putative authorized version. Benedict Nightingale concluded his review: '[Complicite] sometimes prefers physical ado to exploring the mean-ing and feeling embodied in the words. It is uninterested in finding the text below the text. Does it really trust Shakespeare – and should Shakespeare trust it?' (Nightingale 1992).

Nightingale's final question may be meaningless, but it provides excellent exemplification of Worthen's point. We should acknowledge, however, that Complicite's association with an 'anti-text' position is produced, in part, by those who admire their work. Many of those who have celebrated and supported the company over the years are happy to give them a leading role in the resistance to a monolithic textual tradition. In fact, this role seems to be central to the popular understanding of what the company have achieved. Their work is frequently figured as disruptive; a challenge, as Gardner puts it, to 'the spectacle of British theatre, with its English roses and well ordered texts' (Gardner 2002). In similar vein, the director Pierre Audi, an early champion of the company, declares that 'their contribution is to open up the horizons of audiences who don't need to be constantly obsessed with the idea of coming to listen to words, words, words' (O'Mahony 2005). These assertions clearly have more weight as rhetoric than value as considered analysis, but, given the critical consensus, it seems necessary to examine the evidence that Complicite have adopted an 'anti-textual' position.

The exploration of physical expression and corporeal experience is undoubtedly central to the company's work and to McBurney's approach to performance. When asked about the origins of theatre, for example, McBurney cites Edward Gordon Craig's observation, 'Dance is the parent of theatre', describing a journey towards theatre which begins with the expression of internalized emotion through physical action and movement (Giannachi and Luckhurst 1999: 70). Here it is important to remember that three out of four of Complicite's founder members trained at Lecoq's school in Paris. Lecoq's training privileged gesture, touch and movement above verbalization, and the centrality of gesture to his philosophy is indicated by the following aphorism:

> Gesture precedes knowledge
> Gesture precedes thought
> Gesture precedes language (Felner 1985: 150)

The enduring influence of Lecoq's teaching was very apparent at a public workshop McBurney gave at the National Theatre in March 2006, in which he explored scenes and speeches from *Measure for Measure* through a demonstration of Lecoq's seven levels of tension, ensemble movement, and the difficulty of neutral presentation. McBurney's comments on his approach to rehearsal, and on his aims for audience response, also make it clear that embodied experience is crucial in all aspects of the company's work.[20]

These concerns are very much apparent in the company's practice. *A Minute Too Late* (1984, revived 2005) demonstrates the company's

Marcello Magni, Simon McBurney and Josef Houben in Complicite's 2005 revival of *A Minute Too Late*
Photo: Robbie Jack

success in exploring areas of experience in which verbalization fails. It depicts our inarticulacy and embarrassment in the face of death and grief, bringing a sense of the inadequacy and limitations of spoken language to the fore. Gesture and corporeal expression are often used in the piece to signal our desire to avoid referring to death, as when Marcello Magni's ridiculous registrar is suddenly overcome with embarrassment as he realizes that Jozef Houben's undertaker needs a death certificate for his mother. He jerks his head and points upwards as he whispers: 'how did she . . . fall asleep?' Then, rather than name various forms of death, he resorts to miming them. Elsewhere in the show, language can seem terrible in its abstraction. Sitting at home, alone, McBurney's widower flicks through a pamphlet, reading aloud: 'What to do after a death. Department of Health and Social Security. Support and Comfort . . . If the organs have to be donated . . . [. . .] what else has to be done. . . .'.

The language which is present in *A Minute Too Late* often appears empty: rendered meaningless through overuse. For example, the phrase 'I'm so sorry' is compulsively repeated by McBurney's character, whose failure to negotiate successfully the rituals and etiquette which surround death is exploited to hilarious, and eventually poignant, effect. He works his way through a series of scenes and locations, as he moves back and forth across painful memories and nightmarish imaginings, directing his 'I'm so sorry' at the occupants of the graves he steps on in an overpopulated cemetery; at fellow worshippers in church as he struggles with the responses and routines of religious ritual; and finally at Houben's undertaker in the registrar's office. When McBurney's character realizes that the undertaker has just collected a death certificate he begins a sequence of apologies in which both men seek to outdo each other in contrition. They sink towards the floor as they express their regret, squirming downwards until they are grovelling and clawing at the ground in agonies of mutual self-abasement. Here, emotions that are not communicated by hopelessly overworked words are given vigorous physical life.

Despite this effective demonstration of the limitations of language, and the opinion of the section of the critical establishment that seeks to celebrate the company's achievements as a challenge to the perceived British emphasis upon the literary, the company's production history indicates the importance of text in their work. After a handful of early shows such as *More Bigger Snacks Now* (1985), which were solely devised by the company, they went on to draw upon a series of pre-existing texts including Maurice Valency's adaptation of *The Visit* (1989); Shakespeare's *The Winter's Tale* (1992); an adaptation of the stories of Bruno Schulz, *Street of Crocodiles* (1992); *Out of a House Walked a Man* (1994) based on the writings of Russian surrealist Daniil Kharms; a version of a John Berger story, *The Three Lives of Lucie Cabrol* (1994); *Foe* (1996), after J. M. Coetzee's novel; Brecht's *The Caucasian Chalk Circle* (1997); Eugene Ionesco's *The Chairs* (1997); *Light* (2000), based on a book by Torgny Lindgren; *The Elephant Vanishes* (2003), inspired by Haruki Murakami's collection of short stories; and Shakespeare's *Measure for Measure* (2004).

McBurney is unequivocal about the importance of the company's responsiveness to the source material they have selected, and this is particularly apparent in the coverage of the company's development of *Street of Crocodiles*. In an interview for BBC2's *The Late Show* McBurney emphasized the strength of Schulz's influence, arguing that 'The person of Bruno Schulz himself comes across very, very strongly in his writings and you can't avoid an encounter with the man if you're going to read the books.' McBurney's perception of Schulz's centrality led to his decision to include a character – 'the narrator, the poet' – in the production which would represent the author. The decision to name this figure Joseph is also explained by reference to the author: 'I've called him Joseph as he calls himself in his books.' McBurney leaves us in no doubt as to his attentiveness to the authority carried by Schulz's text, as he avers: 'The word is all important. Really. The word in many ways is the basis. Because it is through the word that you make an imaginative leap' (*Late Show* 1992).

This sense of the importance of the source material is communicated by both movement and images in *Street of Crocodiles*. Books figure prominently throughout. The opening scene shows us Joseph sorting through shelves of books, in a reference to the bitter irony of the labour Schulz was assigned by the Nazis before his death: selecting library books for cataloguing or destruction (Complicite 2003: 3). Joseph is captivated by one volume in particular, and, seated centre stage, he lifts it to his face to breathe in its scent, strokes it affectionately, and smiles. Warm lights and rising music signal his absorption as the other characters emerge, immersed in books of their own. Books appear in flight repeatedly throughout the piece, transformed by the performers' simultaneous movements into flocks of birds. The motif embodies both the director's deference to Schulz's work, and the lively, joyous animation of the text realized by the ensemble's synchronicity.

McBurney's description of the preparation for *Street of Crocodiles* also highlights the company's relationship to the text. He notes that although the company started off recounting Schulz's stories in different forms – trying 'simply to read to each other' – objects quickly began to dominate the rehearsal room. He describes this as a mysterious act of possession: 'they seemed to take over the whole process without permission, beyond our control. I remember struggling with the attempt to bring text to the fore with my co-adaptor Mark Wheatley. There were evenings of despair at the apparently unequal nature of the struggle' (Irvin 2003: 80). McBurney's explanation of this turn of events is particularly telling. He places the responsibility for the company's inability to focus upon the text with its author:

In retrospect I realised that Schulz's vision, which evokes the transforming power of the child's eye, necessarily meant that objects and their transmogrification would be central to the process. [. . .] It was the material that pushed us there, the unruly unrepentant skew of Schulz's imagination which was both impetus and goal, and which we were, quite rightly, to be governed by. (76–80)

The assertion that the development processes of the company have been subject to forces outside of the control of the director, the performers or others working on the production – that they have a life of their own – is not unique to *Street of Crocodiles*. Describing the intense four-day period of improvisation and devising which produced *A Minute Too Late* in 1984, McBurney recalls: 'We hardly thought about what we were talking about. The subject simply talked through what we did. We had the strange sensation that the show wrote itself' (76). This statement is intriguing: obviously, the show did not write itself. There may, however, be very good reasons for constructing an elaborate mythology around your creative process and asserting the 'directorial', or even dictatorial, agency of your source material.

Indeed, these narratives can be interpreted as shrewd responses to the continuing critical preoccupation with the text: the 'anti-material, anti-phenomenological, anti-*theatrical* prejudice' identified by Harvie (2005: 117). McBurney is certainly sharply aware of this prejudice. He has observed that the British are 'obsessed with words,' noting, 'we have a habit of retreating into this grey and forbidding castle which is our language to fight off any marauders who dare to suggest that any other form is equal to it.' (Morris 1994). Speaking in 1992, shortly after the critical attack upon *The Winter's Tale*, he suggested that the aural predilection of the average theatregoer reduced their ability to discuss Complicite's work: 'people who are used to dance are more able to talk about our work because they are used to looking, whereas theatre people are used to listening [. . .] so many people are deaf to the articulacy of action and image' (Armistead 1992).

McBurney clearly feels that this is a particular problem with productions of Shakespeare and, after their experience with *The Winter's Tale*, Complicite did not attempt another Shakespeare play for over ten years. Reflecting upon their decision to tackle *Measure for Measure* in an interview with Emma Crichton-Miller, McBurney noted his ambivalence about the way Shakespeare is often interpreted in Britain: 'There is only a tiny proportion of productions of Shakespeare where I come away elated and delighted to have revisited the work. *There is an unspoken code here about how it should be performed*, whereas foreign productions have enormous licence, and Shakespeare is often just the starting point for this great eruption of theatrical delight and invention' (Crichton-Miller 2004, my emphasis). The Shakespearean 'code', of course, had been made explicit in the critical reviews of *The Winter's Tale*, and McBurney seemed to anticipate similar critical

Helen Freshwater

disapprobation for *Measure for Measure*, feeding Crichton-Miller the question, 'What's that bad boy doing with Shakespeare?'

The way in which McBurney went on to answer this rhetorical question is telling. He highlighted the in-depth research into the play's socio-historical moment that he had undertaken with the company, emphasizing his respect for the script – 'I find it [. . .] marvellous, endless, enormously rewarding to engage with the text' – and connecting his decision to take on the production with a readiness to respond to the language: 'I felt I could only go into Shakespeare if I really felt I could mine the language as deeply as possible and come up with an appropriate response' (Neill 2004). Here Worthen's observation that the need to evoke the authority of the text is experienced at least as much by practitioners as it is by scholars and critics seems particularly pertinent. For Worthen, this approach is an attempt to acquire the kind of authority usually associated with authorship. He observes: 'legitimating the author *is* a way of authorizing ourselves' (1997: 191). In McBurney's case, however, the tactic of genuflection before Shakespeare's language – or Schulz's imagination – is resistant to this interpretation. Indeed, Christopher Innes seems to be alone in celebrating McBurney as an *auteur*, or 'a new type of playwright', perhaps because McBurney has not promoted this version of his role within the company (2002: 537). In fact, McBurney takes every opportunity to shift critical attention away from issues of his own achievements as a director and towards the creative input of the performers.

McBurney's emphasis upon this contribution appears to be rather more complex than the usual modest self-effacement that established directors often indulge in. For example, he contends that the moments of immaculate simultaneity produced by Complicite ensembles – such as those which transformed books into birds in *Street of Crocodiles* – should not be thought of as choreography, but should be attributed to the physical discipline of the performers; a discipline acquired through a combination of exceptional, continually renewed commitment, and long periods of preparation through improvisation in rehearsal (Giannachi and Luckhurst 1999: 74). His efforts to move the critical emphasis away from choreography – with its associations of scripted movement and authorship – is also reflected in his insistence upon the importance of the actors' ownership of the material:

> a piece of theatre is, ultimately, in the hands of those who are performing it. The actors. It is they, not the director, who must have a whole

186

piece in their every gesture, hearing the meaning in each word. And to do that I think, as an actor, you have to feel that you possess the piece. And to possess the piece you have to be part of its creation. Involved intimately in the process of its making. (Irvin 2003: 80)

There can be no doubt that performers working with Complicite do make a significant contribution to their work. But one result of the company's combined emphasis upon distancing themselves from technique or method, stressing responsiveness to the source material, and foregrounding the input of the company's performers is the effective obfuscation of McBurney's own creative contribution.

Here, it seems apposite to consider the position of the director within the company more closely: an investigation which Stephen Knapper commences as he draws upon interviews with performers who appeared in *The Noise of Time* (2000). He concludes that it would be incorrect to 'cast McBurney in the role of dictatorial director' and emphasizes the way in which 'actors and technicians are constantly encouraged to explore through improvisation and research and to constantly re-invent material' (Knapper 2004: 68). None the less, the interview material presented by Knapper actually seems to highlight the limitations of the performers' creative contributions. For example, performer Liam Steel comments that the heavy use of multimedia in pieces such as *The Noise of Time* results in the performer becoming 'another technicality alongside music, video and recorded sound'. He continues: 'Your responsibility is not to start expressing yourself' (68). Charlotte Medcalf also observes that McBurney comes to rehearsals 'with a strong sense of some of the shapes that he's going to use and some of the key ideas [. . .] There's always collective feeling about things but in the end it's always going to be Simon's call.' Evidently, devising in this way is not always a comfortable experience. She reports that, towards the end of the rehearsal period,

> you enter into a stage of relationships that become increasingly insecure and volatile [. . .] the decision making process is stalled and stalled and I think underneath it all he knows he's going to return to these key things and he wants to extend and explore as much as possible and at the last minute the decision is made and it slips into line and the whole thing goes back into focus. (69)

Knapper interprets withholding decisions until the last minute and changing content during the run as evidence of the trust (and, indeed, the 'complicity') that develops between performers and director. He reports Steel's observation that this approach gives the performers a 'high status' within the production, but also conveys the insecurity that such an experience involves, as he records Steel's recurring nightmare of 'arriving on stage not knowing what to do' (70). Knapper's interviews seem to show that although the performers make a major contribution to Complicite's creative process, they do not have much control over it.

The Late Show television documentary also offers an intriguing glimpse into the balance between the contributions of the cast and the director in *Street of Crocodiles*. In it, McBurney notes that the process is all about 'looking for that one moment which will get into the show', and describes leading the group through games and physical exercises, observing: 'they hardly know when they're in a scene and not in a scene'. McBurney acknowledges that the performers often found the uncertainty inherent in this technique difficult: 'The main anxiety for the actors is that they don't know what they're doing and they're trusting me [. . .] It's like an enormous leap of faith on their part or else it's kind of down-right lying on my part and I don't quite know which' (*Late Show* 1992). These statements reveal both the importance of this process of preparation and his own creative agency. McBurney's directorial role is also foregrounded by the clips selected by the documentary makers, which present McBurney reassuring individual actors, focusing the group, and demonstrating moments of performance as the cast stand and watch. Viewing these scenes, it is hard not to conclude that the performance is primarily a product of McBurney's fertile imagination, rather than Bruno Schulz's. The potential for slippage between the two is indicated by McBurney's own description of the performance's dream-like quality: 'the beginning is still to my imagination him calling up memory [. . .] The actors themselves are called up [. . .] They form this image almost of spectres that have been conjured up from some rather dark recess of Schulz's imagination' (*Late Show* 1992).

An outsider's perspective on the development of *Street of Crocodiles* certainly provides little support for the assertion that the company were 'governed by [. . .] Schulz's imagination'. Robert Butler's description of rehearsals suggests that the relationship between the text, the performers and the source material can be accounted for in a rather more pragmatic way:

> For a start, there is no script. I saw a list of ideas on a rehearsal room table, but no one else looked at it. The assistant director did offer the

actors cream-coloured cards with neatly typed quotes but only on a take-it-or-leave-it basis. [. . .] If there is a good moment to say something in a scene – that is, use actual dialogue – the director, Simon McBurney, padding round in T-shirt and bare feet, feeds the line. 'Try the one, "I'm away on business . . ."' (Butler 1992)

Butler's report gives little sign that the mysterious forces of Schulz's imagination have possessed the cast. Instead, their director is clearly selecting the dialogue that they use.

How might we interpret McBurney's sustained self-effacement? The director himself attributes his discomfort with the authority traditionally associated with the 'authorship' of the directorial role to his individual disposition. Speaking in 2004 during rehearsals for *Measure for Measure* at the National Theatre, he was keen to highlight his ambivalence about the position of director, and his primary identification with the performer: 'I think of myself as an actor first who happens to have fallen into the profession of directing. And because I am constitutionally disobedient, I am much happier when I am railing against the centre of power rather than being the centre of power that is being railed against' (Crichton-Miller 2004). But McBurney's desire to distance himself from the authority of the traditional director, and to highlight the input of the performer, can be placed in a broader context: it is quite understandable given Complicite's growth from an ensemble, and its continuing dependence upon devised work. Moreover, Deidre Heddon and Jane Milling's survey of the rhetoric that surrounds devising indicates the heavy ideological baggage that the practice carries with it. They report that devising is variously thought of as:

a practical expression of political and ideological commitment; a means of taking control of work and operating autonomously; a de-commodification of art; [. . .] a distrust of words; the embodiment of the death of the author; a means to reflect contemporary social reality; a means to incite social change; an escape from theatrical conventions; a challenge for theatre makers; a challenge for spectators; an expressive, creative language; innovative; risky, inventive; spontaneous; experimental; non-literary. (Heddon and Milling 2006: 4–5)

McBurney's discussion of his reasons for accepting an OBE in January 2005 reflects his awareness of these associations. Expressing ambivalence about the honour – the acme of establishment approval and recognition – he sought to shift the focus away from his individual achievements towards those of the company, maintaining that the award 'honours an act of resistance that grew out of our rediscovery of the revolutionary ideas of previous decades, whereby you create collectively by devising a piece from scratch in rehearsal' (Sierz 2005). This tendency to down-play his own role, and his insistence upon the shared ownership of the work, can be interpreted as a response to the ideological baggage that devising has become loaded with: just as his efforts to assert the company's deference to the authority of the script can be read as an astute negotiation of ingrained critical prejudice.

McBurney is indubitably adept at crafting his public image as a director and presenting a convincing narrative of the company's history in the rounds of promotion and marketing which he is obliged to participate in. The lack of interrogation these accounts receive in the media, however, does little to further our understanding of Complicite's work. Moreover, our failure to question them militates against a genuine appreciation of Complicite's achievements, and elides the complexity of the relationship between text and movement. Clearly, this is not McBurney's responsibility. His statements can be interpreted as an attempt to negotiate both the journalistic tendency to place the script and the body in opposition to each other, and what Worthen describes as a 'related romance'; the tendency amongst performance practitioners to oppose ' "performance" (transgressive, multiform, revisionary) to the (dominant, repressive, conventional, and canonical) domain of the "text" and its minions' (1997: 5).

As Worthen demonstrates, a more nuanced response, which relinquishes the binarism of these approaches, could well commence with an investigation into exactly what we mean by a text (1997: 6); a move which was made in academic circles by theatre semioticians in the 1980s. Indeed, a model of such a response can also be found buried amongst the many interviews and quotations from McBurney which emphasize Complicite's deference to the imagination of the author or the language of the script. Speaking in an interview in 2003, he initially stated that the company 'always begin with a text': but then went on: 'that text can take many forms. [...] it can equally well be a visual text, a text of action, a musical one, as well as the more conventional one involving plot and characters. [...] Action is also a text. As is the space, the light, music, the sound of footsteps, silence and immobility' (Irvin 2003: 80).[21] A wider journalistic engagement with this expanded definition of the dramatic text would challenge the critical investment in tropes of authorship and enable a mature evaluation of the relationship between authority, authorship and interpretation. But given the anti-theatrical prejudice which is still apparent in the judgements of so many of our theatre reviewers, it seems unrealistic to hope that any of these issues will receive considered or sustained analysis in the press in the near future. It seems that a serious public dialogue over Complicite's work, and physical theatre more generally, will have to wait upon a new generation of critics who are better able to respond to the expressiveness of action and image.

In the meantime, analysis of the attitudes that pervade the media's discussion of the work of companies such as Complicite may provide students and scholars with opportunities to examine some of the more substantive issues that its practice presents us with. For example, interrogation of the assumptions which continue to ground assertions about the ultimate authority of the playwright or author would enable a fresh discussion of the definition of a text, whilst examining physical theatre's relationship to the written document would undoubtedly unsettle belief in the 'anti-textual' bias of contemporary performance, as well as allowing us to reconsider the role of the script in relationship to performance.[22] Returning to the question of the definition of the text would also give us the chance to assess the way in which the body itself functions as a sign in performance, and the possibility that gesture and quotidian movement are always already scripted through social convention.[23] Moreover, measuring the claims made by critics and champions of physical theatre against practices in training, rehearsal and performance might allow us to decide whether the ideologies that have come to be associated with physical theatre have made a significant impact upon the operation of traditional creative hierarchies. We might also wish to consider whether the principles which have come to be associated with devising, collaboration and improvisation – identified by Heddon and Milling – have contributed to the development of a transparent method of accounting for the creative contributions of writers, performers and directors. Finally, close examination of audience responses to physical theatre might make it possible to ascertain whether the form has the political agency some commentators claim.[24] One thing is certain, however: continued failure to get to grips with these questions leaves us with an impoverished understanding of contemporary physical theatre in Britain.

Notes

1   An incomplete and inevitably subjective selection of companies that have
    adopted the 'physical theatre' label – or been given it – would include
    Moving Being (1968), the London Theatre Group (1968), Freehold
    (1969), Triple Action (1969), London Mime Theatre (1971), RAT Theatre
    (1972), Shared Experience (1975), the Moving Picture Mime Show (1977),
    Kneehigh Theatre (1980), Trestle Theatre Company (1981), Theatre Babel
    (1982), Théâtre de Complicité (1983), Mime Theatre Project (1984),
    Black Mime Theatre (1984), DV8 Physical Theatre (1986), Volcano (1987),
    Trading Faces (1987), Right Size Theatre Company (1988), the David
    Glass Ensemble (1989), Rejects Revenge Theatre Company (1990), V-Tol
    Dance Company (1991), Frantic Assembly (1992), Told by An Idiot (1992),
    Ridiculusmus (1992), Brouhaha (1993), Bouge de la (1993), HoiPolloi
    (1994), Kabosh Theatre Company (1994), Clod Ensemble (1995), Yellow
    Earth Theatre (1996), Peepolykus (1996), Improbable (1996), Theatre O
    (1997), Cartoon de Salvo (1997), Company F.Z (1998), Shams (2001),
    Gecko (2002), People Can Run Theatre Company (2003), and Tangled
    Feet (2003).
2   An alternative approach is proffered by Lark's attempts to identify com-
    mon generic elements through close semiotic analysis of a range of pro-
    ductions. She concludes that physical theatre presents us with a synthesis
    of expressionism and postmodernism, which uses a range of styles –
    from extreme abstraction to naturalistic quotation – in order to signal
    switches between the representation of internalized experience and ex-
    ternal realities (1999: 236).
3   Challenges have included the argument that the pursuit of a physically
    'neutral' state through actor training is the result of a naïve primitivism
    that leads to the reinscription of existing power structures (Knowles
    2004: 35; Murray 2003: 77). There is also considerable heat in the debate
    over whether physical theatre can still be considered innovative or 'altern-
    ative'. Some assert that it continues to occupy a marginal position in
    Britain (see Dick McCaw in Callery 2001: vii; Chamberlain and Yarrow
    2002: 4; Murray 2003: 35). Others allege that it has been thoroughly
    assimilated and absorbed into the mainstream, having long since lost the
    energy of radical experimentation (Heathfield 2005).
4   There are now several schools dedicated to teaching physical theatre in
    Britain, including the London-based Ecole de Mime Corporel Dramatique,
    the School of Physical Theatre and the London International School of
    Performing Arts (LISPA), as well as Circomedia (Centre for Contem-
    porary Circus and Physical Performance) in Bristol and Liverpool's Hope
    Street International Arts Training and Development. This may explain
    the growing consensus that contemporary physical theatre has a dis-
    tinctive, and easily identified style. Indeed, Heddon and Milling describe

it as 'one of the most recognisable forms of contemporary devised work' (2006: 157).

5 Body art pieces from the 1960s and 1970s by Chris Burden, Vito Acconci and Marina Abramovic, and performances by Stelarc, Orlan and Franko B in the 1990s and beyond, have presented sustained engagement with corporeal experience, but no one could mistake them for physical theatre. Comparison of the two forms may be helpful in establishing physical theatre's specificity. For instance: body art is usually solo, whilst physical theatre is most often produced by a group; it frequently has a gory literalism, in comparison to physical theatre's investment in the creation of a shared imaginary world; its dependence upon reactions of shock, disgust and embarrassment is in sharp contrast to physical theatre's preference for the popular and the playful; and body art's sometimes clinical and rather detached exploration of the limits of artistic experimentation highlights physical theatre's preoccupation with emotional experience.

6 Versions of Lecoq's training are still developing in the teaching which continues at his school in Paris and in the pedagogic practice of ex-colleagues such as Philippe Gaulier, Monika Pagneux and Thomas Prattki, who now work elsewhere (Chamberlain and Yarrow 2002; Murray 2003). Lecoq's work should also be placed in the context of a broader historical move to popularize and modernize the French mime tradition, but unpicking the complex network of contact and collaboration amongst the practitioners who had a share in this development is beyond the limitations of this chapter. Suffice it to say that Jean Copeau, Charles Dullin, Jean-Louis Barrault, Étienne Decroux, Claude Chagrin and Jérôme Deschamps have all been cited as significant sources of influence, and Michel Saint-Denis's foundation of the London Theatre Studio in 1936 and his later collaboration with the Royal Shakespeare Company (RSC) in the 1960s deserve particular mention (Murray 2003: 168).

7 Sanchez-Colberg attests to the influence of Artaud's suggestive, aphoristic writings, and others have commented upon the exposure his ideas received as a result of the production of Peter Weiss's Marat/Sade (1964), which was directed by Peter Brook in collaboration with Charles Marowitz as part of the RSC's Artaudian 'Theatre of Cruelty' season (Sanchez-Colberg 1996: 42; Berkoff 1992: 9; Harvie 2005: 122). A thorough analysis of Artaud's influence upon British theatre has yet to appear, however. Similarly, existing publications on Grotowski's work (such as Grotowski 1975; Wolford 1996; Richards 1995) leave the question of his influence on British theatre unaddressed. Happily, this situation should be remedied by a substantial research project into Grotowski's influence on British theatre-making (being led by Paul Allain at the University of Kent) which will explore his initial work with Peter Brook at the RSC and his contribution to the development of actor training in physical theatre in the UK. This project will conclude in October 2009.

8   The Little Theatre movement was led by Terence Gray at the Cambridge Festival Theatre, and included the work of Peter Godfrey at the Gate Theatre Salon and J. B. Fagan at the Oxford Playhouse. Lark cites Gray's 1926 publication *Dance Drama: Experiments in the Art of the Theatre* as an example of the British engagement with the possibilities of physical theatre. Sadly, as Lark acknowledges, Edward Gordon Craig's visions were largely unrealized, and the Little Theatre movement foundered in the 1930s (Lark 1999: 20).

9   Lark calls for fuller analysis of the impact of American dance companies and choreographers such as Judson Church and Mary Fulkerson; the work and theories of Rudolph Laban; the traditions of German *Ausdruckstanz*; Belgian Wim Vanderkeybus's 'Eurocrash' style; and Pina Bausch's *tanztheatre* (Lark 1999: 14).

10 We should also avoid assuming that playwrights had nothing to teach physical theatre practitioners, as Eugene Ionesco and Samuel Beckett have both been cited as sources of inspiration; and it seems that even the Stanislavskian acting training system – which is usually characterized as the antithesis of physical theatre techniques – requires reassessment, given the influence of Emile Jacques-Dalcroze's eurhythmic techniques on Stanislavski's Method of Physical Action (Callery 2001: 3; Lark 1999: 16).

11 Practitioners such as Steven Berkoff have acknowledged the significance of their exposure to the work of North American companies such as the Open Theatre, the Living Theatre and La Mama, who travelled to London in the 1960s and 1970s (Berkoff 1992: 9–10). Attraction to the types of performance enabled by eastern systems of movement training has a longer history amongst European practitioners, which stretches back to W. B. Yeats's interest in Noh Theatre, Artaud's fascination with Balinese theatre, and Brecht's writing on Chinese performance (Brecht 1964: 91–9). Charges of cultural exploitation and Orientalism have been levelled at these figures – and at later celebrants of intercultural performance such as Peter Brook – but it has now become common practice for western performers to supplement their skills by training in a wide range of eastern disciplines (McCullough 1996: 42–4). A complete history of physical theatre in Britain would, no doubt, add other examples to the above list and also demonstrate links back into the nineteenth century and beyond.

12 As Dick McGraw's introduction to Callery's book notes, 'Someone once said that talking about music is like dancing architecture. I wonder what they would say about a book describing the process of physical theatre. It is incredibly hard to talk about a creative process whose medium of exchange is primarily the body [. . .] Although language is used through the teaching and creative process it plays a secondary role, a supporting role' (Callery 2001: vii).

13 Harvie draws our attention to the wide range of international performance which was presented throughout the UK in festivals, dedicated
seasons, and venues which have policies of international programming,
such as Peter Daubeny's World Theatre Seasons at London's Aldwych
Theatre (1964–73), the Edinburgh International Festival (1947–), the
London International Mime Festival (1977–), LIFT (the London International Festival of Theatre, 1981–), BITE (the Barbican International Theatre
Event, 1998–), and venues including Glasgow's Citizens and London's
Gate.

14 The company also developed relationships with other major British
venues during the 1990s, delivering *Foe* (1996) and *The Chairs* (1997) as
co-productions with the West Yorkshire Playhouse and the Royal Court
Theatre respectively.

15 For example, *The Noise of Time* (2000) was co-commissioned by several
institutions, including New York's Lincoln Center for the Performing
Arts, the Massachusetts International Arts Festival and the Berlin Festival;
whilst *The Elephant Vanishes* (2003) was a co-production with Tokyo's
Setagaya Public Theatre and the Barbican, London.

16 Examples of transfers to the West End and Broadway include the 1995
revival tour of *The Three Lives of Lucie Cabrol* (1994) commencing at
London's Shaftesbury Theatre; a final tour for *Street of Crocodiles* (1992)
including dates at London's Queen's Theatre in 1999; and a 12-week
season at the Golden Theatre in New York for *The Chairs* (1997) in 1998.

17 These have included a film adaptation of *Anything For a Quiet Life* (1987)
commissioned by Channel 4 and broadcast in 1989; a radio production
of *Mnemonic* for BBC Radio 3; and a multidisciplinary installation, *The
Vertical Line*, performed in the disused Aldwych tube station in London
(1999).

18 This introductory page has been updated recently, and now omits the
phrase 'A collaboration between individuals to establish an ensemble
with a common physical and imaginative language'. It will be interesting
to see if this signals a shift in company policy.

19 Gardner's unreflective reiteration of the company's claims fails to draw
out the connection between this rejection of fixed method and McBurney's
exposure to Lecoq's 'via negativa' approach. It is also important to point
out that Complicite's work is, like most physical theatre, tightly discip-
lined in the moment of performance. Their productions may be reworked
during a run, and between tours, but the moment of improvisation
and play is in the process, not in product. Indeed, much of their work
depends upon the performers' strict adherence to a movement score that
has a very specific place within a multilayered aural and visual environment, as Liam Steel's discussion of his experience as a performer in *The
Noise of Time* indicates. A simplistic reading of this might associate the
need for this precision with Complicite's increasing use of technology,

but this element was there from the start: several of the gags in *A Minute Too Late* depend upon the exact timing of sound cues.

20   McBurney explains that his task as a director during the development of a piece is to ensure that the actors are fully aware of its form and themes, but describes this engagement as being primarily physical, rather than intellectual: 'I want them to hold the piece in their hands; [. . .] that understanding is not an intellectual process, it is a physical one, they have to feel it' (Giannachi and Luckhurst 1999: 74). He discusses the source of the company's creativity in phenomenological terms: 'Words emanate from a physical act in the body, and for me the body is where you begin in the rehearsal room' (70). McBurney also makes it clear that he is not seeking an exclusively intellectual response from Complicite's audiences. He explains that the company aims to provide a space 'for people to dream and feel, not merely to assimilate this piece of language or that piece of language. Of course, the language is there, but the language is there to release something in the minds of the audience, not to constrain' (Hemmings 2005: 6).

21   In an earlier interview, McBurney discussed the 'language' of props, observing: 'For me the objects I use are like words on a page; the rules of their movement are like grammar and syntax' (Giannachi and Luckhurst 1999: 77). McBurney's analytical emphasis upon the multiple languages of movement, space, sound and design is similar to that made by theatre semioticians in the 1980s. It seems, however, that this movement has had little impact upon the popular understanding of the definition of a dramatic text, despite controversies over its benefits and limitations (see Melrose 1994; Knowles 2004: 16).

22   It is difficult to imagine another company producing a Complicite show on the basis of the published scripts for *Mnemonic* or *Street of Crocodiles*, for example. So, are these publications oriented towards the past or the future? Are they maps for future performances, or a partial record of an unrepeatable event?

23   Judith Butler's work on the performativity of gender, developed in *Gender Trouble* (1990) and *Bodies that Matter* (1993), encourages us to consider the role of mundane gesture and movement in the construction of identity, as she proposes that those cultural practices which we have come to see as natural expressions of masculinity or femininity are actually internalized codes of behaviour, acquired through a long process of socialization, and secured through the quotidian repetition of social signifiers such as dress, gait and gesture. Within this theoretical model, the most unconscious physical practices, habits and rituals – the way we walk, sit or stand – appear as citations of cultural norms, rather than the creative property of the individual. There are many examples of characters attempting to reproduce conventional and acquired movement in Complicite's work. The scene in *A Minute Too Late* in which McBurney's character struggles to imitate the assured movements of his fellow

worshippers in church makes much of our efforts to follow the 'script' of quotidian gesture.

24 There is no consensus about the political impact of Complicite's work; some scholars have asserted that it has remarkable agency, others that it is apolitical (see Knowles 2004: 49–53; Luckhurst and Holdsworth, p.c., 17 March 2006). Reinelt raises some interesting questions in this regard (2001: 365–87).

Primary reading

Complicite (2003). *Plays 1*. London: Methuen.
For a complete list of Complicite's productions, see the company's website: www.complicite.org/productions/index.html.

Further reading

Armistead, Claire (1992). 'The Slick Art of Sense and Serendipity', *Guardian*, 13 August, 26.
Artaud, Antonin (1958). *The Theatre and Its Double*, trans. Mary Caroline Richards. New York: Grove Press. (Original work published 1938.)
Barthes, Roland (1977). 'The Death of the Author' in *Image-Music-Text*, trans. Stephen Heath. London: Fontana, 142–8. (Original work published 1968.)
Berkoff, Steven (1992). *The Theatre of Stephen Berkoff*. London: Methuen.
Berkoff, Steven (1999). 'Obituary of Jacques Lecoq', *Total Theatre* 11:1, 5.
Billington, Michael (1992). 'Winter's Tale; Lyric Hammersmith', *Guardian*, 4 April, 24.
Brecht, Bertolt (1964). 'Alienation Effects in Chinese Acting' in *Brecht on Theatre*, trans. and ed. John Willett. London: Methuen, 91–9. (Original work published in English in 1936.)
Butler, Judith (1990). *Gender Trouble: Feminism and the Subversion of Identity*. London and New York: Routledge.
Butler, Judith (1993). *Bodies that Matter: On the Discursive Limits of 'Sex'*. London and New York: Routledge.
Butler, Robert (1992). 'Just Don't Bump Into the Actors', *Independent on Sunday*, 2 August, 22.
Callery, Dymphna (2001). *Through the Body: A Practical Guide to Physical Theatre*. London and New York: Routledge.
Carlson, Marvin (1985). 'Illustration, Translation, Fulfillment, or Supplement?', *Theatre Journal* 37:1, 5–11.
Cavenish, Dominic (2003). 'They're the Key to What Is Possible', *Daily Telegraph*, 11 January, 8.
Chamberlain, Franc, and Yarrow, Ralph, eds. (2002). *Jacques Lecoq and the British Theatre*. London and New York: Routledge.

Complicite (2006). www.complicite.org/about, accessed 2 April 2006; updated version accessed 26 May 2006.

Crichton-Miller, Emma (2004). 'The Measure of a Man', *The Times*, 24 May, 14.

Culture Show (2004). BBC2, 25 November.

Esslin, Martin (1999). 'Mask over Matter', *Guardian*, 23 January, 17.

Felner, Mira (1985). *Apostles of Silence: The Modern French Mimes*. Cranberry and London: Associated University Presses.

Foucault, Michel (1977). 'What is an Author?' in *Michel Foucault: Language, Counter-Memory, Practice: Selected Essays and Interviews*, trans. Donald F. Bouchard and Sherry Simon. Ithaca, NY: Cornell University Press, 113–38.

Gardner, Lyn (2002). www.complicite.org/about/review.html?id=55, accessed 25 May 2006.

Giannachi, Gabriella, and Luckhurst, Mary, eds. (1999). *On Directing: Interviews with Directors*. London: Faber and Faber.

Gore-Langton, Robert (1992). 'The Winter's Tale', *Time Out*, 8 April, 115.

Gray, Terence (1926). *Dance Drama: Experiments in the Art of the Theatre*. Cambridge: W. Heffer and Sons.

Grotowski, Jerzy (1975). *Towards a Poor Theatre*. London: Methuen.

Harvie, Jen (2002). 'DV8's *Can We Afford This*: The Cost of Devising on Site for Global Markets', *Theatre Research International* 27:1, 68–77.

Harvie, Jen (2005). *Staging the UK*. Manchester: Manchester University Press.

Heathfield, Adrian (2005). 'Time Wounds', unpublished paper, Performance Studies International Conference, Brown University, 1 April.

Heddon, Deirdre, and Milling, Jane (2006). *Devising Performance: A Critical History*. Basingstoke: Palgrave Macmillan.

Hemmings, Sarah (2005). 'Then and Now' in *On Tour: UK Drama and Dance 2005*. London: British Council, 4–7.

Hewison, Robert (1992). 'Shrewaskew', *Sunday Times*, 5 April, 6.

Hornby, Richard (2002). 'Forgetting the Text: Derrida and the "Liberation" of the Actor', *New Theatre Quarterly* 72, 355–8.

Innes, Christopher (2002). *Modern British Drama: The Twentieth Century*. Cambridge: Cambridge University Press.

Irvin, Polly (2003). *Directing for the Stage*. Mies: RotoVision.

Knapper, Stephen (2004). 'Complicite's Comintern: Internationalism and *The Noise of Time*', *Contemporary Theatre Review* 14:1, 61–73.

Knowles, Ric (2004). *Reading the Material Theatre*. Cambridge: Cambridge University Press.

Lark, Christine (1999). 'The Body Finds a Voice'. Unpublished PhD thesis, University of Surrey.

Late Show (1992). BBC2, 'Théâtre de Complicité, Profiled in Rehearsal for *The Street of Crocodiles*', 21 September.

Lecoq, Jacques (2000). *The Moving Body*, trans. David Bradby. London: Methuen.

198

McCullough, Christopher (1996). *Theatre and Europe: 1957–95*. Exeter: Intellect.

Melrose, Susan (1994). *A Semiotics of the Dramatic Text*. London: Macmillan.

Morris, T. (1994). 'Rebels with Applause', *Sunday Times*, 20 February, 9.

Murray, Simon (2003). *Jacques Lecoq*. London and New York: Routledge.

Nathan, David (1992). 'New Robes for Classic Message', *Jewish Chronicle*, 10 April, 26.

Neill, Heather (2004). 'Simon McBurney, Magic Man', *Independent on Sunday*, 23 May, 14.

Nightingale, Benedict (1992). 'Snap, Crackle but All Too Pop', *The Times*, 4 April, 5.

O'Mahony, John (2005). 'Simon McBurney: Anarchy in the UK', *Guardian*, 1 January, 16.

Reinelt, Janelle (2001). 'Performing Europe', *Theatre Journal* 53:3, 365–87.

Richards, Thomas (1995). *At Work with Grotowski on Physical Actions*. London and New York: Routledge.

Sanchez-Colberg, Ana (1996). 'Altered States and Subliminal Spaces: Charting the Road Towards a Physical Theatre', *Performance Research* 1:2, 40–56.

Sierz, Aleks (2005). 'The Audience Dies Laughing', *Independent*, 26 January, 18.

Spencer, Charles (1992). 'Shakespeare with Fizz', *Daily Telegraph*, 10 April, 19.

Taylor, Paul (1992). 'Empty Gestures', *Independent*, 4 April, 32.

Valdez, Carolina (1999). 'Obituary of Jacques Lecoq', *Total Theatre* 11:1, 8.

Wardle, Irving (1992). 'Sex War Turns to Class Vengeance', *Independent on Sunday*, 5 April, 20.

Wolford, Lisa (1996). *The Grotowski Sourcebook*. London and New York: Routledge.

Worthen, W. B. (1997). *Shakespeare and the Authority of Performance*. Cambridge: Cambridge University Press.

Chapter 10

Verbatim Theatre, Media Relations and Ethics

Mary Luckhurst

An English Etymology

Verbatim theatre has proliferated in Europe and North America since the 1990s, and post-9/11 has become increasingly visible on both mainstream and fringe stages. In the last 10 years it has come to occupy an important political territory in Britain (especially in England) where contentious international and national issues are aired and interrogated. Particularly high-profile shows have included Richard Norton-Taylor's *Nuremberg* (1997), *The Colour of Justice* (1999), *Justifying War* (2003), *Bloody Sunday* (2005) and *Called to Account* (2007), Victoria Brittain and Gillian Slovo's *Guantanamo* (2004), David Hare's *The Permanent Way* (2003) and *Stuff Happens* (2004), Robin Soans's *Talking to Terrorists* (2005), Tanika Gupta's *Gladiator Games* (2005), Gregory Burke's *Black Watch* (2006) and Peter Morgan's *Frost/Nixon* (2006). The reasons for the apparent 'explosion' (Ben-Zvi 2006: 45) of verbatim theatre in the west are complex and seem to be bound up with widespread suspicion of governments and their 'spin' merchants, a distrust of the media and a desire to uncover stories which may be being suppressed, and a western fetishization of representations of 'the real', perhaps most manifest in the obsession with so-called 'reality' television. This chapter will examine the origins of verbatim theatre, track different working methods, consider its relation to the media industries, and reflect on some of the ethical issues implicated in its practice.

The use of the term 'verbatim theatre' is specific to the UK, suggesting that particular political and cultural factors are in operation which make it important to distinguish the working method of this form of documentary theatre from others.[1] As the Latin root of 'verbatim' suggests, the moment of utterance is privileged, and 'verbatim theatre', in its purest sense, is understood as a theatre whose practitioners, if called to account, could provide interviewed sources for its dialogue, in the manner that a journalist must, according to the code of ethics, have sources for a story. The term originated in England and was first coined in an article by Derek Paget in 1987 called '"Verbatim Theatre": Oral History and Documentary Techniques', and it makes for intriguing study. While acknowledging that the German documentary tradition has been a major influence, Paget focuses on tracing a domestic lineage of documentary theatre, citing the British documentary film movement of the 1930s and 1940s, living newspaper theatre, the radio ballads of the 1950s, Joan Littlewood's Theatre Workshop in the 1950s and 1960s, Chris Honer's work in Chester, and crucially, Peter Cheeseman's documentaries at the Victoria Theatre, Stoke-on-Trent, from 1962 to 1984 and then at the New Victoria Theatre, Newcastle-under-Lyme, from 1984 to 1998 (Paget 1987: 317–36).[2] Paget's article is instructive not just because it contains the first definition of verbatim theatre and outlines working practices, but also because it is revealingly framed by the editors of *New Theatre Quarterly*, who position it as a political weapon which can be wielded against the very broadcast media which helped inspire it:

> Quite simply, the form owes its present health and exciting potential to the flexibility and unobtrusiveness of the portable cassette recorder – ironically, a technological weapon against which are ranged other mass technological media such as broadcasting and the press, which tend to marginalise the concerns and emphases of popular oral history. (Paget 1987: 317)

For the editors of *New Theatre Quarterly* verbatim theatre can make important socio-political interventions by projecting voices and opinions which otherwise go unheard into a public arena. This stress on empowering those normally disempowered is a strong undercurrent in the original definition, and continues to be an important factor in many verbatim plays. Its emergence through and reliance on certain forms of technology (voice recording) also makes it distinctive, and, like his editors, Paget links verbatim theatre to the oral history movement, arguing that 'both are operating in and seeking to extend the space left by the "official" recording and reporting media' (Paget

1987: 326). Indeed the playwright Rony Robinson is convinced that Cheeseman's documentaries were the first to make use of oral history (319). It is Robinson who formulates the definition of verbatim theatre offered in Paget's essay:

> a form of theatre firmly predicated upon the taping and subsequent transcription of interviews with 'ordinary' people, done in the context of research into a particular region, subject area, issue, event, or combination of these things. This primary source is then transformed into a text which is acted, usually by the performers who collected the material in the first place.
>
> As often as not, such plays are then *fed back* into the communities (which have, in a real sense, created them), via performance in those communities. In verbatim theatre, the firmest of commitments is thus made by the company to *the use of vernacular speech*, recorded as the primary source material of their play. (317)

Robinson's understanding of the working method is also Cheeseman's: the company conduct and record interviews with local constituencies on a given subject; the company discuss the transcripts and a rehearsal process is begun; interview transcripts are selected by the director and the writer working closely with company actors; the writer edits and collages scenes as part of the rehearsal process; the company actors perform the material back to the community. What is also stressed in Paget's article is the importance of a straightforward aesthetic – actors on stage with economical use of set and props. Locality and community are clearly privileged in this model, and the idea of a community 'owning' its past and present to reaffirm certain identities is very significant. These verbatim plays told local stories, often with biting agendas that attempted to make interventions into local politics – Cheeseman's *The Fight for Shelton Bar* (1974), about a campaign to stop the closure of a steel plant, a case in point. While Cheeseman's plays were composed and performed for the local community, regional politics of course spun out into matters of state policy. A fundamental drive behind such projects was a concern to tell working-class histories and stories, and to bring to the stage narratives that might not otherwise be deemed suitable for dramatic representation. That desire to populate plays with voices and accents previously marginalised or unheard was, of course, part of a wider campaign in 1960s and 1970s theatre, as was the desire for actors to wrest more control from writer and director in the rehearsal room. But these early verbatim practitioners were particularly concerned that local idiom, tics of speech and linguistic markers should not be erased or lost, and were understood at the time to have developed what Robinson refers to as a 'puritanism . . . the meticulous way in which the material had to be collected, had to be transcribed – and certainly at that stage they were using the methodology of linguistics to actually annotate the stuff, so that you can see how you speak it' (Paget 1987: 319). The transcripts were central in the rehearsals.

The privileging of the spoken word, including the qualities of a speech pattern, make this form of documentary theatre distinctive. However, the underlying conviction expressed by these practitioners that verbatim theatre can lay claim to a greater historical veracity is troubling, and Robinson's leap of logic that the plays were 'in a real sense' created by the communities represented is also vexing.[3] Verbatim theatre, like other documentary forms, is always stretched on the rack between a pursuit of 'facts' – a loaded word in its own right – and an engagement with artistic representation. But the purpose of these plays was political, their local success is not in question, and their intention was not unworthy. It is important to understand the seed of their origin, and like his editors, Paget sees verbatim theatre as a means of challenging totalizing narratives purveyed by the media:

> It is not to devalue the plays . . . to compare them to human interest stories in journalism: in celebrating locality, and in seeking out discourse not normally privileged by either the journalistic or the entertainment media, these plays are what might recognisably be called the Stoke tradition of documentary. Particularly in a theatre profession in which success tends only to be recognised when validated by and from London, it is vital that the work of people like Peter Cheeseman and Chris Honer be not just appreciated, but assessed accurately in terms of what they have reclaimed from the margins of local and national experience. (322)

The Tribunal Plays

The term 'verbatim theatre', then, in its original context alluded to a particular kind of working method which was new in the 1960s. From the 1990s, however, the term is applied by some informed practitioners, and more loosely and confusingly by others, to much documentary theatre, from Piscator's model in the 1960s, to plays like

My Name is Rachel Corrie (2005), based on diaries, notebooks and emails, as well as to plays which incorporate both testimony and invented material, such as Hare's *Stuff Happens* and Gupta's *Gladiator Games*. Stephen Bottoms has argued that the distinctions between the usage of 'verbatim theatre' and 'documentary theatre' matter 'because, where the latter might be said to imply the foregrounding of documents, of texts, the term "verbatim theatre" tends to fetishize the notion that we are getting things "word for word," straight from the mouth of those "involved"' (Bottoms 2006: 59).

This stress on authenticity was certainly important in Richard Norton-Taylor's so-called tribunal plays, all produced through the artistic director Nicolas Kent at the Tricycle Theatre in London, which dramatized the edited transcripts of legal inquiries, and testify to the fact that the work of Rolf Hochhuth, Heinar Kipphardt and Peter Weiss has had profound repercussions in Britain.[4] Norton-Taylor's first tribunal play was co-written with John McGrath, founder of the 7:84 Theatre Company, a prominent playwright and theorizer of popular political theatre, and a man in tune with projects such as Cheeseman's, who understood the importance of community politics and oral cultures to a profound degree (DiCenzo 1996, 2006). Their play *Half the Picture* (1994), which dramatized edited transcripts of the Scott Inquiry, otherwise known as 'the arms-to-Iraq' inquiry, attracted widespread attention, was later filmed for BBC2, and was the first play ever to be performed at the House of Commons. The Scott Inquiry exposed the fact that government officials at all levels were aware that British companies were illegally exporting arms to Iraq, allowing Saddam Hussein to build up a war machine, and that they had at first turned a blind eye and then later prosecuted them. It also exposed the fact that ministers were prepared to utter deliberate inaccuracies or, to put it politely, make misleading statements to save their own skins. Time and time again the leader of the inquiry, Sir Richard Scott, expressed his frustration with ministers who he suspected were evading a frank answer to his questions. Indeed, mendacity was upheld as a justifiable course of action and even argued to be a virtue. The Department of Trade and Industry official Eric Beston opined that 'the way in which questions are answered in Parliament tends to be something of an art form rather than a means of communication' (Norton-Taylor et al. 1996: 64). Beston can have had no idea of the prophetic irony of his remark, and while this is a chilling statement to make in a courtroom, the idea that politicians and other figures in the media spotlight borrow from theatrical discourses and performance modes is not new.[5] But it was the claim by two senior Foreign and Commonwealth Office representatives, Sir Robin Butler and David Gore-Booth, which resonated in the media – that failure to reveal all the information could be defended on the grounds that 'half a picture' could be accurate. Sir Geoffrey Howe conceded that the truth had been suppressed because 'Government knows best' (Norton-Taylor et al. 1996: 68). Scott's statement that 'Without the provision of full information it is not possible for Parliament, or for that matter the public, to hold the executive fully to account' (68) ferociously hit the mark and encapsulated the reason why McGrath and Norton-Taylor engaged on their project. The writers dramatized witness statements by Margaret Thatcher, John Major and Alan Clarke, and McGrath 'inserted monologues recording the marginalized voices of those affected by the government's duplicitous actions' (Holdsworth in McGrath 2005: 61–2). The affair threatened to destabilize Major's Conservative government for good, but it survived the play, the television screening, the final Scott Report, and a significant vote in the House of Commons. The government had got away with it. But the power of this form of theatre had been demonstrated as never before in England.

Given the strength of feeling against the press voiced by the 1960s and 1970s generation of verbatim theatre practitioners, it is both ironic and highly significant that Norton-Taylor has worked as a political journalist for the *Guardian* since 1975. He has always sought outlets for his investigative journalism other than the broadsheet, and has written books exploring the abuse of power in public agencies.[6] It is also telling that in 1986 he won the Freedom of Information Campaign Award for journalism and is a member of the Civil Liberties Trust. The stimulus for his journalism is the same as the stimulus for his plays – a desire to expose cover-ups, injustice and corruption in public institutions accompanied with a demand for public accountability. Five other sole-authored plays have followed *Half the Picture*: *Nuremberg* (1996), composed of edited transcripts from the War Crimes Trial, conducted 1945–6; *The Colour of Justice* (1999), compiled from transcripts from the Stephen Lawrence Inquiry (the play moved to the West End, toured nationally, was performed at the National Theatre, and made into a television drama); *Justifying War: Scenes from the Hutton Inquiry* (2003), which interrogated the death of David Kelly; *Bloody Sunday: Scenes from the Saville Inquiry* (2005), which investigated the shooting of 13 civil rights marchers in Londonderry, Northern Ireland, on Sunday 30 March 1972; and *Called to Account* (2007), about Tony Blair and the Iraq question.

The crossover of methodology from his journalistic life into his theatrical career is very clear, and interestingly, Norton-Taylor is unsure about the status of his authorship regarding the tribunal plays: 'I'm not sure whether I'm a playwright or a journalist. David Hare tells me I'm a playwright.'[7] In the published playscripts he is described as an editor. Editing seems an insufficient term to describe the stringent selection and dramatic shaping that he has to do: for the Nuremberg War Crimes Trials over 50 million pages of documents were produced; the Lawrence Inquiry lasted for 69 days, the Saville Inquiry took 2,500 witness statements and heard evidence from 921 witnesses, and the Hutton Inquiry sat for 25 days. Norton-Taylor is candid about the difficulty of brutal choices and in his 'editor's note' to *The Colour of Justice* expounds his intentions. They are explicitly to do with the need for a theatrical dramaturgy and with a desire that more coverage of the case reaches the public realm:

> I set out to include the most telling exchanges for a theatre audience, many of which did not hit the headlines at the time but which reflect the interlocking threads which ran throughout the inquiry – police incompetence, conscious or unconscious racism and stereotyping, and the hint of corruption in the background. And I have included exchanges which reflect the personal tensions between the police and the Lawrence family – for example, Doreen's [Stephen's mother] anger when she saw Detective Chief Superintendent William Ilsley, who supervised the investigation, 'fold up' as he put it, 'screw up' as she said, a piece of paper she handed him containing the names of the suspects.
>
> Above all, I wanted to select evidence to the inquiry which presented as fair, balanced and rounded a picture as possible. It was not an easy task. But if it contributes to a greater understanding of all the issues involved, it was, I hope, worthwhile and valuable. (Norton-Taylor 1999: 6)

Norton-Taylor's journalistic credentials shine through in this last paragraph, but in ironic counterpoint to the dismaying portrait of a police officer flagrantly abusing his position of power. The murder in 1993 of the black teenager Stephen Lawrence in London, and the indifference, corruption and incompetence of police officers involved at all levels of the subsequent investigation, became touchstones for evidence of deep-seated institutional racism in the police force. Enough circumstantial evidence pointed to five white youths, known for their activity in the extreme right-wing British National Party, but police failed to pursue leads, and 'lost' or 'mislaid' files and notes, as well as all too frequently taking refuge in pretexts about poor memory. No prosecution was brought and the Lawrence family filed a civil action against the lead suspects but was unsuccessful. The Inquiry in 1999 found the police actively negligent and racist and concurred with the Lawrences' suspicions about the identity of the perpetrators, but by that time nothing could be done because the civil action had failed. *The Colour of Justice* premiered in the month before the Inquiry proceedings, the MacPherson Report, were published, at a time when the case had already sparked a national outcry. On tour, therefore, the play was performed against the media discourses of the Inquiry's shocking conclusions.

Norton-Taylor's dramatization is a brilliant act of compression and shaping, which packs a devastating polemical punch. Mrs Lawrence's testimony comes towards the end of the play and the constant obstruction that she and her husband endured in trying to force investigation into their son's death makes a harrowing impact:

> Presumably, there is no possibility of me being an intelligent, black woman with thoughts of her own who is able to ask questions for herself. We were patronised and we were fobbed off. As the meetings [with the police] went on, I got more and more angry. I thought that the purpose of the meetings was to give us progress reports, but what actually happened was that they would effectively say: stop questioning us. We are doing everything. That simply was not true, and it led me to believe then and now that they were protecting the suspects. (Norton-Taylor 1999: 118)

What is interesting about Mrs Lawrence's statement is that there is, in the legal proceedings, a freedom permitted in the stating of suspicions and opinion which is much more difficult for the press to venture without being accused of libel. Her surmise that the police, far from upholding the law, may actually be aiding and abetting criminals is quite startling, even though it comes after repeated testimony by officers which exposes them as actively hostile to the case and the family.[8] That her cross-examination should continue a line of innate hostility is horrifying:

Gompertz: Can I ask you something quite different now: your journey home from the hospital on the night in question. You went, did you not, to the Welcome Inn?
Mrs Lawrence: No.

Gompertz:	Where did you go then?
Mrs Lawrence:	Can I ask a question here? Am I on trial here or something here? I mean from the time of my son's murder I have been treated not as a victim. Now I can only tell you or put into my statements what I know of what went on that night. And for me to be questioned in this way, I do not appreciate it.
Macpherson:	Mr Gompertz, I think your discretion should be exercised in favour of not asking further questions. (121)

Equally interesting is Norton-Taylor's decision to end the testimonies not with Neil Acourt, one of the suspects, but with the words of Howard Youngerwood, the crown prosecutor, who argues that he foresaw the failure of the private prosecution and suffered extreme frustration and stress at the inadequacy of the evidence presented to him by the police (139–42). Acourt reveals himself to be little more than a pathological liar and his own words condemn him (132–9): the underlying assumption in the court and in the play is that he is unquestionably guilty of murder. Youngerwood, by contrast, presents himself as the heroic official battling in vain against a noose of police corruption about which he can do nothing. Though we might well question Youngerwood's version of events, in ending the testimony at this point Norton-Taylor seems intent on highlighting systemic failures in legal process – moments when an individual may suspect illegality but is powerless to do anything about it. (Or is he? That question actually hangs quite heavily.) Of course inquiry transcripts inherently interrogate the integrity of the speaker, but in the Stephen Lawrence case the level of systemic failure was overwhelming. A young man was brutally murdered and no serious attempts made to bring anyone to account: it is dramaturgically fitting that Norton-Taylor begins and ends his play in the same way as the court hearing – with a minute's silence for Stephen Lawrence, during which audience members paid their respects by standing.

The Tricycle Theatre itself became a place of campaign and protest, as one of the actors, Thomas Wheatley, has explained: 'The Lawrence family spent a lot of time at the Tricycle.'[9] Norton-Taylor observed that the Tricycle was frequented by 'young black people – people who don't normally come to the theatre.'[10] He is also adamant that the production of the play served a function that the press could not:

The public were not present at the Inquiry, and the vast majority of people are not going to read the Inquiry Report. Press coverage is restricted to column inches and occurs over days, weeks and even months: the intricacies of the proceedings cannot be covered by the broadcast media and their world is a sound-bite medium not suited to the unfolding of long narratives. My point is that dramatising Inquiry transcripts allows for the main details of a protracted story to be drawn together, and the crux of the political agendas to be laid forth. The compression allows the public to get to grips with the salient issues.[11]

For Norton-Taylor the tribunal play offers a different kind of public platform from the press, and a more compact way of disseminating a protracted story. The plays can also hold 'spin' narratives up to scrutiny and provide a means of combating the control of public discourse. For artistic director Nicolas Kent, a tribunal play itself can provide the public platform which he has argued the media have failed to do sufficiently.[12] Norton-Taylor infers that a dramatization of proceedings might provide a more effective focus for public engagement with the issues than coverage in the press. He can, in the way he shapes his plays, make more of a polemical intervention than he is able to do with his journalism. Others have indicated this too, arguing that The Colour of Justice 'should be on every syllabus' and that the dramatization exploded the case 'from being a black family tragedy to being a British tragedy.'[13]

There is no doubt that Norton-Taylor's plays led to the current spate of verbatim plays in Britain. Playwright David Hare is perhaps the most noted convert to the form. Having earlier declared that: 'We cannot quite remember what virtue there is in telling made-up stories rather than in telling true ones' (Hare quoted by Neil Ascherson, Observer, 9 November 2003), he reversed his position after seeing The Colour of Justice, arguing that: ' The play seemed not just a rebuke to the British theatre for its continuing drift towards less and less important subject matter. It also exposed other forms by the sheer seriousness and intensity with which it was able to bring the theatre's special scrutiny to bear' (ibid.). Hare is struck by the political resonance of Norton-Taylor's work, and no doubt by the mass television audience it attracted. But for Hare, its form, the fact that it incorporates real words spoken by real people, also lends it a particular gravitas, and demonstrates a uniquely effective interrogative mechanism, which apparently renders other forms suddenly inferior.

Hare pursued his fascination and went on to pen verbatim plays The Permanent Way (2003) and Stuff Happens (2004), but he is troubled by what he perceives as a possibility that the public may begin to look to such plays as a compensation for their distrust of print and broadcast media:

> Theatre [. . .] is not journalism. The mistake is to imagine that simply because it can incorporate real-life material, so it can be judged by similar criteria. It is certainly true that the recent much publicised flush of British drama on factual subjects is taken by many to be a response to the failures of the press. Audiences at this time of global unease want the facts, but also they want the chance to look at the facts together, and in some depth. Everyone is aware that television and newspapers have decisively disillusioned us, in a way which seems beyond repair, by their trivial and partial coverage of seismic issues of war and peace. Front-page apologies in a couple of the more august American newspapers, admitting professional gullibility, may show late stirrings of conscience, but they are hardly adequate to the laziness and stupidity of the mass American media in the last three years. The fact that journalism is too arrogant to recognise the crisis adds to the crisis. But even if it seems ungrateful to turn away both the attention and the praise which the medium of theatre has attracted by default, it is also important to point out to our new and clamorous public that theatre is not first and foremost a substitute for anything. It is itself, and what it does is unique. (Hare 2004)

This begins as a statement of the obvious, but turns into a warning that while verbatim plays might have more factual integrity than television and the press, they should not be substituted for them. This gives a view of the public as very naïve. How are we to account for the plethora of verbatim theatre in Britain? And surely, the disillusion and distrust is with domestic media forms? Hare makes an important point about looking at the facts together, that theatre offers community and communion. In the case of verbatim theatre audiences come together in an act of collective witness. Those that went to the Tricycle were likely to have been clear about their political position in relation to the material from the outset. In other words, most audience members went to hear a story the basic outlines of which they already knew but which they wanted to hear again, to have confirmed, and to hear in greater detail. And most audience members, as the commercial success of *The Colour of Justice* shows, must have been shocked anew.

Janelle Reinelt, it seems to me, is right when she argues of verbatim theatre that:

> Audiences know that documents, facts, and evidence are always mediated when they are received; they know there is no raw truth apart from interpretation, but still, they want to experience the assertion of the materiality of events, of the indisputable character of the facts – one reason why trials and hearings, given force of law, still have so much resonance . . . I see the potential for this gesture as an ethico-political revolt, as a demonstration of caring, engagement, and commitment. (Reinelt 2006: 82–3)

The Colour of Justice gave rise to the demonstration of a massive public consensus that the police force were no longer credible upholders of the law. *Bloody Sunday* exposed a long suspected and scandalous cover-up amongst government officials and the British military. And *Justifying War*, to a great extent, put the media itself in the dock – Alastair Campbell, Tony Blair's chief spin merchant, is depicted in the play. It exposed the government's and the media's obsession with finding David Kelly, who had allegedly accused Blair's advisers of 'sexing up' intelligence documents to make the case for war against Iraq. The release of Kelly's name led to his pursuit by the media, his use by the government as a fall-guy, his suicide, and ultimately to the toppling from the BBC of director general Greg Dyke, who became the political sacrificial lamb – again causing a national outcry, and very much emphasizing that the BBC's Board of Trustees is in the pocket of the government. Norton-Taylor's scrutiny, it seems, is turning more and more towards the omissions and collusions of his own profession in a time when the British government is seeking to exert an ever tighter control over the media. It might well be that he would concur with Reinelt's argument about the power of verbatim theatre, specifically the theatrical and televised versions of the Stephen Lawrence case, which 'demonstrate the potential explanatory power of performance to shape ideas, question truth claims, sway public opinion, and construct an aesthetics that sometimes functions as an epistemology' (Reinelt 2006: 72).

On Ethics

Set against Cheeseman's plays, Norton-Taylor's tribunal plays demonstrate a shift from the local to the national, and are concerned with miscarriages of justice, the implementation of law, public institutions, and issues related to human rights. They are driven by the stories of the dead, not of the living, and audiences engage in an act of witnessing which is politicized. The dead and the bereaved have also provided the dramaturgical momentum for Hare's *The Permanent Way*, about the privatization of the railways, and *Stuff Happens*, which investigates the American decision to go to war with Iraq. *Gladiator Games, My Name is Rachel Corrie*, and the Liverpool Everyman's production of *Unprotected* (2006), about Liverpool sex workers, also have narratives of the dead at their centre, and *Exonerated* (2002) the stories of those condemned to die on death row. Dennis Woolf's *Beyond Belief* (2004) centred on serial killer Harold Shipman, held responsible for at least 200 deaths. If Cheeseman was focused on the voices of ordinary people, verbatim theatre of the last decade deploys celebrity voices as much as it does ordinary ones. And if the most successful verbatim plays go on to the West End, like *Guantanamo* and *Rachel Corrie*, then others are equally well still performed in and by local communities and concentrate on the topical and often on a trauma narrative. Working practices vary but the interview is the prevalent research tool.[14] Yet the format and processes of interviews vary from subject to subject and certain plays present as very dubious in their claims for a rigorous working process. Hare's *Stuff Happens* may have enscripted into it numerous scenes indicating politicians' dependence on and use of the media as a propaganda machine, but he is remarkably unclear about the demarcation between what he may have read or seen in the media and what he has invented. His 'author's note' declares that: 'What happened happened', that events can be 'authenticated from multiple sources, both private and public' and that 'nothing in the narrative is knowingly untrue'. It is, confusingly, a 'play' not a 'documentary', though Hare states that 'scenes of direct address quote people verbatim' (Hare 2004: n.p.). Politicians such as George W. Bush, Blair and Donald Rumsfeld are named but the 'Journalist' and 'Reporter' are not; furthermore, the media figures are constructed effectively only as voices of conscience who put the politicians under pressure to justify their actions. This is a somewhat romantic construction of the media, to say the least, and as Bottoms has argued 'it becomes impossible to tell where factual reportage stops and political caricature starts: under Hare's all-seeing gaze, both acquire equal status as (dramatic) truth' (Bottoms 2006: 60). The dangers of succumbing to a form simply for fashion's sake are also apparent in Soans's *Talking to Terrorists* (2005), which is unsure of the focus of the material it is investigating. Soans offers an array of seemingly randomly selected 'terrorists' from different cultures caught up in different struggles, and appears to be engaging in making highly suspicious generalizations about them. The justification for producing the play is that no one is listening,[15] another veiled criticism of the inactivity of the press and broadcast media.

In fact, as Bella Merlin, one of the actors in *The Permanent Way*, has revealed, the company 'had no idea that the play would be verbatim theatre' even during the interview stages.

> We were sent out to interview or people came to us. There was no tape recorder, we took copious notes. We came back to the rehearsal room and would then 'be' that character. Max [Stafford-Clark, the director] said to us as actors: 'You have to surrender yourself to the material.' We would prime Max and David [Hare] on what came up in interview, they would ask questions and we would respond in character. After this we would say what we had invented. I saw this process as very close to Stanislavsky's idea of taking actual fact and turning it into what he would have called 'scenic truth'. [. . .] Ethically this was quite an issue for some. David gave everyone a draft of the script (except the politicians!) and they altered it or gave editorial consent. [. . .] As an actor I was combining Brecht and Stanislavsky – even though Max's process is very much Stanislavsky.[16]

This process replicates the methods of producing material used in the 1970s and early 1980s by Joint Stock, a company in which Stafford-Clark and Hare were key figures. But Joint Stock working practices still privileged the writer in the traditional way: they used interviewees and actors to generate a good deal of the raw material, but the writer (in discussion with the director) had free rein over material used and free rein to invent. These Joint Stock methods of sending out actors to interview members of the public or individuals in a particular community are still much in evidence, and are often deployed to train performers in techniques of observation and emulation.[17] Such practices are, however, quite different from Cheeseman's and from Norton-Taylor's, where the writer operates more in the manner of an editor, a task which needs much imagination but does not require the invention of any words. For Joint Stock the playwright was the linchpin of the team.[18]

Thus it is that performances proceeding from very different kinds of working methods are currently marketed as verbatim theatre. The label implies that no words are invented, which suggests that some marketing strategies are perhaps more focused on appealing to fashion than they are interested in certain kinds of integrity to the work (and of course to the interviewees). Merlin's analysis of the process as turning fact into scenic truth is intriguing but even more problematic than truth claims for Norton-Taylor's work: if actors write their own notes and select what they perform back to writer and director, they are from the beginning searching for a character who interests or moves them, and what constitutes 'facts' in such work? All actors 'create' their characters, of course, but with Joint Stock methods actors provide the words on which that character will be based. I am not arguing that the Joint Stock method is less powerful as drama, but I am questioning its current claim to constitute verbatim theatre. Nor did Joint Stock originally have a particular bugbear about the press. They became increasingly interested in the 'shocking and controversial' (Ritchie 1987: 19), sometimes for its own sake, which is a different matter entirely.

If there is a particular set of ethical questions attached to acting, to writing and directing verbatim plays (in its purest form verbatim theatre is performed with actors in a line before the audience), then there are many questions surrounding the extraction of information from interviewees. As Slovo and Brittain found out with *Guantanamo*, interviewees were victims of injustice but were far from inarticulate, and saw the play as an opportunity for their own political campaigning.[19] A novelist, Slovo felt that she needed another hand to amass, select and edit material and turned not to a playwright, but to a political journalist, Victoria Brittain, to be a co-writer. 'The creative process', argued Slovo, 'was in the selection and editing.'[20] But Brittain was also a much more practised interviewer and well versed in the legal protocols of taking down testimony. Esther Wilson, the lead writer for *Unprotected*, was soon confronted by one of the prostitutes she was interviewing: 'She said: "the more upset I get for you, the better" and I said: "well, yes actually."'[21] Tanika Gupta, author, of *Gladiator Games*, found different interviews very challenging for different reasons.[22] The family of the murdered teenager, Zahid Mubarek, were:

> always very suspicious of me. The mother was unable to speak because she was crying so much. I made available every single draft to them and they were very useful on details. [. . .] It wasn't a journalistic process for me. When I interviewed prison officers their response to me was fascinating – they rarely looked at me, but looked instead at the director at my side, Charlotte Westenra, who is blonde and white.[23]

Gupta, then, herself became a target of the institutional racism she was investigating and became 'quite disheartened' that the response of many white people was a desire to have more information about Robert Stewart (the murderer) in the play.[24] David Hare has talked of the 'slither of ice' in his writer's heart on the night that those bereaved by rail crashes caused by corporate negligence came to see the production of *The Permanent Way*.[25] Writer and director Alecky Blythe found the tables turned on her most unexpectedly when she asked the real-life hostage at the centre of her play *Come out Eli!* (2002) for his story a short while after the hostage-taking (during which she had conducted numerous interviews with distressed local residents). According to Blythe, the hostage demanded sex in return for his story. Blythe refused, bought him lunch instead, and wove the attempted blackmail into her play.[26] This is a stark reminder that verbatim plays rely wholly on others to provide the material. Journalists might well pay handsomely for an exclusive, artists do not expect to pay anything.

The lack of clear sources in some verbatim plays is an ethical issue which bothers Stephen Bottoms (Bottoms 2006: 61). Gupta is extremely rigorous in providing all her sources and noting them against the text, clarifying that 'anything unmarked is a dramatisation based on events/hearsay' (Gupta 2005: 32), and providing an interesting model of notation for verbatim plays which incorporate invented material.[27] Alecky Blythe's company, Recorded Delivery, foregrounds the sourcing and research process itself by insisting that actors wear headphones throughout performances. Actors reproduce the exact words and tics of the interviewee they are playing, saying the words after having just heard them on tape (although spectators actually have no idea whether the actor's simulation is accurate or not because access to the tapes is not part of their experience). Essentially the device works in the manner of Brechtian alienation, serving as a constant reminder that actors are presenting material rather than identifying with it. Blythe's manner of performance offers an aesthetics which appear to lend a greater authenticity to her shows, but that appearance is in itself a performance. What is doubly fascinating is that while Blythe seeks a supposed transparency in her performances, she is, like other verbatim practitioners, becoming increasingly concerned to diminish the effect of the microphone in interviews, which makes the situation seem too 'set up', and to reduce its effect on interviewees, who become self-conscious in ways which are not useful for her purposes (Blythe 2006: 4).[28] Blythe wears a small microphone pinned to her clothing and argues that the effect she is after is akin to 'fly on the wall documentary'. At the same time she is clear that she is in the business of representation and that the 'magic of the technique' comes from the audience knowing that they are hearing the words of real people (Blythe 2006: 5). That there can sometimes be a very curious privileging of words above the visual in verbatim theatre is evident from Blythe's *Cruising*, a play about the sex lives of the elderly. Blythe felt no compulsion to attempt any physical veracity and cast actors who were 30–40 years younger than their characters. This certainly added to the alienation effect but it also treated the characters as comic, strongly implying that the subject itself might be difficult to take seriously, arguably reinforcing taboos about the elderly, and prejudging the material for spectators.

Conclusion

Documentary forms have always proved an especially effective way of putting grand narratives and received ideas under scrutiny. In Britain verbatim theatre has lent itself well not just to highlighting the horror and injustice of wars and other traumatic events, but also to the business of scrutinizing institutions, legal processes and human rights abuses. It is not surprising that this theatre is flourishing in Britain at a time when the failing infrastructures of the civil service, the National Health Service and the justice system are constantly in the headlines.[29] Blair's term of office has singularly failed to deliver the domestic agenda for which he was voted in, and has committed the country to a course of action in Iraq which the majority question. Public confidence in the integrity of politicians continues to be disastrously low. In a paradoxical way the media drives verbatim theatre but is also clearly under sustained attack from it. Moguls such as Rupert Murdoch increase their control over the media industry all the time, and it is common knowledge that government spin merchants exist to make interventions which suit the party more than the nation. What verbatim theatre seems to represent is the importance of alternative stories, which symbolize the way that it is still possible for the mechanisms of democracy to function. As Carol Martin has argued, much verbatim theatre is 'made to "set the record straight" or to bring materials otherwise ignored to the public's attention. [. . .] Depending on who you are, what your politics are, and so on, documentary theatre will seem to be "getting at the truth" or "telling another set of lies"' (Martin 2006: 13–14).

Verbatim theatre is currently fashionable not because the British public are more gullible than others, as Bottoms has argued, or because 'most Britons believe in the underlying truth/reality of the news as mediated by the BBC and by newspapers such as the *Guardian*' (Bottoms 2006: 57). It is quite the reverse. It is precisely because the media industries are no longer trusted to put forward dissenting or minority views that verbatim plays thrive. Such plays are not a substitute for the media but offer a powerful alternative way of reflecting on a set of narratives and debating them. Playwright David Edgar may see verbatim theatre as 'an abdication on the part of the writer',[30] a refusal to present your own case, but the public manifestly have a thirst for hearing these narratives, as well as a thirst for hearing them live and as part of a community. Attendance at certain verbatim plays is definitely a demonstration of political credentials and is a sign of how disempowered many feel. It is, of course, unfashionable in these cynical times to claim that theatre can have any political effect, but there is demonstrably mass demand for verbatim theatre, and dissemination of plays such as *The Colour of Justice* indicates as much. Cultural commentator Joan Bakewell has pointed out that the Tricycle's Tribunal productions have gained audiences of 25 million worldwide in their theatrical and televised versions (*Independent*, 17 March 2006).

Victoria Brittain has been very struck by the power of the form on certain individuals:

> As a journalist you don't get anywhere with all your articles but I found *Guantanamo* was a transformational experience for many people, who said extraordinary things to me afterwards. I've had several right-wing lawyers and United Nations dignitaries say to me: 'I'm ashamed I didn't pay attention.' I think you can make small changes with a play like this. Certainly actors have been transformed in the States: some in *Exonerated* have become political campaigners. The experience has absolutely altered their lives.[31]

Martin is right to remind us that 'the paradox of a theatre of facts that uses representation to enact a relationship to the real should not be lost in the enthusiasm for a politically viable theatre' (Martin 2006: 13), but it is also quite clear, as Hesford has argued, that verbatim theatre provides important cultural spaces 'in which to contemplate the ethical and moral questions raised by the repetition of trauma and the violation of human rights.' (Hesford 2006: 39).

Notes

1   Verbatim theatre is simply referred to as documentary theatre elsewhere.
2   Littlewood and Cheeseman were themselves greatly influenced by Brecht and Piscator.
3   Questions abound. Which interviewees, for example, were selected from the unproblematized 'community'? And what of the artfulness of shaping and creating a piece of performance from hundreds of pages of transcripts, especially when much of the material is not suitable for a theatrical event – as director David Thacker points out: 'ninety per cent of what you get is incredibly boring – it's platitudinous' (see Paget 1987: 326).
4   Hochhuth's *The Representative* (1963) explicated the Vatican's complicity in the Holocaust and enjoyed 73 productions in 27 countries in just a few years. Kipphardt's *In the Matter of J. Robert Oppenheimer* (premiered Germany 1964: London 1965: New York 1969) used legal documents to dramatize the case of an American nuclear scientist accused of treason. Weiss's *The Investigation* dramatized transcripts from the Frankfurt War Crimes trial about the atrocities at Auschwitz, and was premiered in 13 different theatres throughout East and West Germany on 19 October 1965. These works were all very contentious and demonstrated that documentary theatre could have significant international impact.
5   See Tracy C. Davis and Thomas Postlewait (2003). *Theatricality*. Cambridge: Cambridge University Press.
6   For example, (1982) *Whose Land Is It Anyway? Agriculture, Planning and Land Use in Britain*. Wellingborough: Turnstone; (1984) *The Ponting Affair*. London: Cecil Wolf; (1988) *Blacklist: The Inside Story of Police Vetting*. London: Hogarth.
7   Norton-Taylor was speaking on a panel 'Tribunal, Testimony and Political Process' at the symposium on 'Verbatim Practices in Contemporary Theatre' held at the Central School of Speech and Drama, London, 13–14 July 2006.
8   Janelle Reinelt has written at length about the role of class as well as racial prejudice in this case (Reinelt 2006).
9   Thomas Wheatley has acted in all Norton-Taylor's tribunal plays, and was speaking at a symposium on verbatim practices (see note 7). He also said that 'For me as an actor this work has been the most fulfilling I have ever done. It is extraordinary to play real people who've said real things. It's very challenging and very daunting. You do less "acting" in these plays: you get inside the language of the person: you *impersonate*, you do not play a character in the traditional sense.'
10 Symposium on 'Verbatim Practices in Contemporary Theatre', 13 July 2006.

11 Norton Taylor: private conversation with author, symposium on 'Verbatim Practices in Contemporary Theatre', 14 July 2006.
12 In the introduction to *Srebenica* (1996) Kent states: ' I was so upset that this testimony to the worst massacre in Europe since World War II was receiving so little public and media attention that the editing of this material into a play for the theatre became a necessity' (Kent 2005: 5).
13 Commentary on the back cover of the published play credited, respectively, to the *Observer* and Trevor Phillips.
14 Some practitioners incorrectly seem to think that a process whereby sources are interviewed is enough to constitute it as a piece of 'verbatim theatre'.
15 Author's and director's note, Soans (2005: n.p.).
16 Merlin was speaking at the symposium on 'Verbatim Practices in Contemporary Theatre', 13 July 2006. Ethics were not a problem for actor Lloyd Hutchinson, speaking at the same symposium, who appeared in *The Permanent Way* and *Talking to Terrorists*. For him *The Permanent Way* was exciting because it was his first verbatim play and it was 'very liberating' to meet the people you would be playing. 'I left ethics to the writers and director.' But his experience on *Talking to Terrorists* was quite different: 'I vowed I'd never do another verbatim play again. It was a woolly subject: one man's terrorist is another man's freedom-fighter.'
17 Directors Mark Wing-Davey and Les Waters, who both worked for Joint Stock, have used these techniques in Britain and America. The Central School for Speech and Drama incorporates these techniques into its acting programmes, as do other drama schools and universities in Britain.
18 David Rintoul, an actor with Joint Stock, believed that 'writers were nurtured at the expense of actors' (Ritchie 1987: 23).
19 Gillian Slovo, symposium on 'Verbatim Practices in Contemporary Theatre', 13 July 2006. Slovo was asked by Nicolas Kent at the Tricycle Theatre to write the play and told that she could not make up any words.
20 Ibid.
21 Ibid., 14 July 2006.
22 *Gladiator Games* was a co-production between the Sheffield Crucible and the Theatre Royal, Stratford, London. The latter is one of the leading theatres for new black and Asian writing in Britain.
23 Ibid., 14 July 2006.
24 Ibid.
25 Ibid., described by Bella Merlin, 13 July 2006.
26 Ibid., Alecky Blythe, 14 July 2006. *Come out Eli!* was produced at the Arcola Theatre and is not published but Blythe is currently writing a film script.
27 Gupta chose to dramatize the murder victim Zahid Mubarek because she wanted to keep the focus firmly on his story (symposium on 'Verbatim Practices in Contemporary Theatre', 14 July 2006).

28   Robin Soans has now completely dispensed with technology for interviews. 'I've done hundreds of interviews and never use anything other than a pencil and notebook. Gadgets go wrong, need constant adjustment, interrupt concentration and put people off' (Soans 2004: 19).

29   Chris Megson studied the relation between verbatim theatre and the pressure on state institutions, which began under Margaret Thatcher, in a paper entitled 'Creative Institution-Building: Verbatim Theatre and Civic Transformation, 1990–2006' given 17 March 2006, University of Aberystwyth.

30   Edgar was speaking at a conference on 'Gagging', University of Hull, 25 March 2006.

31   Symposium on 'Verbatim Practices in Contemporary Theatre', plenary session, 14 July 2006.

Primary reading

Blank, Jessica, and Jensen, Eric (2006). *The Exonerated*. London: Faber and Faber.

Blythe, Alecky (2006). *Cruising*. London: Nick Hern.

Brittain, Victoria, and Slovo, Gillian (2004). *Guantanamo*. London: Oberon.

Burke, Gregory (2006). *Black Watch*. London: Faber and Faber.

Cheeseman, Peter (1977). *Fight for Shelton Bar*. London: Methuen.

Gupta, Tanika (2005). *Gladiator Games*. London: Oberon.

Hare, David (2003). *The Permanent Way*. London: Faber and Faber.

Hare, David (2004). *Stuff Happens*. London: Faber and Faber.

Hochhuth, Rolf (1963). *The Representative*. London: Methuen.

Kent, Nicolas (2005). *Srebenica*. London: Nick Hern.

Kipphardt, Heinar (1968). *In the Matter of J. Robert Oppenheimer*. London: Mermaid.

McGrath, John (2005). *Plays for England*, selected and intro. Nadine Holdsworth. Exeter: University of Exeter Press.

McGrath, John, and Norton-Taylor, Richard (1995). *Half the Picture* in Richard Norton-Taylor, *The Truth is a Difficult Concept*. London: Fourth Estate.

Morgan, Peter (2006). *Frost/Nixon*. London: Faber and Faber.

Norton-Taylor, Richard (1997). *Nuremberg*. London: Nick Hern.

Norton-Taylor, Richard (1999). *The Colour of Justice*. London: Oberon.

Norton-Taylor, Richard (2003). *Justifying War*. London: Oberon.

Norton-Taylor, Richard (2005). *Bloody Sunday*. London: Oberon.

Norton-Taylor, Richard (2007). *Called to Account*. London: Oberon.

Rickman, Alan, and Viner, Katharine (2005). *My Name is Rachel Corrie*. London: Nick Hern.

Soans, Robin (2000). *A State Affair*. London: Methuen.

Soans, Robin (2004). *The Arab-Israeli Cookbook*. London: Aurora Metro.

Soans, Robin (2005). *Talking to Terrorists*. London: Oberon.

Weiss, Peter (1966). *The Investigation*. London and New York: Marion Boyars.

Wilson, Esther, Fay, John, Green, Tony, and Nunnery, Lizzie (2006). *Unprotected*. London: Josef Weinberger.

Woolf, Dennis. *Beyond Belief*. Not published. Premiere: Library Theatre, Manchester, 22 October 2004.

Further reading

Ben-Zvi, Linda (2006). 'Staging the Other Israel: The Documentary Theatre of Nola Chilton', *The Drama Review* 50:3 (T191), 42–55.

Bottoms, Stephen (2006). 'Putting the Document into Documentary', *The Drama Review* 50:3 (T191), 56–68.

DiCenzo, Maria (1996). *The Politics of Alternative Theatre in Britain, 1968–1990: The Case of 7:84 (England)*. Cambridge: Cambridge University Press.

DiCenzo, Maria (2006). 'John McGrath and Popular Political Theatre' in Mary Luckhurst (ed.), *The Companion to Modern British and Irish Drama*. Oxford: Blackwell, 419–28.

Giannachi, Gabriella, and Luckhurst, Mary (1999). 'Peter Cheeseman' in Gabriella Giannachi and Mary Luckhurst (eds.), *On Directing*. London: Faber and Faber, 13–18.

Hare, David (2004). 'Enter Stage Left', *Guardian*, 30 October, review section, 4–6.

Hesford, Wendy S. (2006). 'Staging Terror', *The Drama Review* 50:3 (T191), 29–41.

Irmer, Thomas (2006). 'A Search for New Realities: Documentary Theatre in Germany', *The Drama Review* 50:3 (T191), 16–28.

Lahr, John (2006). 'Human Shield', *New Yorker*, 30 October, 98–9.

Martin, Carol (2006). 'Bodies of Evidence', *The Drama Review* 50:3 (T191), 8–15.

Nichols, Bill (1991). *Representing Reality: Issues and Concepts in Documentary Drama*. Bloomington, IN: Indiana University Press.

Norton-Taylor, Richard, Lloyd, Mark, and Cook, Stephen (1996). *Knee Deep in Dishonour: The Scott Report and its Aftermath*. London: Gollancz.

Paget, Derek (1987). '"Verbatim Theatre": Oral History and Documentary Techniques', *New Theatre Quarterly* 3:2, 317–36.

Paget, Derek (1990). *True Stories? Documentary Drama on Radio, Screen and Stage*. Manchester: Manchester University Press.

Reinelt, Janelle (2006). 'Toward a Poetics of Theatre and Public Events', *The Drama Review* 50:3 (T191), 69–87.

Renov, Michael (1993). *Theorising Documentary*. New York and London: Routledge.

Ritchie, Rob, ed. (1987). *The Joint Stock Book*. London: Methuen.

Mary Luckhurst

Weiss, Peter (1971). 'The Material and the Models: Notes Towards a Definition of Documentary Theatre', trans. Heinz Bernard, *Theatre Quarterly* I.I (January–March), 41–3.
White, Hayden (1987). *The Content of the Form: Narrative Discourse and Historical Representation*. Baltimore: Johns Hopkins University Press.

Part IV

Science, Ethics and New Technologies

Chapter 11

Theatre and Science

David Higgins

Anxieties about the consequences of scientific discoveries and new technologies have been present in western culture for a long time, but became widespread and urgent in the second half of the twentieth century, following the use of atomic weaponry at Hiroshima and Nagasaki in 1945.[1] In the following decades, nuclear conflict between the USA and the USSR, resulting in worldwide destruction, seemed like a very real possibility. Since the end of the Cold War, these anxieties have continued to increase, due not only to geopolitical turmoil and nuclear proliferation, but also to accumulating evidence of global warming.[2] Alongside fears that nuclear weapons may fall into the hands of terrorists, or that conflict in the Middle East may escalate into a nuclear cataclysm, there now exists an increasingly strong body of scientific opinion suggesting that humanity's reliance on fossil fuels is changing the world's climate to an extent that may have negative implications for life on Earth. Furthermore, science's increasing capacity for genetic manipulation is challenging conventional religious and secular ideas about human dignity and identity, and evoking fears of eugenics (breeding people for 'desirable' inherited characteristics and, perhaps, trying to prevent children with 'undesirable' characteristics from being born), leading to ongoing controversies surrounding stem-cell research, 'designer babies', and human cloning.[3] Science, therefore, particularly when it raises dystopian spectres, is now subject to widespread public debate, and it is not surprising that a number of recent plays engage with it (if one includes American drama, then this is a large number).[4] For the purposes of this chapter I will focus on four: *Copenhagen* (National Theatre, 1998) by Michael Frayn (b. 1933); *Arcadia* (National Theatre, 1993) by Tom Stoppard (b. 1937); *An Experiment with an Air Pump* (Royal Exchange Theatre, 1998) by Shelagh Stephenson (b. 1955); and *A Number* (Royal Court Theatre, 2002) by Caryl Churchill (b. 1938). All of these plays reveal anxieties about science, even though they also testify, in different ways, to its excitement and potential for positive effects.

Michael Frayn, *Copenhagen*

The most successful recent play dealing with science is undoubtedly Michael Frayn's *Copenhagen*. Its first production, directed by Michael Blakemore, ran for almost three years, receiving several awards and glowing reviews in the process. Blakemore's New York production of 2000 was similarly well received, and, in 2002, a film version was broadcast in Britain by the BBC and in the United States by PBS.[5] The play's success is remarkable given the complexity of its themes: epistemology, ethics and quantum physics. It concerns a meeting in Copenhagen in September 1941 between two of the greatest physicists of the twentieth century, Niels Bohr and Werner Heisenberg. Once close friends and colleagues, who together had come up with the so-called Copenhagen Interpretation of quantum physics in the late 1920s, they were now on opposing sides in the Second World War. Heisenberg was leading the German team attempting to build a nuclear bomb, whereas the Danish Bohr (who was half-Jewish) found his country occupied by the Nazis.[6] From the perspective of the afterlife, the two men and Bohr's wife, Margrethe, try to work out exactly why Heisenberg wanted to meet Bohr and to agree on what they discussed. Was Heisenberg on a spying mission, trying to find out if Bohr knew anything about the Allied nuclear programme? Was he seeking Bohr's help with regard to achieving nuclear fission? Or was it that he had moral qualms about helping the Nazis and sought the advice of his former mentor? For Frayn, though, there can be no definitive answer to Margrethe's opening question, 'But why?' (Frayn 2002: 3).

Two linked scientific areas are crucial to *Copenhagen*: quantum physics and nuclear fission. Quantum physics developed in the early twentieth century as a way of describing the behaviour of subatomic particles (neutrons, electrons and protons), which did not seem comprehensible by using classical (Newtonian) physics. Heisenberg is best known for his so-called 'Uncertainty Principle', which, along with Bohr's theory of Complementarity (suggesting that light sometimes behaves like a wave and sometimes like a particle), make up the Copenhagen Interpretation of quantum physics. Put in its simplest terms, Heisenberg claimed that whereas in classical physics it is possible to be precise about the position and momentum of a particle, in the quantum world, the more one knows about a particle's position, the less one knows about its momentum, and vice versa. Frayn attempts to encapsulate this, and to bring in Bohr's theory, in the following passage:

Heisenberg: Listen! Copenhagen is an atom. Margrethe is its nucleus. About right, the scale? Ten thousand to one?
Bohr: Yes, yes.
Heisenberg: Now, Bohr's an electron. He's wandering about the city somewhere in the darkness, no one knows where. He's here, he's there, he's everywhere and nowhere. Up in Faelled Park, down in Carlsberg. Passing City Hall, out by the harbour. I'm a photon. A quantum of light. I'm despatched into the darkness to find Bohr. And I succeed, because I manage to collide with him. . . . But what's happened? Look – he's been slowed down, he's been deflected! He's no longer doing what he was so maddeningly doing when I walked into him!
Bohr: But, Heisenberg, Heisenberg! You also have been deflected! If people can see what's happened to you, to their piece of light, then they can work out what must have happened to me! The trouble is knowing what's happened to you! Because to understand how people see you we have to treat you not just as a particle, but as a wave. I have to use not only your particle mechanics, I have to use the Schrödinger wave function.
Heisenberg: I know – I put it in a postscript to my paper. (68–9)

This description of the movements of people as symbolizing quantum behaviour ingeniously inverts the central conceit of the play, which is to suggest that the uncertainty (or, better, the indeterminacy) prevalent in the quantum world also applies to human behaviour.[7] And, significantly, both comparisons serve to suggest that the apparently abstract world of theoretical physics isn't really that abstract at all: it is inextricably connected not only with political and technological change, but also with the paths and patterns that make up individual lives. As Margrethe puts it, 'everything is personal' (73).

One might complain that the whole point of quantum physics is that larger physical objects, including people, *do not* behave in the way Heisenberg describes – Bohr is *not* an electron, Heisenberg is *not* a photon – and that all this uncertainty applies only at the subatomic level. Frayn, though, is suggesting that there is a parallel between the uncertainty of quantum physics and 'epistemological uncertainty' of human behaviour, as he explains in an interview:

> It is extremely difficult (not to put it more strongly) to know why people do what they do, and it's also extremely difficult to know why one does what one does oneself. [. . .] What the play is suggesting is that there is some sort of theoretical barrier in the way of our ever knowing. It's not a practical difficulty; there is a theoretical difficulty – as there is in knowing precisely about the behaviour of particles. (Wu 2000: 214–15)

Copenhagen is a success, simply, because Frayn *makes* this parallel work through the constant questioning and bickering of the characters, as Heisenberg's visit is replayed again and again. There is plenty of information available about the Heisenberg–Bohr meeting, and the play's characters desperately want to get to the truth, but certainty is not possible: memory is unreliable; motivation is murky; evidence is contradictory; interpretation is subjective. The meeting, so overdetermined by personality and politics, may have had a crucial impact on the outcome of the war and the future of humanity – 'preserved, just possibly, by that one short moment in Copenhagen' (94) – but will never be precisely described or understood. In the context of current media speculation about the possibility of US military action in the face of Iran's refusal to suspend its programme of uranium enrichment, Frayn's 'just possibly' painfully emphasizes the fragility of a world with nuclear weapons, and the unimaginable pressures on individuals like Bohr and Heisenberg.

Nuclear fission occurs when an atomic nucleus (consisting of neutrons and protons) splits into fragments; this causes a massive chain reaction as neutrons fly off and split other nearby nuclei. Within less than a millionth of a second, there is an enormous release of energy. The only natural element that can be split is uranium-235; this makes up less than 1 per cent of natural uranium, over 99 per cent of which is the non-fissionable isotope uranium-238. According to Thomas Powers, it was Bohr who first realized early in 1939 that it wasn't uranium that fissioned, but the 235 isotope (Powers 2000a: 56).[8] This led, in effect, to three questions. How much U-235 would be required to sustain a nuclear reaction? Was it feasible to separate such a quantity from natural uranium? And, if feasible, how long would the separation process take? Most physicists, including Bohr himself, seem initially to have believed that building a nuclear bomb would be virtually impossible, although there was also anxiety about the rapid publication of papers on fission and the possibility that Hitler might seek to make nuclear weapons (Powers 2000a: 56–66). A question raised by the play, and hotly debated by its critics, is whether or not Heisenberg calculated (at some point during the war), or at least attempted to calculate, the amount of uranium-235 needed to set off a nuclear explosion. Perhaps, the play suggests, he failed to make the calculation and assumed that it would be an impossibly impractical amount because, as he puts it, '*I* wasn't trying to build a bomb', although that again, he concedes, begs the question, 'why did I come to Copenhagen?' (86).[9]

Frayn's initial inspiration for *Copenhagen* came from reading Powers's *Heisenberg's War* (2000a, first published 1993). This includes the contentious and widely criticized claim that Heisenberg deliberately sabotaged the Nazi nuclear programme by being deceitfully pessimistic to his bosses about the chances of achieving nuclear fission: 'Heisenberg did not simply withhold himself, stand aside, let the project die. He killed it' (Powers 2000a: 479). Frayn's willingness at least to consider this possibility, and his apparent sympathy for Heisenberg, have led to criticism, most notably from Paul Lawrence Rose, author of *Heisenberg and the Nazi Atomic Bomb Project* (1998). In the postscript written to coincide with the New York production in 2000, Frayn makes it clear that he believes Rose to be excessively harsh on Heisenberg, and not always reliable in his use of evidence (107–10). Responding to the New York production, though, Rose reiterated his view that Heisenberg was 'a brilliant but weak man, whose shallow moral character allowed him to be easily corrupted by his nationalist German sympathies into colluding with Nazism', and who met Bohr to try to pick his brains about the Allied nuclear programme and the feasibility of a nuclear weapon (Rose 2000a).[10] Heisenberg had no moral doubts about arming the Nazis with atomic weaponry, but simply thought it unfeasible, because he 'had miscalculated, first the mass of a U235 bomb, and second, the time and scale for the production of plutonium' (Rose 2000b).[11] Rose's occasionally self-righteous tone, his apparent hatred for Heisenberg, and his off-the-mark claim that *Copenhagen* supports a pernicious moral relativism can make it hard to sympathize with him, but he does have a point when he claims that Frayn shows a disregard for historical accuracy. It may well be that the conflicting accounts of the meeting, and our obvious inability to access Heisenberg's mind, mean that it is impossible to be certain about his attitude to the Nazi nuclear project. However, this does not necessarily mean that some hypotheses are not better supported than others. Despite Frayn's use of Margrethe to question and challenge Heisenberg's attempts to explain and justify himself, *Copenhagen* seems to suggest that, bearing in the mind the limits of our knowledge, it is *equally* possible that Heisenberg enthusiastically supported the project, or that he was unenthusiastic about it and dragged his feet, or that he sabotaged it. For Rose, this manifests a dangerously irresponsible, postmodernist attitude to history. It seems reasonable to concede this point, whilst at the same time noting that *Copenhagen* is a play, not a historical documentary, and that its audiences have been and will be capable of making the distinction.

Tom Stoppard, *Arcadia*

Copenhagen was not the first play to use quantum theory as a metaphor for the uncertainties of human behaviour. Tom Stoppard tried something similar in describing the deceit and bluffing of Cold War spies in *Hapgood* (1988), but with considerably less critical and commercial success than Frayn, due, in part, to a confusingly complex plot.[12] *Arcadia* (1993), however, which dizzyingly connects the themes of chaos theory, entropy, and romanticism versus classicism, in a story of academic backbiting, sexual desire and personal tragedy, is often described as Stoppard's best play. It is set in Sidley Park, a country house in Derbyshire owned by the Coverly family, and its events take place in two historical periods: 1809–12, and the present. It begins with the adolescent Thomasina Coverly and her young tutor Septimus Hodge engaging in a discussion that amusingly combines sex and mathematics, and this sets the tone for the rest of the play. Thomasina, we later discover, is an unappreciated child prodigy who has 'discovered' the second law of thermodynamics (entropy) and some aspects of chaos theory, and who dies in a fire in 1812. The present-day plot is concerned principally with the research of the

historian Hannah Jarvis, the ambitious literary academic Bernard Nightingale, and the biologist-mathematician Valentine Coverly. Hannah is
studying the hermit who lived in the gardens of Sidley Park in the
early nineteenth century (he later turns out to have been Septimus);
Bernard is a Byronist who ends up wrongly claiming that during a
stay at the house, Byron shot and killed a guest (Ezra Chater) in a
duel; and Valentine is using the house game books in order to study
fluctuations in the grouse population over two centuries.

Hannah's interest in the hermit, a madman who spent his days
drawing 'cabalistic proofs that the world was coming to an end',
stems from her view of him as a symbol of

> the whole Romantic sham [. . .]. It's what happened to the Enlighten-
> ment, isn't it? A century of intellectual rigour turned in on itself.
> A mind in chaos suspected of genius. In a setting of cheap thrills and
> false emotion. [. . .] The decline from thinking to feeling. (Stoppard
> 1993: 27)[13]

Bernard, as a professional (and private) Romanticist, can hardly be
expected to concur, and, arguing with Valentine, ends up attacking
the Enlightenment belief in scientific progress and the utility of scientific
knowledge:

> Oh, you're going to zap me with penicillin and pesticides. Spare me
> that and I'll spare you the bomb and aerosols. But don't confuse progress
> with perfectibility. A great poet is always timely. A great philosopher is
> an urgent need. There's no rush for Isaac Newton. We were quite
> happy with Aristotle's cosmos. Personally, I preferred it. [. . .] I can't
> think of anything more trivial than the speed of light. Quarks, quasars
> – big bangs, black holes – who gives a shit? (61)

What matters to Bernard is the inner world of thought and feeling;
knowledge of the wider universe is essentially pointless. However,
despite his considerable wit and intelligence, Bernard is depicted as a
self-serving bully who completely misinterprets the evidence about
Byron and Chater because he is blinded by ambition. His disdain for
larger truths is shown to be a defective personality trait, rather than
an intellectual position. His polarization of science and literature is
palpably absurd, as the play makes clear by successfully intertwining
the two; so, though, is Hannah's polarization of the classical and the
romantic, and of thinking and feeling. Rightly or not, before *Arcadia*,
Stoppard was often characterized by critics as being overly interested

in ideas, to the detriment of character and emotion; the play can be seen as a typically self-reflexive riposte to this view.[14] As the plot progresses, the reserved thinker Hannah finds out that 'feeling', however misplaced or confusing, is an inescapable part of existence: Valentine's silent brother Gus falls in love with her and the plays end with them waltzing alongside Septimus and Thomasina, as the two spots of time movingly coalesce. Furthermore, chaos theory, as it appears in *Arcadia*, suggests that the ordered universe of the Enlightenment that Hannah so respects is itself something of a 'sham', or at least inadequate as a way of explaining human behaviour and the patterns of nature.

Stoppard values chaos theory because, in his own words, it 'is precisely to do with the unpredictability of determinism' (Gussow 1995: 84). It seeks to describe through mathematics the behaviour of 'non-linear' systems; that is, systems (such as a population of grouse) that seem to fluctuate randomly even though the starting conditions are known and there are no random parameters.[15] It is important to note that 'chaos', here, does not mean 'randomness', but simply the impossibility of making long-term predictions about such systems. In *Arcadia*, chaos theory is contrasted with deterministic Newtonian physics, which relies on the theoretical predictability of cause and effect: the same initial conditions will always lead to the same outcome. The problem, though, is that it is impossible to measure initial conditions with complete accuracy, and chaotic systems manifest extreme sensitivity to initial conditions: tiny variations at the start will lead to massive, unpredictable variations later on (this is why long-term weather forecasts are so hit and miss). As Valentine explains:

> We're better at predicting events at the edge of the galaxy or inside the nucleus of an atom than whether it'll rain on auntie's garden party three Sundays from now. Because the problem turns out to be different. We can't even predict the next drip from a dripping tap when it gets irregular. Each drip sets up the conditions of the next, the smallest variation blows prediction apart, and the weather is unpredictable the same way, will always be unpredictable. [. . .] It's the best possible time to be alive, when almost everything you thought you knew is wrong. (48)

Thomasina's insight is that the complex systems and forms of the universe *can* be expressed mathematically, not by using Euclidean geometry, but through iterated algebra ('feeding the solution back into the equation, and then solving it again' [44]): 'if there is an equation for a curve like a bell, there must be an equation for one like a bluebell, and if a bluebell, why not a rose? [. . .] I will plot this leaf and deduce its equation' (37). The problem is that she lacks the computational power to be able to iterate her equations enough times. Valentine is engaged in a similar project: he is attempting to come up with the equation which, when iterated, would explain the fluctuations in the grouse population at Sidley Park. By pushing Thomasina's equations through his computer 'a few million times further than she managed to do with her pencil', he comes up with 'the Coverly set', an allusion to the famous Mandelbrot Set of fractals, which shows how the iteration of a simple equation can lead to highly complex images, revealing 'islands of order' (76) in a mass of complex and seemingly random data.

Perhaps chaos theory is not necessarily as anti-Newtonian as Stoppard suggests; it seems to have more to do with the *epistemological impossibility* of predicting the behaviour of certain systems, rather than suggesting that they don't ultimately behave in a deterministic way. But this doesn't much matter; like Frayn's, Stoppard's main emphasis is on a rough parallel between a revolutionary scientific theory and the behaviour of human beings. This is encapsulated in an exchange between Valentine and his sister Chloë:

Chloë: [. . .] The future is programmed like a computer – that's a proper theory, right?
Valentine: The deterministic universe, yes.
[. . .]
Chloë: But it doesn't work, does it?
Valentine: No. It turns out the maths is different.
Chloë: No, it's all because of the sex.
Valentine: Really?
Chloë: That's what I think. The universe is deterministic all right, just like Newton said, I mean it's trying to be, but the only thing going wrong is people fancying people who aren't supposed to be in that part of the plan.
Valentine: Ah. The attraction that Newton left out. All the way back to the apple in the garden. (73–4)

Arcadia is full of misplaced and/or unconsummated desire: Thomasina and Septimus; Septimus and Lady Croom; Gus and Hannah; Bernard and Chloe; and so on. What Thomasina calls, innocently, 'the action of bodies in heat' (84) gives the lie to the mechanistic universe of the Enlightenment, both literally – through thermodynamics (see below) – and metaphorically, through sexual desire. This might suggest that Stoppard is 'coming out' as a Romantic: certainly, *Arcadia* represents chaos theory as a more humane, open-ended science than Newtonian physics, one that actually describes 'the ordinary-sized stuff which is our lives, the things people write poetry about' (48), thereby destroying Bernard's argument that science has nothing to do with humanity.[16]

The other scientific idea crucial to *Arcadia* is 'entropy', which is presented as similarly anti-Newtonian. Early in the play, Thomasina notes that when stirring jam into rice pudding, 'the spoonful of jam spreads itself round making red trails [. . .]. But if you stir backward, the jam will not come together again. [. . .] You cannot stir things apart' (4–5). Some physical processes only go one way and, like the jam in a rice pudding, disorder in a closed system tends to spread as energy dissipates. As Valentine explains to Hannah:

> Heat goes to cold. It's a one-way street. Your tea will end up at room temperature. What's happening to your tea is happening to everything everywhere. The sun and the stars. It'll take a while but we're all going to end up at room temperature. (78)

Later in the play, Thomasina fully formulates this principle when considering why the 'heat engine' of the gardener Mr Noakes can't produce enough energy to run itself: 'Newton's equations go forwards and backwards, they do not care which way. But the heat equation cares very much, it goes only one way' (87). What we are left with, then, is a vision of the heat-death of the universe (ironically prefiguring Thomasina's own 'heat-death'), which, by the end of play, Thomasina has managed to communicate to Septimus (93). This, along with Thomasina's death, seems to be what sends him mad.

The theme of science versus literature is also important here: whereas Bernard quotes from Byron's 'She walks in beauty' as a way of attacking scientific interest in the wider universe (61), Hannah quotes, aptly, from Byron's 'Darkness' in response to Valentine's explanation of entropy:

> The bright sun was extinguished, and the stars
> Did wander darkling in the eternal space,
> Rayless, and pathless, and the icy earth
> Swung blind and blackening in the moonless air . . . (79)

Again, this makes Stoppard's point that the imagination, as well as reason, has a role to play in understanding and representing scientific ideas. That these ideas may sometimes lead to bleak imaginings is apparent in the comic *Arcadia* just as much as in the seemingly far more serious *Copenhagen*. Both of them have at their heart a vision of 'total and final darkness' (Frayn 2002: 79), and describe the terrible pressure that such a vision can bring to bear on human beings.[17] They are, in part, manifestations of *fin-de-siécle* angst by writers who were children when the atomic bomb was dropped, and who grew to maturity during the Cold War.

Shelagh Stephenson, *An Experiment with an Air Pump*

Unabashedly influenced by *Arcadia*, Shelagh Stephenson's *An Experiment With An Air Pump* also moves between the Romantic period (1799) and the present day (1999), refers to the tension between science and literature, and explicitly engages with the *fin de siécle*. Stephenson's particular focus, though, is the ethics of stem-cell research and gene therapy. Her title comes from Joseph Wright's painting *An Experiment on a Bird in the Air Pump* (1768), which depicts a wizard-like scientist, surrounded by spectators, performing an experiment to show the formation of a vacuum by withdrawing air from a flask containing a cockatoo.[18] Stephenson draws on the theatricality of this scene by starting with a tableau of the play's Romantic-period characters in a similar situation, and projecting images of the painting above the audience. An explanation is provided by one of the modern characters, the geneticist Ellen, who has loved the painting since she was a child:

> Because it has a scientist at the heart of it, a scientist where you usually find God. [. . .] As a child enraptured by the possibilities of science, this painting set my heart racing [. . .]. I wanted to be this scientist [. . .]. I wanted to be God. (Stephenson 2003: 139)

This is the central theme of the play: the power and responsibility of the scientist and the danger of hubris: 'the ethics of dabbling with life and death' (140). The Romantic-period plot concerns the relationship between a radical Enlightenment scientist, Joseph Fenwick (who seems to be based loosely on Joseph Priestley), and his family, and that between one of his acolytes, the physician and anatomist Thomas Armstrong, and Fenwick's servant Isobel Bridie. The present-day plot concerns the relationship between Ellen and her recently redundant English-lecturer husband Tom, who live in what was Fenwick's house. Ellen is having an 'ethical crisis' (171) about whether to take up a job in a company that employs her younger scientist friend Kate. The job would involve stem-cell research, which uses the cells of 14-day-old embryos that are 'left over' following *in vitro* fertilization (that is, fertilization in a laboratory). The purpose of such research would be to help the process of discovering genetic 'defects' in the womb and correcting them. She eventually decides to take the job. This crisis is juxtaposed with the discovery of human bones in the house; the audience later discover that these are the remains of the servant Isobel, who tries to hang herself when she discovers that Armstrong, whom she believed (with good reason) to be in love with her, is only fascinated and aroused by the prospect of examining her deformed back. Isobel is still barely alive when discovered but Armstrong finishes her off by suffocating her (227).

There are a number of reasons why stem-cell research is controversial. Some religious groups argue that an embryo has the moral status of a person from the moment of conception, and therefore that using embryonic stem cells for scientific research is tantamount to murder. Other opponents focus on the possible consequences of gene therapy; for example, that it may lead to misplaced attempts to 'cure' complex mental disorders such as manic depression, and also to discrimination on the basis of genetics:[19]

Tom: I mean, where's it all leading? If you can eventually determine the genetic code of any given foetus, all I know is that's going to lead to trouble. Can you imagine what insurance companies will do with that information? Mortgage companies? Health insurers? [. . .]

Ellen: Oh for God's sake Tom, d'you think I don't worry about these things? [. . .] It's easy to have rarefied ethics if all your job involves is decoding bits of Shakespeare. It's not so bloody easy if you're trying to move genetics into the twenty-first century. All you have is moral principles, Tom. You don't have any solutions. (188–9)

Ellen makes a strong point here, but, generally speaking, the play is not even-handed or sympathetic in its portrayal of science and scientists. Fenwick is well-intentioned, but dangerously arrogant and hubristic, and Armstrong is an amoral monster who is incapable of empathizing with others (he tells his colleague Roget that 'I've never had a moral qualm in my life, and it would be death to science if I did' [207]). Kate, although she is not a murderer, seems to have similar attitudes to Armstrong's, caring nothing for the consequences of knowledge, or how it is obtained: 'for me it's all potential, it's all possibility, everything's there to be unravelled and decoded. [. . .] I want to eat up the world, I want to tear it apart and see what it's made of' (224). Ellen is much more sympathetic, and, unlike Kate and Armstrong, does not believe that science is 'value-free' (223) – but ultimately she decides to take the job because of the emotional and intellectual excitement of discovery.

Stephenson, then, is suspicious of Enlightenment claims that the pursuit of knowledge is an unmitigated good, and that scientists are disinterested strivers after truth. Mary Shelley's *Frankenstein* (1818) is an influence here, and we might also recall Wordsworth's lines from 'The Tables Turned' (1798), 'Our meddling intellect / Misshapes the beauteous forms of things; / – We murder to dissect' (Wordsworth and Coleridge 1991: 106). Armstrong literally murders to dissect, and some opponents of stem-cell research argue that it is effectively doing the same. Stephenson's suspicion seems at least partly to be based on her sense that the Enlightenment belief in scientific and social progress has its roots in Christian millenarianism. It is fitting, therefore, that the play is set in 1799 and 1999. When Fenwick talks early in the play about having a programme of scientific lectures that show that we are 'march[ing] towards a New Jerusalem with all our banners flying' (144), he is not talking metaphorically. Tom, arguing with Kate about the idea of 'curing' mental illness through gene therapy, points out that 'dinosaurs' like him, with their interest in the past, know 'that the Messiah's not coming' (225). As the characters enter the new century at the end of the play, rather than feeling 'hope and anticipation', they are (as Fenwick admits when standing next to Isobel's open coffin) 'groping blindly over the border in a fog of bewilderment' (231). Fenwick is shocked and disturbed by Isobel's death, and Tom is troubled by the fact that the bones he's discovered are missing ribs and the upper vertebrae. The audience know that this is because Armstrong must have taken them for study. Isobel stands for the horrors of treating people as means rather than ends, and is an expression of Stephenson's dystopian fears that modern geneticists may seek to do just that; fears that, through the device of the time-shift, she is able to link to long-standing taboos about the use of the human body in medical research (Marshall 1995).

Caryl Churchill, *A Number*

Like *An Experiment, A Number* is concerned with the possible consequences of genetic research; unlike Stephenson, however, Churchill *shows* those consequences through a piece of dystopian science fiction. The play, though, is not really about science *per se*; rather, cloning is the basis for considering the themes of responsibility and human identity. Since British scientists created Dolly the sheep in 1996 – the first mammal to have been cloned successfully from an adult cell – there has been intense public interest in the possibility of human cloning and the likely consequences of such a development. It is important to distinguish here between therapeutic cloning, in which scientists take stem cells from a cloned embryo with the aim of using them to treat illness, and reproductive cloning, which would produce a person who was genetically identical to another human being. One widely used argument against cloning is that it could turn human beings into commodities by allowing the creation of individuals for a particular purpose, such as treating a sick person, or replacing a dead loved one. A related argument is that cloned individuals are likely to feel inferior to other people and to have identity problems. These are the themes of Churchill's play. Each of the five scenes is an encounter between a manipulative and deceitful old man, Salter, and one of his cloned sons (each son is played by the same actor). In the first scene, Bernard (B2) has discovered that he is one of a number of clones created from the cells of Salter's first son Bernard (B1), who Salter, lying, tells him was killed in a car crash. In the second, the psychologically disturbed B1 confronts Salter about the serious neglect he suffered as a child, after his mother died when he was two (Salter 'sent him away' at the age of four and replaced him with B2) and finds out about the existence of B2. Next, B2 tells Salter that he has encountered B1 and has decided to leave the country as he fears B1 might kill him. In the fourth scene, B1 tells Salter that he's followed B2 to wherever he was hiding and murdered him (as is typical of *A Number*, precise details are not given), and the play ends with Salter meeting Michael Black, another cloned son, for the first time, following the (offstage) suicide of B1.

The violent deaths of B1 and B2 are both a consequence of, and a metonymy for, their feeling that the existence of other genetic clones destroys their individuality:

B2:   Because there's this person who's identical to me
Salter: he's not
B2:   who's not identical, who's like
Salter: not even very
B2:   not very like but very something terrible which is exactly the same genetic person
Salter: not the same person
B2:   and I don't like it. (Churchill 2004: 39)

On the other hand, the happily well-adjusted Michael Black says that he is not made 'frightened' or 'angry' by the news that he has 'a number' of clones; rather, he is 'fascinated'. This disturbs Salter, who sees losing one's uniqueness as the same as 'losing your life' (60). Black, though, finds it 'delightful' that 'all these very similar people [are] doing things like each other or a bit different or whatever we're doing' (61). He seems less individualistic than the other three characters, with a happy and close-knit family; his identity depends on connections, rather than differences:

> We've got ninety-nine per cent the same genes as any other person. We've got ninety per cent the same as a chimpanzee. We've got thirty per cent the same as a lettuce. Does that cheer you up at all? I love about the lettuce. It makes me feel I belong. (62)

Perhaps there is a suggestion here that modern genetics and cloning might have a positive effect by diminishing our selfish individualism (exemplified by Salter) and emphasizing our connectedness to other people, and to all living things. That is, in contradistinction to the anxieties of *An Experiment*, that it might make us care *more*, rather than *less*. However, it is difficult to know how seriously to take Black; his trivial remarks earlier in the scene about liking 'banana icecream' (59), and the example of the lettuce, jar uneasily with the grim events of the rest of the play and its emphasis on the dreadful consequences of Salter's actions.

A Number is, among other things, an economical meditation on the effects of heredity and environment on identity. Why has B1 ended up as a disturbed and dangerous individual? The play keeps coming

back to a primal scene from his childhood that suggests Salter's neglect of him after his mother died:

B1:   You know when I used to be shouting.
Salter: No.
B1:   When I was there in the dark. I'd be shouting.
Salter: No.
B1:   Yes, I'd be shouting dad dad
Salter: Was this some time you had a bad dream or?
B1:   shouting on and on
Salter: I don't think I
B1:   shouting and shouting
Salter: No
B1:   And you never came, nobody ever came. (31)

Later in the play, Salter admits, without being very specific, not only
that he did ignore B1 in the night, but also that he neglected (and
possibly abused) him to the extent that he became a 'disgusting thing'
(51, 61). It is cruelly fitting that, after the suffering of his infancy, B1
is now stalking the streets giving B2 'nightmares' (40). Despite being
genetically identical, they are very different characters: B2 suggests of
B1 that it's 'his childhood, his life, his childhood' that has 'made him
a nutter' (37). The problem with this sort of cause-and-effect argument, though, as B2 realizes, is that it suggests that we should not be
held responsible for our actions. The argument he has applied to B1
can also apply to his father. It is not Salter's fault that he mistreated
B1 and was a good father to B2 – it is just how he is because of
heredity and/or upbringing: 'maybe it was a genetic, could you help
drinking we don't know or drugs [. . .] and of course all the personal
all kind of what happened in your own life your childhood [. . .] so
probably I shouldn't blame you' (43). Salter feels that he should be
held responsible, blamed for B1 and praised for B2, but B2 argues
that freedom is just a feeling we have, not a reality, because we have
no control over our identity: 'who you are does freely not forced by
someone else but who you are who you are itself forces or you'd be
someone else wouldn't you?' (45).

It is this theme of personal responsibility that links all four plays.
Our actions may be determined by causal processes that we don't
fully understand; they may have effects that we cannot fully predict;
the motivations behind them, *or even the actions themselves*, may be
impossible to reconstruct with any certainty – and yet, despite all this,

most of us feel like we have free choices, and want these choices to be understood and judged. Thus, Heisenberg endlessly re-enacts his visit to Bohr; Hannah and Tom argue about the ethics of stem-cell research; and Salter created B2 in a misplaced attempt to put right the wrongs he had done to his first son. *Arcadia*'s emphasis is somewhat different, for, unlike the other three plays, it is *not* greatly concerned with the consequences of new technologies. Responsibility, though, is still an issue here; Septimus, we are led to believe, blames himself for Thomasina's death, although not sleeping with her was probably the 'right' thing to do. Even in everyday life, decisions made with the best of intentions may have negative consequences. The problem that affects Heisenberg and Hannah in particular is that their passion for science and, indeed, their responsibility to 'truth' may conflict with their responsibility for the possible effects of their discoveries. Science is not morally neutral: the question, though, is how much can we expect any individual to deal with the problems presented by the inevitable imbrication of scientific work with other forces – politics, commerce, desire. This is what *Copenhagen* so brilliantly articulates, and it seems fitting to end this chapter with Michael Frayn's remarks on Heisenberg:

> I am astonished by the ease with which British and American commentators have condemned him. People who were never called upon to make any great moral decisions in their life find it so easy to condemn Heisenberg for not taking a heroic stand. I think you can admire people who are heroes, but you can't *require* people to be heroes – otherwise there's no point in admiring them when they *are* heroic. (Wu 2000: 224)

Notes

Thanks to Brian Baker and Ashley Chantler for their comments on an earlier draft of this chapter.

1   See John Hersey (2002). *Hiroshima*. London: Penguin.
2   Mark Maslin (2004). *Global Warming: A Very Short Introduction*. Oxford: Oxford University Press.
3   I. Wilmut and R. Highfield (2006). *After Dolly: The Uses and Misuses of Human Cloning*. London: Little, Brown.
4   An extensive list of plays depicting science can be found at http://web.gc.cuny.edu/sciart/StagingScience/staging_science.htm#list, accessed 15 April 2006. Recent British plays dealing with science that are not

discussed here include Howard Brenton, *The Genius* (1982); Mick Gordon, *On Ego* (2005); Tony Harrison, *Square Rounds* (1992); Terry Johnson, *Insignificance* (1982); Stephen Poliakoff, *Blinded by the Sun* (1996); Arnold Wesker, *Longitude* (2002); and Hugh Whitemore, *Breaking the Code* (1986). There have also been three successful British versions of Brecht's *Life of Galileo*, by Howard Brenton, David Hare, and David Edgar.

5   PBS have a set of web pages devoted to *Copenhagen*, including interviews, information about the scientific and historical context, and so on: www. pbs.org/hollywoodpresents/copenhagen/index.html, accessed 12 April 2006.

6   Bohr escaped from Denmark in 1943 and ended up working on the Allied nuclear programme.

7   For a discussion of the limitations of the translated term 'uncertainty', see Frayn (2002: 99–100).

8   Bohr's insight followed experiments by Otto Hahn and Fritz Strassman and calculations by Lise Meitner and Otto Frisch during 1938; see Powers (2000a: 44–55).

9   Powers argues that Heisenberg, and a couple of other German scientists, thought in 1941 that a nuclear reactor might be used to produce the highly fissionable plutonium, but kept this quiet from the Nazi authorities (Powers 2000a: 99–102).

10   It should perhaps be noted that, according to Powers, Heisenberg was not a member of the Nazi party, does not appear to have been an anti-Semite, and was attacked a number of times in the late 1930s for his association with 'Jewish' physics (Powers 2000a: 35–43).

11   This quotation is from a letter to the *New York Review of Books*, responding to Thomas Powers's review of *Copenhagen* (Powers 2000b). Powers replied in detail to this letter, taking issue with a number of Rose's points (Powers 2000c). Frayn writes thoughtfully on some of Rose's criticisms, as well as those of others, in a 'Post-Postscript' to the 2002 edition of *Copenhagen* (Frayn 2002: 133–46). There are some complex issues of evidence and interpretation involved here, as well as a huge amount of information, and my discussion above is inevitably simplified and limited.

12   Stoppard revised the play for the New York production in 1994 in order to make the plot clearer. For *Hapgood*, see Edwards (2001: 171–176; Fleming 2001: 175–190; Gussow 1995: 78–83; Jernigan 2003: 4–17). Stoppard has also engaged with science in an early work, *Galileo* (originally an unproduced screenplay), which was written in the early 1970s (but not performed until 2004); see Fleming (2001: 66–81).

13   She relates this theme to the history of the Sidley Park garden, which by the early nineteenth century had been changed from an ordered, geometrical landscape into a pseudo-wilderness in which a mad hermit was a fitting ornament.

14   For love and science in *Arcadia*, see Zeifman (2001: 186–92).

15 Stoppard's main source for chaos theory is Gleick (1997, first published 1988). For detailed discussions of chaos theory in *Arcadia*, see Edwards (2001: 176–84; Jernigan 2003: 20–31; Kramer and Kramer 1997: 1–4; Vees-Gulani 1999).

16 The notion that the Romantics were against science *per se* is one of the great myths of intellectual history. It is simply that they were suspicious about the mechanistic and deterministic aspects of some Enlightenment thought.

17 For an interesting discussion of entropy and fear in twentieth-century literature, see Cartwright and Baker (2005: 243–63).

18 This can be viewed online on the website of the National Gallery, London: www.nationalgallery.org.uk/cgi-bin/WebObjects.dll/Collection Publisher.woa/wa/work?workNumber=NG725, accessed 16 April 2006.

19 For more information about these issues, see National Bioethics Advisory Commission (1999). This can be found online at www.georgetown.edu/research/nrcbl/nbac/pubs.html, accessed 20 April 2006.

Primary reading

Churchill, Caryl. (2004). *A Number*. London: Nick Hern.
Frayn, Michael. (2002). *Copenhagen*. London: Methuen.
Stephenson, Shelagh. (2003). *Plays: 1*. London: Methuen.
Stoppard, Tom (1993). *Arcadia*. London: Faber and Faber.
Tom Stoppard Papers (University of Texas, Austin).

Further reading

Cartwright, John H., and Baker, Brian (2005). *Literature and Science*. Santa Barbara: ABC-CLIO.
Edgar, David (2005). 'The Italian Job', *Guardian*, 26 October, 18–20.
Edwards, Paul (2001). 'Science in *Hapgood* and *Arcadia*' in Katherine E. Kelly (ed.), *The Cambridge Companion to Tom Stoppard*. Cambridge: Cambridge University Press, 171–84.
Fleming, John (2001). *Stoppard's Theatre*. Austin, TX: University of Texas Press.
Gleick, James (1997). *Chaos: A New Science*. London: Minerva.
Gussow, Mel (1995). *Conversations with Stoppard*. London: Nick Hern.
Jernigan, Daniel (2003). 'Tom Stoppard and Postmodern Science: Normalizing Radical Epistemologies in *Hapgood* and *Arcadia*', *Comparative Drama*, 37, 3–35.
Kramer, Prapassaree, and Kramer, Jeffrey (1997). 'Stoppard's *Arcadia*: Research, Time, Loss', *Modern Drama* 40, 1–10.

Marshall, Tim (1995). *Murdering to Dissect: Grave-robbing,* Frankenstein *and the Anatomy Literature.* Manchester: Manchester University Press.

National Bioethics Advisory Commission (1999). *Ethical Issues in Human Stem Cell Research.* Rockville, MD.

Orthofer, M. A. (2002). 'The Scientist on the Stage: A Survey', *Interdisciplinary Science Reviews* 27, 173–83.

Powers, Thomas (2000a). *Heisenberg's War.* New York: Da Capo Press.

Powers, Thomas (2000b). 'The Unanswered Question', *New York Review of Books,* 25 May, 4–7.

Powers, Thomas (2000c). Reply to Paul Lawrence Rose. *New York Review of Books,* 19 October, 65–6.

Rose, Paul Lawrence (1998). *Heisenberg and the Nazi Atomic Bomb Project.* Berkeley: University of California Press.

Rose, Paul Lawrence (2000a). 'Frayn's *Copenhagen* Plays Well, at History's Expense', *Chronicle of Higher Education,* 5 May, B4.

Rose, Paul Lawrence (2000b). 'Heisenberg in Copenhagen' [letter], *New York Review of Books,* 19 October, 65.

Stewart, Victoria (1999). 'A Theatre of Uncertainties: Science and History in Michael Frayn's "Copenhagen"', *New Theatre Quarterly* 15, 301–7.

Vees-Gulani, Susanne (1999). 'Hidden Order in the "Stoppard Set": Chaos Theory in the Content and Structure of Tom Stoppard's *Arcadia*', *Modern Drama* 42, 411–16.

Wordsworth, William, and Coleridge, Samuel Taylor (1991). *Lyrical Ballads.* London: Routledge.

Wu, Duncan, ed. (2000). *Making Plays: Interviews with Contemporary British Dramatists and Directors.* Basingstoke: Macmillan.

Zeifman, Hersh (2001). 'The Comedy of Eros: Stoppard in Love' in Katherine E. Kelly (ed.), *The Cambridge Companion to Tom Stoppard.* Cambridge: Cambridge University Press, 185–200.

Chapter 12

From the State of the Nation to Globalization: Shifting Political Agendas in Contemporary British Playwriting

Dan Rebellato

What is political theatre? When Mark Ravenhill's *Some Explicit Polaroids* opened in 1999, Sarah Hemming in the *Financial Times* noted with some surprise that she was 'watching a piece of political theatre – a rare beast on the stage these days' (Hemming 1999). The sentiment was echoed by other theatre critics, and their comments, taken together, tell us something intriguing about the way that political theatre is still understood in Britain. When, for example, Benedict Nightingale remarks that Ravenhill's play was 'the return of a dramatic genre long out of fashion [. . . the] state-of-England play' (Nightingale 1999), we can see that political theatre is most easily recognized when it conforms to a model of theatre developed in the 1970s: the state-of-the-nation play. As those reviews indicate, state-of-the-nation plays are not often written any more, which produces the associated argument that political theatre in Britain is in decline.[1]

This model of political theatre and the story of its decline continues to dominate critical and academic responses to contemporary playwriting. But against this gloomy reading, I want to argue that the political context in which the state-of-the-nation play was developed has changed, and as a consequence political theatre has changed. I want to suggest that British playwriting continues to respond to its political

245

surroundings with remarkable imaginative power and that the critics, with their outdated dramaturgical models, are looking for political theatre in all the wrong places.

The state-of-the-nation play

There is no established formal definition of the state-of-the-nation play, yet it is a term with some critical currency and a readily agreed core group of plays to which it applies. Typical examples are *Magnificence* (Royal Court, 1973), *The Churchill Play* (Nottingham Playhouse, 1974; RSC: Warehouse, 1979), *Weapons of Happiness* (National Theatre: Lyttelton, 1976) and *Epsom Downs* (Joint Stock, 1977) by Howard Brenton; *Destiny* (RSC: The Other Place, 1976) and *Maydays* (RSC: Barbican, 1983) by David Edgar; and *Plenty* (National Theatre: Lyttelton, 1978) by David Hare. Into this category one can draw plays by writers who wrote in that style only briefly, e.g. Robert Bolt's *State of Revolution* (National Theatre: Lyttelton, 1977), Barrie Keeffe's *Frozen Assets* (RSC: Warehouse, 1977), and Howard Barker's 'state-of-England' plays, which included *Claw* (Open Space, 1975), *Stripwell* (Royal Court, 1975) and *The Love of a Good Man* (Sheffield Crucible, 1978). The techniques were put to use by Edgar in his adaptation of *Nicholas Nickleby* (RSC: Aldwych, 1980), and arguably became part of the *mise en scène* for such RSC hits as *Les Misérables* (RSC: Barbican, 1985).

There are clear distinctions of tone, style, even of political view, between these writers, which the general label can smother. None the less, it will be useful for what follows to offer a provisional list of attributes most of which are shared by these plays, and which correspond to the particular political ambitions of their authors.

State-of-the-nation plays tend to be (a) large-cast plays, with (b) a panoramic range of public (and sometimes private) settings, employing (c) epic time-spans (years rather than hours or days), and (d) usually performed in large theatres, preferably theatres with a national profile. The grand scale of these plays represents a belief that the domestic rooms of the mainstream naturalist theatre represent a conservative and highly individualistic view of the world. In keeping with the socialist convictions of most of these writers, they wanted to show, in David Hare's words, 'the undulations of history [. . .] a sense of movement, of social change' (1991: 32), in which not individuals but whole classes of people were the protagonists, and the entire nation was the stage.

There were antecedents, in the generational scale of the Wesker Trilogy (Belgrade Theatre, Coventry, 1958–60), or indeed in the acknowledged influence of Shakespeare and his contemporaries.[2] However, in the spirit of this generation's determined historicism, it is important not to cast the net too wide and thereby blur the extent to which this work was developed in relation to the specific social and political conditions of its time.

The emergence of the state-of-the-nation play must be seen in the context of the rise and fall of working-class militancy in the 1970s. The first half of the decade saw a wave of trade-union radicalism that grew up around the Industrial Relations Act of 1971 and culminated in a series of strikes by mineworkers in 1972 and 1973. Socialist theatre workers, wishing to support the emergence of a socialist consciousness, needed to develop forms that could respond immediately and with great clarity to events as they unfolded. For this purpose they turned to agitprop, a form of theatre that developed in the 1920s as a means of disseminating a revolutionary analysis of society.

In the early 1970s, agitprop took the form of cartoon-like, often comic, episodic plays that deliberately eschewed any trace of individual psychology to force attention to the larger forces at work. It was quick to write, was adaptable to changing political circumstances, and at its best offered a direct point of information – 'how many working people have time to sit down and read an Act of Parliament? Providing information is an important function of political theatre' (Edgar, quoted in Itzin 1980: 141) – and communicated with a popular energy and appeal that was quite separate from the aesthetic ambitions of the conventional theatre.

However, with the collapse of the Heath administration, and the re-election of a centrist Harold Wilson government, the militancy subsided. In these new circumstances, playwrights had the opportunity to reflect anew on the merits of agitprop as a political tool. Part of the problem with agitprop – and something that became particularly evident at a time of 'class retreat' – is that it finds it hard to connect with the issue of consciousness. Agitprop works in a visually conceptual way: the top-hatted Victorian mill-owner represents the capitalist class as such, not any particular member; similarly, performers might find themselves representing historical forces, social conflict, a governmental system. David Edgar once, only half-jokingly, confessed, 'I had a fantasy at that time that I wanted to do a play which had no people in it at all, in which everybody was either an aeroplane or a graph of labour migration from the north west during the 1960s'

(Edgar et al. 1979: 8). In other words, actors were embodying objects of the understanding. But the visual and experiential is deliberately eliminated, with the result that agitprop offered little help in coordinating our understanding of the world with our experience of it.

Moving beyond these limitations involved an accommodation with realism. The argument against realism was that it individualized problems, the walls separating the characters from historical processes; their relationships, their problems, their concerns, ideas, lifestyles were visually isolated from at least some crucial determining forces. So the task became to socialize realism, to place recognizable human beings against the background of the historical and social forces that carry them forward.

An article in the theatre programme for *Destiny* argued that what Edgar had achieved in his play was to place the bourgeois drama in dialectical relation to agitprop theatre, and thus create a synthesis of individual motives and societal forces (Nuttall et al. 1977: 38). The result was the state-of-the-nation play, which tended to focus on specific, fully realized individual characters (Jed in *Magnificence*, Susan in *Plenty*, Major Rolfe in *Destiny* and Peter Singer in *Singer* are among the most memorable roles in post-war political theatre), but always against a greater sense of history in motion. Their personal feelings, desires and anxieties are set against a backdrop that enriches, rather than simplifies, the character portraits. The structure of the plays still derives from agitprop (cf. Itzin 1980: 146; Edgar et al. 1979: 16; Edgar 1988: 171–2) while the texture of the scenes owes more to realism.[3]

In this ability to hold together the public and the private in its grand visions of Britain and Britishness, the state-of-the-nation play reflects the structure of the nation-state. This was the basic building block of a system of geopolitical organization dating back to the Peace of Westphalia of 1648 that ended the Thirty Years War. Under the Westphalian system, the world is divided into nation-states that mutually recognize each other's sovereignty over their internal territorial domains. Together they form a balance of power and have collective jurisdiction over the globe (Watson 1992).

Two things are brought together in the nation-state. The state is a unit of public political organization and it bears responsibility for justice, reason and law; the nation on the other hand binds people together through shared temperament, language, history, culture, landscape and so on. These two aspects roughly correspond to the two forces at work in the state-of-the-nation play; the conceptual structures of agitprop have an affinity with the judicial generality of the state, while the experiential immediacy of realism finds its equivalent in the sensuous particularity of the nation. This helps us see more clearly what is politically and dramatically distinctive about the state-of-the-nation play. The personal is the means of experiencing the conceptual, while the conceptual structure is a way of understanding the personal.

Plenty traces the decline and fall of Susan Traherne from the intensity of experience as a British intelligence operative dropped behind enemy lines during the Second World War, through the bathos of peacetime, a marriage of dwindling interest, and finally her descent into something like madness by the early 1960s. All of this is played out against some key landmarks of post-war British social and political history: the Festival of Britain in 1951, the Suez crisis of 1956. We understand her growing alienation from people and places through the compromise and apathy of Britain's political class, and we experience that compromise and apathy through our intense engagement with Susan's individual trajectory.

This coordination of private and public, nation and state, operates at a thematic level, as these plays often diagnose an imbalance of nation and state as a primary ill. In *Destiny*, Major Rolfe's speech that explains why he has become an English fascist is explained as a shift of loyalty to the protectors of nation over the state that failed to protect his son (Edgar 1987: 377–8). In *The Churchill Play* the closing down of state-wide political freedom is theatrically felt as the closing down of individual liberty and in the desecration of the countryside. That the nation-state should be held up in this way is unsurprising since for at least two centuries it has been a primary focus for political aspiration: from the European nationalist movements of the nineteenth century, through the anti-colonial movements of the mid-twentieth, right up to formation of regional assemblies in Britain and the struggle for a Palestinian homeland, political struggles have focused their ambitions on the territorial coincidence of nation and state.

As the 1970s turned into the 1980s, several factors conspired to make state-of-the-nation plays less writable. For one thing, they were expensive to stage and in a climate of Thatcherite cuts in arts subsidy and the rise of business sponsorship, cast sizes of 20 or more became harder to defend. There were, also, criticisms from within the left of the sexual politics of these plays (e.g. Wandor 1980).

But underlying some, if not all, of these challenges lay a deeper global shift. In Howard Brenton's *The Romans in Britain* (National Theatre, 1980), an envoy from the neighbouring tribal leader, Cassivellaunel, tries to warn that the Romans are coming.

It is an army of red leather and brass.
It is a ship.
It is a whole thing. It is a monster. It has machines. [. . .]
They have come from the other side of the World. And they are one.
One whole. [. . .]
Understand. The Romans are different. They are – (*He gestures, trying to find the word. He fails. He tries again.*) A nation. Nation. What? A great family? No. A people? No. They are one, huge thing. (Brenton 1989: 18, 20)

His failure to find the right words suggests the unimaginable scale of this technology of destruction, this entirely new system of human organization. The play's premiere was roughly contemporary with the emergence of a new political phenomenon, also of unimaginable scale, involving a vast and growing totality of technology and people: globalization.

Globalization

There are many competing definitions of globalization. Some stress the speed and volume of our communications, others the blending and clashing of world cultures; I want to adhere to a more narrowly economic definition. In other words, by globalization, I mean global neo-liberalism, the global extension of capitalism under neo-liberal policies.

In the early seventies, a series of worldwide economic shocks transformed the international economy. Richard Nixon's decision to abandon the convertibility of the dollar to gold kicked away what had been the central support of currency stability since the Second World War. Currencies could now rise and fall without ceiling or safety net. Almost at the same time OPEC (the Organization of Petroleum Exporting Countries) increased the price of oil threefold, which meant a huge increase in industrial running costs in all the petroleum-importing (or 'NOPEC') countries. To meet their short-term obligations they were forced to take out loans. As it happened, the banks had huge amounts of money to lend, in the form of petrodollars (the petroleum profits being made by OPEC countries, denominated in dollars and deposited in northern banks). Nixon's action had been de facto to devalue the dollar, so, as the decade wore on, the developing countries, principally in Africa and South America, which had taken out large dollar-denominated loans, found it harder and harder to plan or repay their debts. Loans were added to loans and between 1973 and 1982 the indebtedness of the non-petroleum-exporting developing world increased fivefold (Ellwood 2001: 43).

Between 1981 and 1983 a succession of South American countries experienced a calamitous currency crisis and reported that they were likely to default on their loans. The IMF (International Monetary Fund), bereft of its former responsibility for managing the currency system anchored to the dollar, suddenly found a new role, handling the consolidation and renegotiation of its outstanding loans.

As a result the debt negotiations included strings. 'Structural adjustment' is the polite term for the forcible imposition of neo-liberal policies on vulnerable states: it meant a programme of sweeping privatization, trade liberalization, deregulation, significant cuts to government expenditure and a preference for interest-rate controls as the main lever of economic management. These policies forcibly opened the economies of the developing world to the global market, unifying the world's economy dramatically, and creating vast new sources of raw materials and labour, which saw a swathe of northern-hemisphere international corporations becoming truly global ones. This exacerbated industrial changes in the developed world, with manufacturing jobs being rapidly exported to countries where the labour was more competitive (lower-waged), the tax environment more business-friendly (cheaper), and health and safety standards more relaxed (or just lax).

The global expansion made possible by the neo-liberalization of the world's economies has allowed global corporations and global currency traders to accumulate economic power that is rapidly overtaking that of states. An Institute for Policy Studies report produced in 2000 showed that of the 100 largest economies in the world, only 49 are countries; the rest are corporations (Anderson and Cavanagh 2000). The comparison of corporate turnover with GDP is not the whole story, but it does remain startling that General Motors has a larger economy than Denmark, or that Wal-Mart's annual sales are greater than the combined GDP of Pakistan, Peru and Hungary.

The balance of power between states and capital has certainly shifted. Conducted across computer networks, traded in offshore financial centres, weightlessly transacted in virtual space, capital can move against countries now with extraordinary speed and power; the French government in 1981, the British government in 1992, the Asian tigers in 1997. Foreign exchange trading in the world's financial centres exceeds a trillion dollars every day, more than all the world's currency reserves, and almost twenty times the GDP of the OECD countries.

251

Dan Rebellato

Through this power, transnational corporations can play states off against each other by setting internal transfer prices to exploit the cheapest tax regimes, and through the game of regulatory arbitrage create the conditions for what Leo Panitch calls 'competitive austerity' (1994: 89), as governments engage in a race to the bottom, competing with each other to offer the least resistance to the path of profit. It is a group of twenty-first-century institutions playing cat and mouse with a seventeenth-century system of geopolitical organization.

One of the other effects of this has been to shake nation apart from state. In an attempt to retrieve some regulatory authority over global capital, states are compelled to join forces and create supranational jurisdictions, potential superstates, like the European Union, the African Union, OPEC, the UN and so on. Meanwhile, in the same period, and partly due to a desire to create local-level institutions that can protect regional diversity, countries have been fragmenting into smaller and smaller devolved units. So nations are getting smaller and more numerous, while states are getting larger and fewer. Nation – in the jargon – is being unbundled from state.

The state-of-the-nation play mirrored the nation-state in its mapping of the political onto the personal, and the general onto the particular. But if the values of nation and state no longer coincide at the territorial level, this raises a problem for the state-of-the-nation play.

Beyond the state-of-the-nation play

In 1983, two plays, both by state-of-the-nation writers, show the values of nation becoming dramatically uncoupled from those of state. In January, David Hare's *A Map of the World* (National Theatre) – a play very much about the early phases of globalization – is set at a UNESCO conference on global poverty and we watch a row brewing over the political responsibility of writers. The first half shows these issues unwinding through a complex series of theatrical frames that requires us continually to adjust our sense of what we are watching and from whose perspective we are watching it. But it takes an odd turn in the second half when the two antagonists in the debate confront each other and Peggy, an actress who is hanging around the conference for some reason, offers herself as the prize to whoever wins the argument. It's an unsatisfactory narrative turn, to put it mildly, and it's been criticized for that, but one way of understanding it is as a metonymic working through of a crisis in the solidity of the nation-state. Here we see the personal and the particular – values associated with nation – being subordinated to rational argument – a value associated with the state.

Meanwhile, in October of the same year, Howard Barker's *A Passion in Six Days* opened at the Sheffield Crucible. It is also set at a conference, this time the Labour Party annual conference, and in a pivotal scene in the play, the idealist John Axt proposes a motion to conference that 'Love, family, parenthood, marriage, are the primary experiences of the human animal, it is there that socialism must work its transformations if changes in our economic life are to have any meaning' (Barker 1985: 31). By proposing a socialism of personal relations, Axt is trying to bring more closely together the private and public, and, by analogy, the values of nation and state. The proposal, however, is noisily derided and shouted down. To one of his next plays, *The Castle* (RSC: The Pit, 1985), Barker gives the epigraph, 'what is Politics but the absence of Desire?' (1990: 197), as if the imaginative experience of that conference had confirmed to him that socialism cannot be reconciled with sexual politics, that the state was sundered from nation. Almost from here on, Barker pretty much abandons any attempt to coordinate the two, preferring an ever more intense focus on the irruptive qualities of desire.

What we see here is a parting of the ways. The state-of-the-nation play – understood as a play properly addressing itself to, and founding itself in, the values of the nation-state – ceases to operate. One shift in the state-of-the-nation play is to locate it in an institution and bypass the nation-state as such, hence plays about Fleet Street (*Pravda*), the City (*Serious Money*, Royal Court, 1987) and, recently, the privatized railways (*The Permanent Way*, Out of Joint, 2003). David Hare's 'state-of-the-nation trilogy', meanwhile, *Racing Demon* (1990), *Murmuring Judges* (1991) and *The Absence of War* (1992; all National Theatre), actually comprises a 'state-of-the-state' trilogy, anatomizing the church, the judiciary and the executive respectively, and the nation as such barely comes into it. The characters in those plays personify neither the nation nor the state; they are just individuals within the state. Compared with *Plenty*'s thoroughgoing integration of Susan's story with post-war history, the personal stories – for example the subplot about a gay vicar in *Racing Demon* – are cursory and cuttable, incompletely linked to the grander debates running through the play (Hare 1990: 69–71). And perhaps the reason why the trilogy is so suffused with a sense of defeat and stasis is because the nation-state no longer provides a site of hope and liberation.

The problem, increasingly, is that old-style state-of-the-nation plays can't cohere dramatically any more; their analysis of state is hamstrung by trying to couple it to nation – because patterns of power and injustice extend well beyond the boundaries of nation – while the focus on nation is improperly widened to state level, and the particularity is lost. To express that less abstractly, the problem with Peter Flannery's *Singer*, which shares many features of the state-of-the-nation play, is that when he writes well about history, he writes badly about the protagonist, and when he writes well about the protagonist he travesties the history. In David Hare's *The Absence of War* – a fictionalized account of the Labour Party in the run-up to the 1992 general election – it seems to me that a similar problem emerges; the more truthful the play is about its hero, the more unpersuasive its analysis of the politics, and vice versa. We might well accept the story of a man straitjacketed by advisers and speechwriters, but the idea that Labour lost in 1992 because Neil Kinnock wasn't allowed to speak his mind is risible.

Conversely, one might see the raft of plays that tried to engage with the natural landscape – like Caryl Churchill's *Fen* (Joint Stock, 1983), Sue Glover's *Bondagers* (Traverse Theatre, 1991), Rona Munro's *The Maiden Stone* (Hampstead Theatre, 1995) or Stuart Paterson's *King of the Fields* (Traverse Theatre, 1999) – as plays about nation, isolated from the state. Similarly, there are plays about the lived experience of a particular city that do not care to locate that city within a sense of the wider state – plays like Jim Cartwright's *Road* (Royal Court, 1986), Chris Hannan's *The Evil Doers* (Bush Theatre, 1990) or David Harrower's *Kill the Old, Torture their Young* (Traverse Theatre, 1998). And others that investigate the resources of local language, or tradition, or memory; a play like Caryl Churchill's *The Skriker* (National Theatre: Cottesloe, 1994) addresses all of these things, without seeming obliged to expand or contract its imaginative limits to anything resembling the boundaries of the territorial state.

The critics perhaps saw a state-of-the-nation play in Ravenhill's *Some Explicit Polaroids* (Out of Joint, 1999) because it ranges panoramically across London, alternating between private and public spaces: a hospital, an airport, the terrace of the House of Commons. Its subject – a far-left activist, Nick, emerging from prison after 15 years for kidnapping and torturing Jonathan, an international currency trader – was inspired by Ernst Toller's *Hoppla! Such is Life!* (Theater am Nollendorfplatz, Berlin, 1927), whose fusion of agitprop with naturalism was a precursor of the state-of-the-nation play. The subject also recalls the second half of Brenton's *Magnificence* in which Jed, after being imprisoned for squatting, plans to kill the housing minister. In the event, this attempt at a situationist gesture is amateurishly bungled, part of Brenton's lament for the corrosion of the counter-culture and its political firmness of purpose. In the climactic scene of *Some Explicit Polaroids*, Nick and Jonathan meet; in place of the scene we might imagine, revenge of one on the other, they in fact discover that they are 'rather nostalgic about the time we spent together . . . when I hated you. I knew where I stood' (Ravenhill 2001: 310–11). In a sense, they are nostalgic for a time when one could write state-of-the-nation plays.[4]

Writing the Global

Caryl Churchill's *This is a Chair* (Royal Court, 1997) takes the collapse of the political system and turns it into theatrical form. The play comprises eight scenes, each of which is given a grand title addressing a major theme of public political debate. The scenes that are played out under these titles, however, bear no obvious connection with their suggested topics. 'The War in Bosnia', for example, introduces a scene in which Mary turns up late for a dinner-date and has to admit she has double-booked herself. In 'The Labour Party's Slide to the Right' we watch the aftermath of a man jumping from the window of a third-floor flat. This dissonance between the general and particular is, in a sense, the rendering in theatrical form of the drifting apart of nation from state.

It is not quite true to say that there are no connections of any kind between the titles and the scenes. The experience of watching the play is often to find very distant resonances between one and the other. One scene, for example, depicts a family dinner table, the parents encouraging their daughter to eat her food. The title, 'Pornography and Censorship', exerts a gravitational pull on the scene, and the father's lines, 'Have a special bite of daddy's' and 'if you don't eat your dinner you know what's going to happen to you' (Churchill 1999: 11), take on a sexually suggestive tone – one that recedes when the same scene is repeated, word for word, later in the play under the title 'The Northern Ireland Peace Process' (28). The play offers both an experience of radical dissonance and an affirmation of the desire to build connections between the general and the particular.

Crucially, it is the aesthetic form of the play that engenders this complex experience, in particular that kind of aesthetic experience usually referred to as 'the sublime'. In such experiences, according to Kant's influential formulation in *Critique of Judgment*, the sublime is an experience both of displeasure and of pleasure before objects of overwhelming scale or power. We experience displeasure because the sight before our senses is simply too big to take in as a whole and therefore strikes the imagination (which processes our visual experience) as infinite; meanwhile our understanding none the less recognizes that all objects are finite. The clash between the understanding and the imagination causes the displeasure. The pleasure comes from the recognition that however great and powerful objects of the experience may be, the power of our understanding is greater still, and always able to assert itself over those objects: 'that is sublime which even to be able to think of demonstrates a faculty of the mind that surpasses every measure of the senses' (Kant 2000: 134).

Whilst *This is a Chair* does not necessarily offer an experience of the sublime as such, it does stage radical dissonance between objects of the understanding (the titles) and objects of experience (the scenes). This is a reasonably clear instance of such dissonance, but there are several other instances of contemporary plays which contain deliberately clashing or contradictory elements that make the play hard to submit both to the imagination and to the understanding. In Martin Crimp's *Attempts on Her Life* (Royal Court Upstairs, 1997) we are presented with 17 scenarios in which the only consistent link is the name Anne (and variations on it). This figure is never seen and remains a conceptual object; however, it is virtually impossible to reconcile what we learn about her through the scenes with the idea of a single offstage figure suggested by the repeated name and the title. In Sarah Kane's *Blasted* (Royal Court, 1995) what we see happening and what we understand to be happening are pulled radically apart as the Leeds hotel room that we have been watching appears to be in the centre of a civil war somewhere overseas.[5]

In their stagings of sublime dissonance, these plays are responding keenly to transformations in the world around them, and to complete the explanation that links their dramaturgy to globalization, it is worth pursuing the Kantian analysis a little further. In one sense, the nation-state was a way of coordinating and realizing our fundamental ethical commitments. The influential Kantian ethical model holds that our moral commitments must be both universal, in that they must apply universally and disinterestedly, and also particular, in that they are founded on the irreducible and irreplaceable value of each person for their own sake, measured against no external standard. (Other ethical traditions – consequentialist or Aristotelian – might express these values differently but agree that a version of both of these conditions should be met.)

The nation-state holds these two levels together because the state is ideally the site in which universalist moral principles are realized (maintaining distributive justice, upholding human rights, equality before the law, etc.) while the nation is where you experience and express respect for places, traditions, the land, the people and so on as ends and values in themselves. Our local and universal commitments sometimes come into conflict but, in a properly functioning nation-state, they can, all things being equal, be resolved. An example of this would be a progressive and redistributive tax system which respects particular circumstances but also general principles of justice.

But if, as in the era of globalization, nation and state do not map effectively onto one another, it is harder and harder for the nation-state to be an adequate means of realizing our ethical commitments. This is why it is at the level of aesthetic form that these plays respond to the world. They are staging our world's current inability to hold together the two vital principles of ethical judgement, which is a matter of the form of our judgements, not their content. None the less, in their evocation of the sublime or quasi-sublime experiences, they also affirm the desire to express ethical judgement in the world, and the possibility of this judgement even against overwhelming odds (cf. Kant 2000: 145–6). Put more simply, the plays dramaturgically hold apart the understanding and the imagination but aesthetically affirm the possibility of their reconciliation. The theatre that responds most fundamentally to the geopolitical crisis is that which most acutely explores the limits of aesthetic pleasure.

This should serve as an answer to those commentators who see in the theatre a retreat from politics in the decline of the state-of-the-nation play. It is a common complaint by *soi-disant* political critics that these plays engage in what Vera Gottlieb called the 'artistic treatment of individuals in an increasingly vague or undefined context' (2004: 413). The implication is that by abstracting people from their particular circumstances these writers mystify their real relations with the world. Michael Billington of the *Guardian* has a persistent tendency to criticize playwrights for not specifying exactly where their plays take place.[6] However, one might propose instead that these writers are offering a vision of ethical judgement and responsibility in a state where politics has failed us.

Indeed, what we see, time and again, through plays of the global-ization era, is the imaginative boundaries of the playwright sweeping beyond the arbitrary boundaries of the outmoded nation-state. In Robert Holman's *Rafts and Dreams* (Royal Court Upstairs, 1991), we watch a couple getting to know their new neighbour; offstage, in their garden, an old tree-stump is being dug up. At the end of the first half they get the roots up and discover underneath it an underground lake. As the second half begins, we discover that the water has risen and flooded the entire world. The bulk of the second half takes place on a raft several thousands of feet of water above land.

The successive scenes of Caryl Churchill's *Far Away* (Royal Court Upstairs, 2000) take us from a local act of brutality to a state apparatus of televised trials and public executions and finally to a world engaged in global conflict, in which national boundaries are erased by a Hobbesian war of all against all. This play, in the sublime questions it asks about relations between the scenes, echoes the deterritorialization of Kane's *Blasted*; a violent slippage of place signalled by its first stage direction, which places the action in a hotel room 'so expensive it could be anywhere in the world' (2001: 3).

David Greig's *The Cosmonaut's Last Message to the Woman He Once Loved in the Former Soviet Union* (Paines Plough, 1999) and *San Diego* (Tron Theatre Company, 2003) display a globetrotting dramaturgy that sweeps us from continent to continent – and, in the former play, into orbit around the earth – in a way that resembles the panoramic mode of the state-of-the-nation play, but curious echoes – a phrase, a memory, a vision – pass between the intertwined stories in a way that does not obey the causal logic that organizes the geography. The deterritorializing quality of these plays perhaps expresses a growing sense that territory is no longer an adequate focus for political aspira-tion, that the forces that threaten us require the bursting of national boundaries in favour of a more cosmopolitan sense of ourselves as global citizens with rights and obligations that span the world. Kant characterizes such a right as the sense that 'a violation of right on one place of the earth is felt in all' (1999: 330). The refusal of these writers always to specify the location of their plays may be a refusal to let ethical judgement stop at national boundaries: even when these writers are addressing contemporary issues they want to get at the fundamental ethical issues beneath. So Pinter does not mention the Kurds in *Mountain Language*, Kane does not mention Bosnia in *Blasted*, Greig does not mention Afghanistan in *The American Pilot* (RSC: The Other Place, 2005). We do not know where Philip Ridley's *The Pitch-*

fork Disney (Bush Theatre, 1991) takes place, or Kane's *Cleansed* (Royal Court, 1998), or Crimp's *Fewer Emergencies* (Royal Court Upstairs, 2005). This is a pre-political strategy, appropriate for an age in which the national political institutions are being overpowered by global capital, and the international institutions that might give contingent force to our developing cosmopolitan sense have not yet been built.

The state-of-the-nation play continues to stand in certain critics' imaginations as the pinnacle of political playmaking in Britain. Its emergence was in response to a particular socio-political conjunction and its decline was also. It would be a mistake to believe, however, that the decline of the state-of-the-nation play is anything other than the disappearance of a form whose usefulness had passed and whose purchase on contemporary reality had diminished. Globalization has created dramatic and new conditions – and it is a testament to the abiding power of the political tradition that the rules of political theatre have been transformed in response. Where realism seemed essential, now a kind of non-realism seems so; where politics was the object, now it is ethics; where once playwrights proclaimed 'messages first' (Brenton and Hammond 1973), now aesthetic experiment may be the right means to achieve an effective political response to the challenges of a consumer culture and a marketized world.

Notes

1   This was obviously the view of Peter Wilby, the editor of the *New States-man*, the leading magazine of the left, who briefly dropped the theatre review column in September 2003 because there weren't enough political plays going on: 'If there [were] a new play by David Hare every week, then we would have one, but there isn't' (Lister 2003). David Hare is, of course, one of the more distinguished exponents of the state-of-the-nation play.
2   They had an explicit influence on these writers, who sometimes referred to themselves as 'New Jacobeans' (e.g. Brenton and Mitchell 1987: 198) and insisted on the freedom to write with the kind of variety of style and texture of their Renaissance predecessors (Brenton et al. 1975: 13; Hare and Prowting 1997: 6). David Hare remarks that when he and Brenton wrote *Pravda* (National Theatre: Olivier, 1985), 'we wanted to rewrite *Richard III*' (1991: 135). These aspirations were recognized and confirmed by the theatres. In 1977, Barrie Keeffe wrote *A Mad World, My Masters* (Joint Stock, 1977) inspired by Thomas Middleton's city comedy of the same name. In 1983, David Edgar was brought in as dramaturg on Howard Davies's

Dan Rebellato

production of Shakespeare and Fletcher's *Henry VIII* (Chambers 2004: 119), and a year after *Pravda*, Howard Barker's rewrite of Middleton's *Women Beware Women* opened at the Royal Court. At the end of the decade, Peter Flannery's *Singer* (1989) opened at the RSC's Swan Theatre, designed in emulation of an Elizabethan inn-yard theatre, with a text that consciously drew on Elizabethan dramatic devices to set its scene.

3 The distance that these writers have moved from the schematics of agitprop may be witnessed in the frequency with which they resort to showing people preparing agitprop plays as a shorthand for the naïvety of the post-1968 generation; see *The Churchill Play* (Brenton 1986: 142), *Teendreams* (Edgar 1991: 111–13), *Maydays* (Edgar 1991: 261) and *Singer* (Flannery 1989: 64–5). The moment of street theatre in Brenton's *The Genius* (Royal Court, 1983) is presented slightly more affectionately (1989: 200–1).

4 Although there was no conscious influence of *Magnificence* on *Some Explicit Polaroids*, Ravenhill is certainly familiar with that tradition, and indeed, at Bristol University in 1987, acted in a production of *Teendreams* rewritten for the Drama Department by David Edgar.

5 This change is ambiguous, though the dialogue between Ian and the Soldier certainly suggests that he is no longer in Britain: 'don't know what the sides are here', Ian admits (Kane 2001: 40), and remarks that his Welsh accent has been replaced by an English one because 'I live there' – not 'here'. The soldier, noting his disorientation, notes sardonically 'haven't been here long have you' (41).

6 See, for example, his *Guardian* reviews of David Greig's *The American Pilot*, which accuses him of 'calculated geographical imprecision' (7 May 2005), and of Mark Ravenhill's *The Cut*, in which he dourly notes that the play is 'intended as a political fable' (1 March 2006) and does not consider this a strength.

Primary reading

Barker, Howard (1980). *The Love of a Good Man*. London: John Calder.
Barker, Howard (1985). *A Passion in Six Days and Downchild*. London: John Calder.
Barker, Howard (1990). *Collected Plays. Vol. One*. London: John Calder. (Includes *Claw* and *The Castle*.)
Bolt, Robert (1977). *State of Revolution*. London: Heinemann.
Brenton, Howard (1986). *Plays: One*. London: Methuen. (Includes *Magnificence*, *The Churchill Play*, *Weapons of Happiness* and *Epsom Downs*.)
Brenton, Howard (1989). *Plays: Two*. London: Methuen. (Includes *The Romans in Britain*.)
Brenton, Howard, and Hare, David (1985). *Pravda*. London: Methuen.
Cartwright, Jim (1990). *Road*. London: Methuen.

Churchill, Caryl (1996). *Plays: Two*. London: Methuen. (Includes *Fen* and *Serious Money*.)

Churchill, Caryl (1997). *Plays: Three*. London: Nick Hern. (Includes *The Skriker*.)

Churchill, Caryl (1999). *This is a Chair*. London: Nick Hern.

Churchill, Caryl (2000). *Far Away*. London: Nick Hern.

Crimp, Martin (1997). *Attempts on Her Life*. London: Faber and Faber.

Crimp, Martin (2002). *Face to the Wall and Fewer Emergencies*. London: Faber and Faber.

Edgar, David (1987). *Plays: One*. London: Methuen. (Includes *Destiny*.)

Edgar, David (1990). *Plays: Two*. London: Methuen. (Includes *Nicholas Nickleby*.)

Edgar, David (1991). *Plays: Three*. London: Methuen. (Includes *Maydays* and *Teendreams*.)

Flannery, Peter (1989). *Singer*. London: Nick Hern.

Glover, Sue (2001). *Bondagers*. London: Methuen.

Greig, David (2005a). *The Cosmonaut's Last Message to the Woman He Once Loved in the Former Soviet Union*. London: Faber and Faber.

Greig, David (2005b). *The American Pilot*. London: Faber and Faber.

Hannan, Chris (1991). *The Evil Doers*. London: Nick Hern.

Hare, David (1990). *Racing Demon*. London: Faber and Faber.

Hare, David (1991). *Writing Left-Handed*. London: Faber and Faber.

Hare, David (1993a). *Absence of War*. London: Faber and Faber.

Hare, David (1993b). *Murmuring Judges*. London: Faber and Faber.

Hare, David (1996). *Plays: One*. London: Faber and Faber. (Includes *Plenty*.)

Hare, David (1997). *Plays: Two*. London: Faber and Faber. (Includes *A Map of the World*.)

Hare, David (2003). *The Permanent Way*. London: Faber and Faber.

Harrower, David (1998). *Kill the Old, Torture their Young*. London: Methuen.

Holman, Robert (1991). *Rafts and Dreams*. London: Methuen.

Kane, Sarah (2001). *Complete Plays*. London: Methuen.

Munro, Rona (1995). *The Maiden Show*. London: Nick Hern.

Paterson, Stuart (1999). *King of the Fields*. London: Nick Hern.

Pinter, Harold (1998). *Plays Four*. London: Faber and Faber. (Includes *Mountain Language*.)

Ravenhill, Mark (2001). *Plays: One*. London: Methuen. (Includes *Some Explicit Polaroids*.)

Ridley, Philip (1991). *The Pitchfork Disney*. London: Methuen.

Toller, Ernst (1928). *Hoppla! Such is Life!* London: E. Benn.

Further reading

Anderson, Sarah, and Cavanagh, John (2000). *Top 200: The Rise of Corporate Global Power*. Washington, DC: Institute for Policy Studies.

Brenton, Howard, and Hammond, Jonathan (1973). 'Messages First: An Interview with Howard Brenton', *Gambit: International Theatre Review* vi:23, 24–32.

Brenton, Howard, and Mitchell, Tony (1987). 'The Red Theatre under the Bed', *New Theatre Quarterly* iii:11, 195–201.

Brenton, Howard, Itzin, Catherine, and Trussler, Simon (1975). 'Petrol Bombs through the Proscenium Arch', *Theatre Quarterly* v:17, 4–20.

Chambers, Colin (2004). *Inside the Royal Shakespeare Company: Creativity and the Institution*. London: Routledge. Edgar, David (1988). *The Second Time as Farce: Reflections of the Drama of Mean Times*. London: Lawrence and Wishart.

Edgar, David, Barker, Clive, and Trussler, Simon (1979). 'Towards a Theatre of Dynamic Ambiguities', *Theatre Quarterly* ix:33, 3–23.

Ellwood, Wayne (2001). *No-Nonsense Guide to Globalization*. London: Verso and New Internationalist.

Gottlieb, Vera (2004). '1979 and After: A View' in Baz Kershaw (ed.), *The Cambridge History of British Theatre. Vol. 3: Since 1895*. Cambridge: Cambridge University Press, 412–25.

Hare, David, and Prowting, Janet (1997). 'Writing for His Time' (interview), programme for *Skylight*. London: Vaudeville Theatre, 5–9.

Hemming, Sarah (1999). 'Review: *Some Explicit Polaroids*', *Financial Times*, 19 October, 20. (Reprinted *Theatre Record* 19, 1356.)

Itzin, Catherine (1980). *Stages in the Revolution: Political Theatre in Britain since 1968*. London: Methuen.

Kant, Immanuel (1999). *Practical Philosophy*. Cambridge: Cambridge University Press.

Kant, Immanuel (2000). *Critique of the Power of Judgment*. Cambridge: Cambridge University Press.

Lister, David (2003). 'A Dramatic Move, but it is Wrong and Misguided', *Independent*, 13 September, 20.

Nightingale, Benedict (1999). 'Review: *Some Explicit Polaroids*', *The Times*, 16 October, 21. (Reprinted *Theatre Record* 1999, 1354.)

Nuttall, Jeff, Campbell, Ken, Stafford-Clark, Max, Howard, Roger, Calder, John, and Gill, Anton (1977). 'Gambit Discussion: Political Theatre', *Gambit: International Theatre Review* 31, 13–43.

Panitch, Leo (1994). 'Globalisation and the State' in Ralph Miliband and Leo Panitch (eds.), *Between Globalism and Nationalism*. London: Merlin, 60–93.

Wandor, Michelene (1980). 'Sexual Politics and the Strategy of Socialist Theatre', *Theatre Quarterly* ix:36, 28–30.

Watson, Adam (1992). *The Evolution of International Society: A Comparative Historical Analysis*. London: Routledge.

Chapter 13

Theatre for a Media-Saturated Age

Sarah Gorman

Seeking to monitor significant theatrical developments of the 1990s, Andy Lavender observed an 'aesthetic' shift in theatre-making, towards new forms of writing, new ways of 're-imagining' the theatre space and 'the increasing presence of multi-media performance' (1999: 180). Certainly, the sheer volume of multimedia work taking place across the country during the past twenty-five years,[1] and the incorporation of multimedia techniques into mainstream British theatre productions, suggests that contemporary theatre practitioners are keen to exploit the opportunities afforded by new technologies.[2] Focusing on Forced Entertainment's CD-ROM *Nightwalks* (1998), Blast Theory's interactive 3D game *Desert Rain* (1999) and Stan's Cafe's 'film screening' *It's Your Film* (1998),[3] this chapter will explore a number of performative and ontological questions raised by the proliferation of mass-media communication and the inclusion of multimedia technologies in contemporary performance; questions informed by and in dialogue with recent developments in performance and postmodern theory that form the backdrop to this chapter.

Over the past twenty-five years multimedia work has galvanized a great deal of critical attention within the field of theatre and performance studies, with the different manifestations of digital technology in computing, internet and recording technologies resulting in diverse critical and theatrical responses. Philip Auslander, for example, has returned to Walter Benjamin's pursuit of the *auratic*[4] in order to argue that contemporary understandings of 'live-ness' and 'mediatization' are based on distinctions that were unperceivable prior to the invention of analogue and digital recording technologies (Auslander 1999: 51). Jon McKenzie has explored the 'virtual' in performance and considers how the interface between human and technology in virtual reality simulations problematizes the distinction between human and technological performance (McKenzie 2003: 170). Meanwhile, discussing the Wooster Group's use of technology, Jennifer Parker-Starbuck has pointed to the emergence of a genre of 'cyborg theatre', which dramatizes the post-human body. (Parker Starbuck 2004: 219).

For companies such as Blast Theory, digital film-making and global positioning technologies enable them to produce interactive, inclusive online events. Other companies, including Forced Entertainment, use digital and new media technologies to create independent or tangential projects that sit alongside, or feature as part of, a new theatre project. In addition, Stan's Cafe employs a range of twentieth- and twenty-first-century media technologies and a number of low- and hi-tech innovations in their work. In some way each of these companies invites the spectator to explore and question the viewing conventions and expectations they bring to theatre events. In particular they often heighten the spectator's sense of disorientation by destabilizing the viewer's ability to distinguish between the real and the simulated, the live and the mediatized. Above all, these companies do not celebrate the incorporation of new technologies for their own sake, but rather respond to the notion that these innovations, and importantly, *the discourse surrounding these innovations*, have had a profound effect upon the understanding of western ontology; that is, what it means to live in a 'digital age'. The preoccupations emerging from this work, if they cohere at all, appear to share a concern with the attempt to question and legitimate the continued pursuit of the 'real' and 'authentic' in the representational realm.

Philip Auslander uses a quotation from Forced Entertainment's *A Decade of Forced Entertainment* (1994) as an introduction to his text *Liveness*. The quotation reads, 'why would you make live work in an age of mass communication? Why work in more or less the only field which still insists on presence?'[5] This question preoccupies the companies discussed in this chapter as each argues for the continued relevance of live theatrical performance in a 'media-saturated' culture.[6] From this, I will argue that their impetus to 'reimagine' the theatre space and to produce 'new forms of writing' can be interpreted as a response to the cultural shift which has emerged in what Roger Luckhurst has termed 'The Third Industrial Revolution – the digital one' (Luckhurst 2004: 787).

The 'digital revolution' marks a revolution in the speed and efficacy of information exchange. It also marks a move away from analogue recordings, which record data according to linear progression onto electronic tape. Digital recording technology enables sound, voice, text and image signals to be converted into binary code, which can then be compressed, manipulated or edited by computer and transmitted through high-speed internet and satellite connections. Digital media is also non-linear, so can be easily accessed at any point of the recording, rather than by scrolling through a tape from beginning to end.[7] In terms of mass-media communications, the revolution in digital technology facilitates the almost instantaneous exchange of information and screening of events between distant geographical locations. Innovations in digital technology in western societies have resulted in an unprecedented level of private and public usage of mobile telephones, personal computers, satellite navigation, internet file sharing and virtual gaming environments as well as almost constant access to contemporary news footage and publicly accessible online documentation. As McKenzie points out, 'more profoundly than the alphabet, printed book and factory, such technologies as digital media and the internet allow discourses and practices from different geographical and historical situations to be networked and patched together, their traditions to be electronically archived, played back, their forms and processes to become raw materials for other productions' (McKenzie 2001: 18). The sense that the human perception of time has 'speeded up' and that space between temporal instances appears to have 'diminished' in a postmodern age is articulated by philosophers such as Jean Baudrillard and Paul Virilio, who insist that successive innovations in print media, digital and warfare technology have caused a fundamental shift in the way contemporary societies negotiate the interrelationship between reality and representation. For instance, in *The Ecstasy of Communication* (1988) Baudrillard argues that the proliferation of news satellites positioned in space across the globe has enabled western civilization to receive information from previously 'distant' countries almost instantaneously, thereby causing the conception of the physical distance (space) between countries to decrease.[8] This point is further developed by Virilio in his 1995 essay 'Speed and Information: Cyberspace Alarm!', in which he argues:

Real time now prevails above both real space and the geosphere. The primacy of real time, of immediacy, over and above space and surface, is a fait accompli and has inaugural value (ushers a new epoch). Something nicely conjured up in a (French) advertisement praising cellular phones with the words: 'Planet Earth has never been this small'. This is a very dramatic moment in our relation with the world and for our vision of the world. [. . .] To have reached the light barrier, to have reached the speed of light, is a historical event which throws history in disarray and jumbles up the relation of the living being towards the world. (Virilio 1995: 1)

The companies discussed in this chapter are undoubtedly influenced by critical writings about altered perceptions of time and space in a postmodern age. I also consider that they are informed by Baudrillard and Jean Francois Lyotard's writings on the 'real' and the 'representable'.

Baudrillard holds that it is no longer possible to represent 'reality' in any meaningful way, as the overabundance of represented images has emptied the project of significance and meaning. He writes that:

All Western faith and good faith became engaged in this wager on representation: that a sign could refer to the depth of meaning, that a sign could be exchanged for meaning and that something could guarantee this exchange – God of course. But what if God himself can be simulated, that is to say can be reduced to the signs that constitute faith? Then the whole system becomes weightless, it is no longer itself anything but a gigantic simulation – not unreal, but a simulacrum, that is to say never exchanged for the real, but exchanged for itself, in an uninterrupted circuit without reference or circumference. (Baudrillard 1994: 5–6)

Baudrillard's essay 'The Precession of Simulacra' (1994) is significant to the discussion of the performance work in question, as it countenances the project of representation as problematic in the age of instantaneous media exchange. The 'weightless' value system and the uninterrupted circuit of simulation he invokes appear potent metaphors to employ when setting out to address and critique the ontological implications of the loss of the 'real'.

Addressing a more specific question of aesthetics, Lyotard has developed Kant's philosophy of the sublime to argue that a postmodern art-work should frame the project of representation as one of impossibility.[9] In *The Postmodern Condition: A Report on Knowledge* (1979), Lyotard attempts to arrive at an understanding of 'the postmodern'. He writes:

> The postmodern would be that which [...] puts forward the un-presentable in presentation itself; that which denies itself the solace of good forms, the consensus of a taste which would make it possible to share collectively the nostalgia for the unattainable; that which searches for new presentations, not in order to enjoy them but in order to impart a stronger sense of the unpresentable. (Lyotard 1979: 81)

Lyotard is responding to a societal shift which he considers to be marked by innovations in 'technology' and 'techniques of economic redeployment'. He questions who will have access to the (digital) data stored in myriad 'machines', and suggests that the 'old poles of attraction represented by nation states, parties, professions, institutions and historical traditions are losing their attraction' (1979: 14). In his pursuit of a postmodern aesthetics Lyotard calls for a dissolution of the grand narratives[10] represented by 'nation states' and 'historical traditions' and to work instead to 'invent allusions to the conceivable which cannot be presented', be 'witness to the unpresentable' and to 'wage war on totality' (1979: 81–2). In marking the 'powerlessness of the faculty of presentation' and the 'nostalgia for presence felt by the human subject' Lyotard could be seen to be setting out a challenge for contemporary artists. Indeed, the more conventional stage work of the companies in question is often framed through an 'attempt strategy' whereby the figures on stage attempt to represent, or attempt to allow meaning to emerge, or attempt to locate the 'real'. These attempts regularly break down and reveal the project of representation to be one marked by failure and impossibility.

Liz Tomlin has been particularly critical of the work she considers to have been produced to correspond with aspects of postmodern cultural theory. She writes:

> In much of this 1990s experimental theatre the post-modern temptation to accept everything as simulation, to believe that nothing exists beyond mediated representations that cannot hold any claim to 'truth', led to a political stalemate. At its best, there was a charm in the performers' heroic efforts to find meaning and significance in a post-modern void, which the audience might recognise as its own. At its worst, this theatre reached the depths of pessimism as, obsessed with its own inadequacy, it spiralled deeper and deeper into meta-theatrical angst,

unable to gesture towards anything beyond its own ever-decreasing field of self-reference. (Tomlin 2004: 502–3)

Tomlin's critique does not appear to allow for the possibility that some examples of this performance work could be understood to adopt a critical relationship to the theory and aesthetics of postmodernism/ the digital. I argue that rather than being 'tempted' to 'accept everything as simulation' these artists are often galvanized to critique, rather than celebrate, postmodern aesthetics.

In addition to heeding Tomlin's critical voice, it may also be wise to reiterate a warning about constructing cultural artefacts as deterministically and radically responsive to new philosophies. For instance, Luckhurst points to the 'aggressive' claims made by George Landow about the possible 'cultural effects' of hypertext as a radical art-form. Luckhurst writes that the celebration of 'radical' hypertext by the academic community resulted in hypertext becoming 'not only an "embarrassingly literal embodiment" of Roland Barthes' idea of the "death of the author", but also somehow of Derridean textuality, Deleuzian rhizomatics, Bahktinian multivocality *and* Kristevian intertextuality all at the same time' (Luckhurst 2004: 793). Landow, being one of the first academics to investigate the relationship between an emerging aesthetic form and a body of poststructuralist ideas, is perhaps unfairly castigated for arguing for the urgency of the connections between new philosophies and a new art-form. I propose that the following performance work can be read through the lens of postmodern philosophy, with the possibility that it may stand as a critique of that work, rather than being necessarily guided by it.

Forced Entertainment

Forced Entertainment is a Sheffield-based collective that continues to produce on average one full-length theatre piece each year and in addition, has, since 1993, created durational performances, net art, installations, CD-ROMs, video and performance lectures which enable a theme introduced via the theatre work to be explored in a different medium. Many of Forced Entertainment's early theatre pieces used cinema as a reference point for intertextual narratives and scenarios, and Tim Etchells, the artistic director of the company, has revealed that '[w]e've talked a lot about growing up in a house with the TV always on in the corner of the room' (Etchells 1994: 109).

Preoccupations with mediatization, popular TV and film genres, and urban landscapes (specifically Sheffield as a city) have been articulated through a number of different art-forms utilized by the company.

The interest in cinema and the city has resulted in a number of collaborations with photographer Hugo Glendinning. *Red Room* (1994), *Ground Plans for Paradise* (1994), *Frozen Palaces* (1998) and *Nightwalks* celebrate the multiple narratives of city dwellers in a largely visual form which developed out of, but stood independent of, the theatre work. *Nightwalks* was released as an interactive CD-ROM in 1998, and offered the participant the opportunity to explore a number of deserted cityscapes and negotiate his or her way through a sequence of navigational panoramas by clicking on the links embedded within the images. Using Quick Time Virtual Reality, a number of photographs are superimposed to create the illusion of a 360-degree panorama. This effect was also used in *Frozen Palaces*, with an interior setting to enable the participant to move through the 'frozen' aftermath of domestic upheaval. Attempting to identify the unsettling nature of these works, Gabriella Giannachi suggests that:

> Invited to navigate and make sense of this textual world, the viewer finds that their navigation is at best circular and that explanation is impossible. [. . .] It is therefore from the clash of the live and mediated, and, more specifically, the clash between the possibility of movement innate in the construction of the work of art as installation and the condition of immobility derived from its existence as photographic still that the sense of illusion and estrangement experienced by the viewer originates. (Giannachi 2004: 39)

Giannachi appears to be suggesting that it is the hybrid quality of the work, as neither pure photograph nor pure installation, that the spectator finds unnerving. However, much of the unnerving aspect of the work could be attributable to the construction of the images themselves. They are presented against a backdrop of a looped sample of music. As the participant waits to move into the next virtual landscape, a number of images are flashed onto the screen in rapid succession. These include close-ups of money changing hands, a gun, scribbled notes, a man being grabbed from behind, a prostrate body lying on a cobbled street, a sheet of paper set on fire. The landscapes within the navigable panorama are all photographed at night, and include images of deserted back-streets, industrial waste-ground, empty car parks and dark alleyways. These images appear to borrow visual

Nightwalks by Forced Entertainment
Photo: Hugo Glendinning

vocabularies from detective books such as those by Raymond Chandler and make visual reference to Hitchcock's forays into film noir. Significantly, the detective and film noir genres are both predicated upon an internal drive towards plot resolution and narrative closure. Interestingly, in *Nightwalks*, each panorama offers only one possible point of transition between virtual spaces. The cursor is designed to change shape once it is pointed at a designated site; however, this occurs only once in each scenario. As a result, the participant experiences a comparatively linear, cyclical journey, one that might visually resemble a Möbius strip rather than a causal linear progression.[11]

The cyclical narrative journey denies any sense of definite resolution and appears at odds with the references to detective stories elsewhere. At the risk of making what Luckhurst might consider to be an overdeterministic claim about the relationship between postmodern theory and multi-narrative art forms, I would like to argue that the deferral of closure in *Nightwalks* does amount to what Lyotard might term a refusal of 'the solace of good forms' (Lyotard 1979: 81). The goal-oriented nature of the linear causal narrative ensures that closure is attainable, solving the indeterminacy of previous narrative enigmas. However, in this virtual game the participant is led back to the beginning of the journey, so no final sense of resolution or containment is conferred. Although it could be said that *Nightwalks* represents a very basic encounter with a virtual world, and was perhaps designed before 3D gaming software was readily accessible, it does seem unusual that the options for exploration are limited in each scenario. Marie-Laure Ryan points to an apparent consensus emerging in the field of narratology when she writes: 'thanks to the properties of reactivity, interactivity, volatility, and modularity, every run of a digital text can be turned into a performance of different virtualities. Out of

270

a limited number of elements, the computer allows the creation of a vast number of versions' (2004: 415). Forced Entertainment's encounter with this particular digital text, then, appears to forego the creation of multiple narratives in favour of a single, cyclical narrative.

The lack of recognizable contiguity between sites is also at odds with the recognized characteristics of hypertext, as Ryan states 'The placement of links or the timing of user action in a well-designed narrative or informational system cannot be a random act, unless the point is to signify randomness itself' (2004: 418). It is possible that Forced Entertainment's exploration of this alternative output is designed to 'signify randomness itself'; however, I would argue that the subversion of this form points to a rejection of the proposition that multi-variant narratives are necessarily cause for celebration. Adrian Heathfield has drawn parallels between *Nightwalks* and Lyotard's call for a postmodern aesthetic, noting that 'what's important about the role of the spectator here and the use of space is that the freedom to roam that you are ostensibly given is shown to be prescribed, to be an illusion. Again the spectator meets the limits of representation, or here the limits of what can be seen' (Heathfield in Glendinning et al. 2000: 21). Here the 'limits of representation' can be understood to refer to Lyotard's call to 'invent allusions to the conceivable which cannot be presented' (Lyotard 1979: 81). The amalgamation of a traditionally goal-driven genre and a customarily manifold method of navigation creates a productive tension to underscore the expectations the participant brings to this particular mode of viewing. The absence of a clear point of closure and the indeterminate relationship between images render the discrete images equivalent or equal in status. The combinatory equivalence between images and the possibility of endlessly pursuing the sequence of images could also be understood, if approached from the perspective of Baudrillard's 'radical negation of the sign', to point to a 'circuit' of simulations which endlessly refer to another simulation equally bereft of any totalizing meaning.

In engaging with a digital art-form, Forced Entertainment are pursuing the question of art in a digital age in order to confront the troubling realization that the 'equivalence' of signs, the refusal to mark one sign as more meaningful than others, points to a frustrating cycle of repeated, ultimately meaningless, images. Given that, as Landow argued, hypertext appeared to represent an inherently 'multilinear, laterally networked, democratic and interactive' (Landow 1997: 21) form, it would appear that any rejection of the form's multivalence stands as a critique of the proposition that it can be understood to be 'democratic'. *Nightwalks*, then, could be understood to critique the notion that the plural narrative possibilities ostensibly offered by hypertext offer cause for celebration. Instead this piece points the viewer towards a realization of the emptiness and meaninglessness of an endlessly circulating narrative. For Tomlin, this may have amounted to pessimistic defeatism, but it does underscore the negative evaluation embedded within Baudrillard's relativization of the sign.

Stan's Cafe

Stan's Cafe is a Birmingham-based company which works across a range of art-forms, but continues to identify itself primarily as a 'theatre company'. Installation pieces which consistently enjoy popularity on the international touring circuit include *It's Your Film*, initially conceived in 1998, *The Black Maze* (2000) and *Of All the People in the World* (2003).

It's Your Film is a performance installation which invites the audience member to witness a three-minute live performance for an audience of one. The audience member is invited to take his or her place in a small purpose-built booth and to look towards what appears to be a flat screen, but which is in fact a small aperture designed to replicate the ratio of a cinema screen in miniature. The performance and viewing space are reduced to zero visibility then, once in motion, the piece features a number of brightly illuminated images shown in rapid succession. An amalgamation of live action, video and slide projection and the use of Pepper's Ghost (angling mirrors offstage to produce the illusion of an actor's presence on stage) enable the company to give the illusion that these images are two-dimensional projections and so can be faded in and out as part of an absent, pre-recorded image. In addition, static images appear to pan sideways offscreen, or appear as if superimposed. A film noir-esque sound-track and the back-projection of a retreating landscape, viewed as if through the rear window of a car, reiterate the film noir aesthetic by inviting associations with early Hitchcock. Narrative clues (revealed through momentary glimpses of faces and figures) suggest a story of frustrated or lost love. The montage of images includes the sudden illumination of a match, as it is struck to light a cigarette; this action throws a male face into relief against the darkness of the interior of the performance space. The audience also witness a ring being removed from a finger, a love letter torn to shreds, and a detective working late at his desk (he holds up a slide to the light for closer scrutiny).

As with Forced Entertainment's *Nightwalks*, the pleasure of this piece comes in part from the recognition of the imperative to identify with the role of detective, and in part from a sense of wonderment about the level of virtuosity required to render such precise cinematic images in 'real time' and 'real space'. As with much of Forced Entertainment's work, the spectator is unsure as to which body of viewing conventions to draw upon in reading this piece. The knowledge of the proximity of live actors suggests the piece should be read as theatre, but the two-dimensional illusion of the images suggests that this is cinema. As a result, the spectator undergoes a kind of physiological disorientation. The visual vocabulary, the sound-track and the narrative clues are equally reminiscent of a recognizable film genre. It is only the slight shudder of the booth, the sound of sweeping and furniture movement, the rasp of flats being manoeuvred into place which evidence the labour involved in producing these images. *It's Your Film* is designed to draw the spectators' attention to the creation of the illusion. It also foregrounds the human labour behind the creation of the cinematic illusion. Although much of the action is 'live', the spectator must constantly draw comparisons between pre-recorded film footage and the live construction of these images, in the present moment. The piece does not invite the spectator to believe in the live images as cinematic illusions, but rather relies for its success upon the constant comparison between the viewer's recollection of a pre-recorded cinematic image and of a live theatre event. If we can identify the moving figures behind the screen as 'real' figures, then we might understand this piece as a theatrical rebuttal of Baudrillard's assertion that '[i]t is *now impossible to isolate the process of the real, or to prove the real*' (Baudrillard 1994: 21). Although a discourse of simulation could be seen to be brought into play by the company's decision to experiment with the construction of illusion, the piece does not support the idea that 'illusion is no longer possible'; rather it indulges in a certain celebration of theatrical mastery or virtuosity in bringing it into being. If the distinction between representation and simulation depends upon whether the originator is 'feigning' or 'pretending', then the company are unashamedly 'pretending' to be caught on celluloid.

Stan's Cafe could be seen to be responding to Baudrillard's proposition that it is impossible to 'prove the real' by raising the stakes in *It's Your Film*, heightening the similarity between the pre-recorded image

Graeme Rose in *It's Your Film* by Stan's Cafe
Photo: Ed Dimsdale

and the live image. With the noise of moving feet and shifting flats, the real not only remains present throughout the piece, but serves as a reminder of the origin of the illusion. Rather than forging a relativistic equivocation between the live and the mediatized, the simulated and the real, Stan's Cafe work to critique the notion that the real is impossible to identify. The piece acknowledges the significant hold that popular cultural forms have upon contemporary society, and yet it refuses to homogenize, and so relativize, the filmic with other pre-recorded media in order to question whether the proliferation of mediatized images necessitates the disappearance of the real.

Blast Theory

Blast Theory are a London-based collective, led by Matt Adams, Ju Row Farr and Nick Tandavanitj. The company use a range of online, mobile and digital technologies in a range of theatre, installation, site-specific and online events. *Desert Rain* began as a response to Baudrillard's hyperbolical 1991 essay 'The Gulf War Did Not Take Place'.[12] In his drive to make a typically extreme (and largely unsubstantiated) assertion about the impact of mediatization upon the contemporary North American and northern European experience, Baudrillard argued that, given the change in the nature and mode of operation of contemporary warfare, the Gulf War itself could be called into question.

> Since this war was won in advance, we will never know what it would have been like had it existed. We will never know what an Iraqi taking part with a chance of fighting would have been like. We will never know what an American taking part with a chance of being beaten would have been like. [. . .] But this is not a war, any more than 10,000 tonnes of bombs per day is sufficient to make it a war. Any more than the direct transmission by CNN of real time information is sufficient to authenticate a war. (Baudrillard 1995: 62)

Taking its name in part from 'Operation Desert Storm', a key initiative of the first Gulf War (January to March 1991), *Desert Rain* foregrounds the relationship between recent communication and surveillance technology and the celebration of warfare and violence in contemporary computer and console games. In terms of a history of warfare, 'Operation Desert Storm' has been recognized as a landmark battle in its integration of new technologies.[13]

Working with Nottingham University's Mixed Reality Lab, Blast Theory created a unique mixed media installation for an audience of six. The participants are treated as intelligence operatives, asked to remove and store personal belongings and don specialist clothing, and given a briefing on the nature of their task. Each participant is given the name of their 'target' and a credit-card-sized swipe card with a close-up of part of their target's face. The target relates to a 'real' person who participated in the 1991 Gulf War in a variety of ways, but the participant can only discover the true nature of their target's role once they have found them in the virtual landscape and been given a second swipe card with a full facial image of their quarry. Each participant is zipped into an individual participation pod, and a wide curtain of water is activated to create a screen of rain between the participants and the rest of the studio. A virtual motel room and then a virtual desert landscape are projected onto the rain curtain, which acts as a vacillating and deliberately imperfect screen. By applying pressure to the customized footboards the participants are able to leave the motel room, enter the virtual desert space and negotiate their way around the landscape. On successful completion of their task, the player is rewarded by being shown interview footage of the 'targets' involved in the war.

The company also place a small container of sand in the pocket of each participant's jacket. A section of text on the outside of the packet provides the answer to a question the participants have been asked at the outset, that of 'how many Iraqi casualties were there during the Iraqi war?' The text estimates the figure at 100,000. This text is followed by a quotation from General Colin Powell, cited in the *New York Times*, 23 March 1991, which reads: 'It's really not a number I'm terribly interested in' (Blast Theory and Mixed Reality Lab 2002: 16).

In his essay 'The Gulf War Did Not Take Place', Baudrillard sets out to draw attention to the inequality between the Allied forces and the Iraqi forces. For Baudrillard the Allied forces' weaponry and access to satellite surveillance gave them an unfair advantage over the Iraqi forces, and it is for that reason that he calls for the identification of this conflict as 'warfare' to be brought into question. In his introduction to Baudrillard's collected essays on the subject, Paul Patton asserts that:

> Baudrillard's argument in 'The Gulf War did not take place' is not that nothing took place, but rather that what took place was not a war. [. . .] The disparity between US and Iraqi forces with regard to method and military technology was so great that direct engagement rarely took place, and when it did the outcome was entirely predictable. (Patton 1995: 17)

The inclusion of footage from actual combatants and the reminder of the Iraqi death toll invites the participants of *Desert Rain* to occupy a critical position, and to question not only the 'manner in which these [events] were portrayed' but the manner in which real wars are used to inform popular computer games.[14]

Blast Theory's piece alludes to the aircraft pilots' increased level of dislocation from the reality of warfare by employing immersive virtual reality technologies similar to those used in real-life combat training. However, at no point does the game imply that the war was without real consequences; rather it reminds the participants of the number of Iraqi casualties. In addition, the participants are further reminded of the repercussions of the event in the 'real world' as they view footage of soldiers, medical crew and journalists actually posted

Ju Row Farr in *Desert Rain* by Blast Theory
Photo: Dirk Hessaker

in Iraq during the first Gulf War. I would argue that both Blast Theory's performance and Baudrillard's influential essay reject the notion that 'nothing exists beyond mediated representation' (Tomlin 2004: 502–3). Although Baudrillard puts forward this assertion in much of his related work, as Patton has pointed out, Baudrillard's Gulf essays differ from his previous works in that they 'advance no universal claims about the collapse of the real into its forms of representation, but rather make specific ontological claims about aspects of present social reality, such as the virtual war which results from the strategy of deterrence and the virtual informational war which we experience through the media' (Patton 1995: 16–17). Baudrillard's change in strategy, in acknowledging 'present social reality', moves away from a more generalized critique of a culture dominated by mass media to a specific critique of what he perceives to be the ethical corruption of the Allied forces in determining an imbalanced conflict as an equally pitched 'war'. It is this political injustice that Blast Theory seek to underline in their 3D simulation of virtual warfare. Consequently, *Desert Rain* should not be dismissed as apolitical or relativistic, but instead seen to have encouraged a wider understanding of these political issues. The transformation of 'Operation Desert Storm' into an interactive computer game, rather than trivialize the event, enables the company to explore Baudrillard's political opposition to this as an 'electronic' war, which he argues 'involves new forms of deception by means of electronic interference and falsified signals' (Patton 1995: 6). Participants are invited to experience how surveillance of the virtual landscape through specially designed headsets distances them from face-to-face combat, as it does the 'authentic' soldiers'.

In conclusion, each company discussed in this chapter has created a hybrid performance that creates a productive tension between the spectator's expectations of form and the actual experiential challenges presented by form. In the case of Forced Entertainment's *Nightwalks*, the expectation that the CD-ROM will provide the customary opportunities to create multiple narrative excursions through the virtual environments is reversed as the participant is offered a singular, cyclical pathway. In *It's Your Film*, Stan's Cafe challenge the viewer's expectations of a live theatrical event through the framing and presentation of ostensibly two-dimensional images, apparently projected upon a flat screen. The viewers comes to realize the cinematic images are being constructed before their eyes, but the mastery of the illusion means that the viewers must constantly remind themselves that this is live rather than pre-recorded image. On the surface, Blast Theory's *Desert Rain* offers an escapist, recreational experience, as the participants begin to play a computer game using virtual reality headsets and foot paddles, yet empirical data from the 1990s Gulf conflict problematize the normalization of battle histories being incorporated into computer gaming scenarios.

Theorists mapping the change presaged by the digital revolution have pointed to the impossibility of both accessing and representing the 'real', and the impossibility of participating in meaningful exchange. Tomlin has suggested that 1990s experimental theatre work engaging with these theories became ensnared by their reductive pessimism. However, by reading for signs of resistance, rather than approbation, it is possible to ascertain a sense of scepticism about and resistance to the proposition that the digital age presages the disappearance of the real. Each of the selected pieces provokes a crisis in the spectator's sense of expectation about what the identified art-form should offer, and forces the viewer to re-evaluate their own proximity to the 'real'.

Notes

1 Complicite's revival of *Mnemonic* at the National Theatre (2002–3) made use of data projection and live and pre-recorded footage; Tom Stoppard's *Coast of Utopia* trilogy, also at the National (2002), used video projection of virtual computer-generated landscapes; the musical *Sinatra*, produced at the Palladium (2006), features live performers who interact with rare film footage of Sinatra.

2 This is not the first time that new technologies have instigated significant aesthetic shifts. For example, Victorian theatres incorporated hydraulic technologies to create water spectacles in the late nineteenth century on the English stage; see M. R. Booth (1981). *Victorian Spectacular Theatre 1850–1910*. London: Routledge and Kegan Paul. Piscator also used film projection in his work in early twentieth-century Germany; see E. Bentley, ed. (1997). *The Theatre of the Modern Stage*. New York: Applause, 471–3.

3 Forced Entertainment was founded in 1984, whilst Blast Theory and Stan's Cafe were both founded in 1991. The companies chosen for discussion represent a selection from a wide range of small- to medium-scale experimental theatre companies working in Britain between 1980 and 2006. The limited scope of this chapter inevitably results in the contributions of many UK companies going unmarked. Companies and artists such as Third Angel, Moti Roti, Ronald Fraser Monroe, desperate optimists, Insomniac Productions, Index Theatre Co-op, Doo-Cot, Shunt, Station House Opera, Imitating the Dog, Uninvited Guests, Gary Stevens, Fiona Templeton, Bobby Baker, Graeme Miller, Gob Squad and Brith Gof have all created work which could be understood to negotiate a re-evaluation of authenticity, mediatization and simulation as part of their pursuit of 'reality' in a digital age.

4 Benjamin writes: 'Mechanical reproduction threatens to detach the re-produced object from the domain of tradition by bringing it wholly into our own time without, at the same time, bringing the associations it gathered in the course of its history' (1973: 220–1).

5 The quotation is published in Etchells (1999: 44).

6 Blast Theory website: www.blasttheory.co.uk/bt/about.html; Etchells (1994: 109).

7 See www.sharpened.net/helpcenter/answer.php?62 for an introduction to the difference between analogue and digital recording.

8 For discussions of the contribution of digitization to a postmodern culture and aesthetics see Gaylard (2004); Lovejoy (1997).

9 Lyotard posits that Kant's theory relies upon the moment when 'the imagination fails to present an object which might, if only in principle, come to match a concept' (Lyotard 1979: 78).

Sarah Gorman

10 Lyotard writes that in 'postindustrial society' and 'postmodern culture
     [. . .] the grand narrative [of legitimating knowledge] has lost its cred-
     ibility' (1979: 37).
11 *The Collins English Dictionary* (1992) defines the Möbius strip as 'a one-
     sided continuous surface, formed by twisting a long narrow rectangular
     strip of material through 180° and joining the ends' [C19: named after
     August *Möbius* (1790–1868), German mathematician who invented it]'.
12 Translated into English in 1995 by Paul Patton.
13 See Oppenhiem (1991: i). Oppenhiem writes that Allied forces had access
     to US spy satellite pictures, which enabled clear observation of Iraqi troop
     movement. Also see Michael Heim (1993). *The Metaphysics of Virtual Reality*.
     Oxford: Oxford University Press, 113. Heim writes that, 'Virtual environ-
     ments are now incorporated into operational warplanes, filtering the real
     scene and presenting aircrew with a more readable world.'
14 See for example *Battlefield 1942* (2002) and *Battlefield Vietnam World War
     Two Model* (2004) by Electronic Arts; *Call of Duty* (2004) by Activision.

Primary reading

Blast Theory (1999). *Desert Rain*. Blast Theory website: www.blasttheory.co.uk/
     index.php.
Forced Entertainment (1998). *Nightwalks* (CD-ROM). Forced Entertainment
     website: www.forcedentertainment.com.
Stan's Cafe (1998). *It's Your Film*. Stan's Cafe website: www.stanscafe.co.uk.
Documentation of Forced Entertainment, Blast Theory, and Stan's Cafe's work
     can be found in the British Library Sound Archive.

Further reading

Auslander, Philip (1999). *Liveness: Performance in a Mediatized Culture*. London:
     Routledge.
Baudrillard, Jean (1988). *The Ecstasy of Communication*. New York: Semiotext(e).
Baudrillard, Jean (1994). 'The Precession of Simulacra' in *Simulacra and Simu-
     lation*, trans. Sheila Faria Glaser. Ann Arbor, MI: University of Michigan
     Press, 1–42.
Baudrillard, Jean (1995). *The Gulf War Did Not Take Place*, trans. Paul Patton.
     Bloomington, IN: Indiana University Press.
Benjamin, Walter (1973). *Illuminations: Theses on the Philosophy of History*.
     London: Fontana.
Blast Theory and Mixed Reality Lab, eds. (2002). *Desert Rain: A Virtual Reality
     Game/Installation*. Nottingham: Blast Theory.

280

Etchells, Tim (1994). 'Diverse Assembly: Some Trends in Recent Perform-ance' in Theodore Shank (ed.), *Contemporary British Theatre*. London: Macmillan, 106–22.

Etchells, Tim (1999). *Certain Fragments: Contemporary Performance and Forced Entertainment*. London and New York: Routledge.

Gaylard, Gerald (2004). 'Postmodern Archaic: The Return of the Real in Digital Virtuality', *Postmodern Culture* 15:1. Available online at: www3.iath. virginia.edu/pmc/text-only/issue.904/15.1gaylard.txt.

Giannachi, Gabriella (2004). *Virtual Theatres: An Introduction*. London and New York: Routledge.

Glendinning, H., Etchells, T., and Forced Entertainment (2000). *Void Spaces*. Sheffield: Sheffield Site Gallery.

Helmer, Judith, and Malzacher, Florian, eds. (2004). *Not Even a Game Anymore*. Berlin: Alexander.

Landow, George (1997). *Hypertext, 2.0: The Convergence of Contemporary Literary Theory and Technology*. Baltimore: Johns Hopkins University Press.

Lavender, Andrew (1999). 'Turns and Transformations' in Vera Gottlieb and Colin Chambers (eds.), *Theatre in a Cool Climate*. Oxford: Amber Lane Press, 179–90.

Lovejoy, Margaret (1997). *Postmodern Currents: Art and Artists in the Age of Electronic Media*. Englewood Cliffs, NJ: Prentice Hall.

Luckhurst, Roger (2004). 'Ending the Century: Literature and Digital Tech-nology' in Laura Marcus and Peter Nicholls (eds.), *The Cambridge History of Twentieth Century English Literature*. Cambridge: Cambridge University Press, 787–805.

Lyotard, Jean François (1979). *The Postmodern Condition: A Report on Knowledge*, trans. G. Bennington and B. Massumi. Manchester: Manchester University Press.

McKenzie, Jon (2001). *Perform or Else: From Discipline to Performance*. London and New York: Routledge.

McKenzie, Jon (2003). 'Virtual Reality: Performance, Immersion and the Thaw' in Philip Auslander (ed.), *Performance: Critical Concepts in Literary and Cultural Studies. Vol. 1*. London: Routledge, 168–88.

Oppenhiem, I. D. (1991). *Gulf: Diary of the Micro Chip War*. Shoreham: Century Press.

Parker-Starbuck, Jennifer (2004). 'Framing the Fragments: The Wooster Group's Use of Technology' in Johan Callens (ed.), *The Wooster Group and Its Traditions*. Brussels: Peter Lang, 217–30.

Patton, Paul (1995). 'Introduction to *The Gulf War Did Not Take Place*' in Jean Baudrillard, *The Gulf War Did Not Take Place*, trans. Paul Patton. Bloomington, IN: Indiana University Press, 1–6.

Ryan, Marie-Laure. (2004). 'Multivariant Narratives' in Susan Schreibman, Ray Siemens and John Unsworth (eds.), *A Companion to Digital Humanities*. Oxford: Blackwell, 415–30.

Sarah Gorman

Tomlin, Liz (2004). 'English Theatre in the 1990s and Beyond' in Baz Kershaw (ed.), *The Cambridge History of British Theatre. Vol. 3.* Cambridge: Cambridge University Press, 498–512.

Virilio, P. (1995). 'Speed and Information: Cyberspace Alarm!', trans. P. Reimens, in *CTheory*, www.ctheory.net/text.file.asp?pick=72, accessed 16 June 2004.

Index

283

Index

Williams, Tennessee 31, 38, 46
  A Streetcar Named Desire 46
Wilson, Esther 212, 214, 221
  Unprotected 212, 214, 221
Wilson, Harold 247
Wing-Davey, Mark 219
Woolf, Dennis 212, 221
  Beyond Belief 212, 221
Wooster Group (the) 264, 281
Worthen, W. B. 179–80, 186, 189, 199

Wrights & Sites 99–101, 105
  Exeter Mis-Guide, An 99, 105
  Misguide to Anywhere, A 101, 105

yardies 55, 56
Yeats, W. B. 32, 39, 40, 46, 194
Yellow Earth Theatre 192
York Millennium Mystery Plays 97

Zadek, Peter 167